Pragmatism and the Philosophy of Sport

Pragmatism and the Philosophy of Sport

Edited by Richard Lally, Douglas Anderson, and John Kaag

LEXINGTON BOOKS
Lanham • Boulder • New York • Toronto • Plymouth, UK

Published by Lexington Books
A wholly owned subsidiary of The Rowman & Littlefield Publishing Group, Inc.
4501 Forbes Boulevard, Suite 200, Lanham, Maryland 20706
www.rowman.com

10 Thornbury Road, Plymouth PL6 7PP, United Kingdom

British Library Cataloguing in Publication Information Available

Library of Congress Cataloging-in-Publication Data

Pragmatism and the philosophy of sport / edited by John Kaag, Douglas Anderson, and Richard
Lally.
p. cm.
Includes bibliographical references and index.
ISBN 978-0-7391-7840-9 (cloth : alk. paper) -- ISBN 978-0-7391-7841-6 (electronic)
1. Sports--Philosophy. 2. Pragmatism. I. Kaag, John J., 1979- II. Anderson, Douglas. III. Lally, Dick.
GV706.P65 2013
796.01--dc23
2012033849

Printed in the United States of America

Contents

Introduction: Pragmatism and the Seasoned Practitioner

Richard Lally, Lock Haven University

I. PRAGMATISM: GETTING TO KNOW THE COURSE

As many historians and commentators have pointed out, pragmatism began in the interactions among the participants of the "Metaphysical Club," an informal philosophy group, in Cambridge, MA in the 1870s. Among these participants were Charles Sanders Peirce and William James, who have come to be identified as the founders of the pragmatic movement. Peirce first identified the idea of pragmatic meaning in his 1876 essay "How to Make Our Ideas Clear," and James first used the word "pragmatism" in technical fashion in a talk he gave to Berkeley's Philosophical Union in 1898. As a method of inquiry and a general outlook on the practice of philosophy, pragmatism was then inherited by a number of thinkers including John Dewey and F.C.S. Schiller. Dewey brought pragmatism forward into the twentieth century and, most recently, there has been a linguistic version of pragmatism introduced by Richard Rorty that goes by the popular name of "neo-pragmatism." Meanwhile, a number of thinkers who were politically marginalized with the ascent of Anglo-American philosophy in American universities carried on the classical pragmatic tradition. Among these were most notably John E. Smith of Yale University and John J. McDermott of Texas A & M University. Our present work relating pragmatism and the philosophy of sport draws heavily on the classical pragmatic tradition and, to a lesser extent, on some themes from the neo-pragmatic movement. I do not believe that pragmatism provides any one sort of answer to questions regarding sport and movement, but I do believe it is a useful idea for conducting inquiries into the meanings, practices, cultural uses, and truths of sport and movement. I therefore begin with an overview of the importance of pragmatism for our immediate purposes.

The experiences an individual undergoes during training and competition shape her worldview in a fashion that is unique. Rigorous aspects of endurance sport, for example, lend a raw-boned feel to daily life that is outside normal experience. This unusual quality, and the power it has to mold an individual, deserves a more detailed examination than it has

1

received up to this point. This connection between athletic practice and experience and philosophical outlook is one of the themes at the core of this work. To get at this connection, I will employ pragmatism and James's radical empiricism as guides to our method. As Christopher Hookway maintains,

> Pragmatism is a form of empiricism that employs a much richer under-standing of experience than is familiar from the work of Hume and from twentieth-century logical empiricists. We can see this clearly in William James's radical empiricism.[1]

This approach involves a thick and phenomenological description of lived experience of the sort provided by writers such as Henry Bugbee and George Sheehan. It also requires a search for meaning in the midst of human practices, a pragmatic feature of inquiry central to both James and Dewey.

Early in the twentieth century, James noted the inadequacy of philo-sophic concepts to grasp the full meaning of human experience.[2] A "con-ceptual map," James asserted, "remains superficial through the abstract-ness, and false through the discreteness of its elements; and the whole operation, so far from making things appear more rational, becomes the source of gratuitous unintelligibilities. Conceptual knowledge is forever inadequate to the fullness of the reality to be known."[3] To address this concern, he developed his pragmatically oriented radical empiricism, which sought to elicit concepts from the thickness of experience in gener-al by paying direct attention to one's own experience and to the lived experience of others. What some critics of his *The Varieties of Religious Experience* took to be unprofessional scholarship came to serve as an im-portant contribution to the American version of phenomenological in-quiry. James's radical empiricism subsequently informed a number of American philosophical projects from W.E. Hocking's *The Meaning of God in Human Experience* to Henry Bugbee's *The Inward Morning*. And, of course, it also brings philosophical importance to earlier work in American thought including Jonathan Edward's "Personal Narrative," Thoreau's *Walden*, and Margaret Fuller's *Woman in the Nineteenth Century*.

In describing radical empiricism James speaks of how a person has authority when making claims of truth—in our case, claims about sport and its power to cultivate the individual. For James the experiencer is the original knower: The experiencer of such a situation possesses all that the idea contains. He feels the tendency, the obstacle, the will, the strain, the triumph, or the passive giving up, just as he feels the time, the space, the swiftness or intensity, the movement, the weight and color, the pain and pleasure, the complexity, or whatever remaining characters the situation may involve.[4] His brand of pragmatism relied on two types of knowing that are integral elements of radical empiricism—the first being knowl-edge of acquaintance, and the second, knowledge about. The athlete, we believe, has a Jamesian knowledge of acquaintance that generates living personal truths, allowing the individual to make claims about the world and the self that have worth. These claims are based on lived experience and form an intimate catalogue of knowledge on which the individual relies for guidance. And while it is possible for the individual to be deceived, or to misinterpret experience, the pragmatists saw this process as the fundamental means by which the individual comes to know the universe and her place in it. What must be avoided in pragmatic inquiries such as this one are individual truth claims that dogmatically resist and stand in opposition to all other testimony. James's second type of knowing guards against such trouble.

Knowledge about, according to James, advocates the validity of a catalogue of knowledge that can be discussed in a shared context larger than one individual's life. Dewey develops this, pushing James's radical empiricism in the direction of what he calls *shared experience*. This allows individual claims that are corrigible to be ratified or rejected through testing. For example, if a runner claims that a personal best can be attained in the marathon by limiting the length of the longest training run to less than fifteen miles, the general community of runners can test that claim. The pragmatic method is public and experimental. As Dewey argues, "An education based upon the pragmatic conception would inevitably turn out persons who were alive to the necessity of continually testing their ideas and beliefs by putting them into practical application, and of revising their beliefs on the basis of the results of such application." [5]

This approach, which combines both knowledge of acquaintance and knowledge about, is appealing because James manages to preserve the worth of both personal experience and the developing beliefs of a tradition. And while knowledge of acquaintance is irrefutable when based only on one individual's testimony, the informed community can reject the claim on the basis of knowledge about. This aspect of pragmatism is of critical importance because it allows individual experience to count, while maintaining the normative authority of the existing tradition.

An example will help to clarify this aspect of Jamesian pragmatism as it relates to this project. I run the trails of State College, Pennsylvania and know some truths of those trails. A corresponding map is only of worth to us if it jibes with the catalogue of perceptual truth that we have created. As a result, we become sources informed well enough to validate an externally generated picture of what has been experienced by others. The beauty of this conception of knowledge is that we need not remain Robinson Crusoe-like solipsists, cut off from all others. There is room at our table for Friday, if he is a seasoned practitioner like myself. I can listen to his testimony and together we can generate a shared version of the truth. In *Democracy in Education*, Dewey makes this point in a more general way. Men live in a community in virtue of the things which they have in common and communication is the way in which they come to possess things in common. What they must have in common in order to form a community or society are aims, beliefs, aspirations, knowledge—a common understanding—like-mindedness, as the sociologists say.[6] We can develop these communally held beliefs through a sharing of individual percepts, which can then be used in conceptual form to validate or reject the assertions of other practitioners. Over time a tradition develops that enriches the practice and allows individual athletes to share their truths with others who have similar experiences. James describes how this process occurs in the following way: "New truth is always a go-between, a smoother-over of transitions. It marries old opinion to new fact so as ever to show a minimum of jolt, a maximum of continuity."[7]

However, within this Jamesian conception, it is important to note that as the tradition develops, primary importance is still given to individual experience, regardless of the communal institutions that may be spawned subsequently. In conducting my present investigations, I have given primary importance to the experiences of the individual while being mindful of the final validating authority of the community. This focus on individual testimony within the radically empirical method gives pragmatic examinations a style that is noticeably different from more traditionally analytic philosophy. With this in mind, the next section describes the radically empirical approach to experience and its relevance to this project.

II. THE STYLE OF A RADICALLY EMPIRICAL STUDY

Radical empiricism is well suited for an examination such as this one because it encourages numerous approaches to the study of experience, including narration and biography. James believed that these personal accounts captured the thickness of experience more effectively than generalized concepts. In compiling *The Varieties of Religious Experience*, James utilized biography and firsthand testimony to communicate a greater sense of the whole of experience than would have been possible through the exclusive use of abstract concepts. In doing so, he realized that this approach is open to criticism by those within philosophy more comfortable with traditional logical analysis. In lecture one of *The Varieties of Religious Experience* he addresses this likelihood:

> our theory should allow that a book may well be a revelation in spite of errors and passions and deliberate human composition, if only it be a true record of inner experiences of great-souled persons wrestling with the crises of their fate, then the verdict would be more favorable. You see that the existential facts by themselves are insufficient for determining the value; and the best adepts of the higher criticism accordingly never confound the existential with the spiritual problem.[8]

A similar use of descriptive narration in this project should allow us, at times, to get closer to the marrow of the lived experience than would be possible through the removed stance of philosophic analysis. With that in mind, I will attempt to heed what James once told his audience:

> The man who knows governments most completely is he who troubles himself least about a definition which shall give their essence. Enjoying an intimate acquaintance with all their particularities in turn, he would naturally regard an abstract conception in which these were unified as a thing more misleading than enlightening. And why may not religion be a conception equally complex?[9]

I take a similar approach in this investigation of pragmatism and sport. Many of the most insightful experts in any given field are those who dwell within the lived practice, be it politics or athletics. Thus, I will look at the particular experiences of individuals who have trained for and competed in sport, as I believe these people are less likely to accept an abstract description of their practices that is without some grounding in lived experience.

III. PRAGMATIC USES

While it is important to remember the passion that led to the scholarship, it is also necessary to be mindful of the fact that conclusions reached through a pragmatic investigation are tentative. In remaining true to pragmatism and radical empiricism, the conclusions I draw regarding pragmatism and endurance sport must be thought of as temporarily useful. In the future, other investigators will modify the claims made here, expanding and improving on the work of this project. As pragmatic investigators, we must welcome this inevitability. Rather than attempting to construct a philosophic argument that is impervious to outside attack, we must accept the risks of dialectic and the vulnerability that comes with tentative conclusions. Therefore, I will regard certainty within the philosophic process, more as an animating force behind human action than as the outcome of a cleverly constructed argument. Bugbee took a similar approach in writing *The Inward Morning*, and spoke directly to this point when he wrote: "Perhaps the last thing we should demand of an interpretation of certainty is that it show how we are entitled to some credo, once-for-all incontrovertibly."[10] His assertion squares with pragmatism's belief that inquiring is always ongoing, never final.

I believe the adoption of a Bugbee-like certainty, or a tentative certainty, is necessary when reading the chapters that follow. We need an attitude closer to faith than close-mindedness, a basis for action "rather than arrival at a terminus of endeavor."[11] If we can find the confidence to live with a partial description, that claims only to touch truth, rather than capture it, we may "open ourselves to the meaning of life in the wilderness and be patient of being overtaken in our wandering by that which can make us at home in this condition."[12]

The radically empirical method employed here is not unique within contemporary philosophic discourses. Other recent trends in philosophy have made it acceptable, even professionally wise, to consider art, literature, music, and sport as viable arenas for philosophic insight.[13] Richard Rorty, as a disciple of James, most notably turns to literature and personal experience as avenues of philosophical inquiry. Stanley Cavell, a nonpragmatist, is also exemplary, having turned some of his philosophical energies to the task of disclosing cultural meaning in Hollywood film. Moreover, Cavell's work stands in a philosophical tradition in which it is acceptable to present one's own voice as a valid form of scholarship. Both Rorty and Cavell are familiar with Bugbee's work and might agree with his assertion that, "In a sense to write your own words, to write your own inner voice, is philosophy. But the discipline most opposed to writing, and to life, is analytic philosophy."[14] As Ed Mooney points out, and James knew, radical empiricism is not new in the history of philosophy: "since Augustine and Plato, philosophy has been a testament and confession, not just an impersonal report."[15]

As a radically empirical investigation, this project is an attempt to disclose the features of sport that provide meaning for our personal and cultural lives. It assumes that sport is a dynamic process, not a static institution. It aims at the truth that the poetic aspects of existence offer us, rather than at the fully abstracted world constructed by the pure intellect. Therefore, the chapters that follow "will not be set up like the solution of a puzzle, worked out with all the pieces lying there before the eye. It will be more like the clarification of what we know in our bones."[16]

IV. PRAGMATIC THEMES

Just as James's radical empiricism informs my method of inquiry, pragmatism informs the content of our descriptions and analyses. Pragmatism is a philosophic theory that differs from traditional philosophy in its rejection of all assertions thought to be absolute or generated independently of human experience. According to James, true ideas "are those that we can assimilate, validate, corroborate and verify. False ideas are those that we can not."[17] Furthermore, once an idea is experienced as true it still must demonstrate its worth as an instrument of action if it is to be valued. James describes the process by which a truth claim evolves from the mere untried hypothesis to a belief that is workable, but provisionally so. In other words, true claims demonstrate their validity by producing their intended effects. As a result, within pragmatism all human undertakings are viewed as attempts to orchestrate the outcomes of our interplay with the universe. The pragmatists believed this was achieved through an ongoing process of testing that was carried out in the world of action.

This intimate connection between thought, action, and outcome runs against some other traditional depictions of intellectual investigations of the world—namely, idealism, rationalism, or any outlook that takes inquiry to be its own end. The possession of truth, so far from being here an end in itself, is only a preliminary means towards other vital satisfactions. If I am lost in the woods and starved, and find what looks like a cow path, it is of the utmost importance that I should think of a human habitation at the end of it, for if I do so and follow it, I save myself. The true thought is useful here because the house which is its object is useful. The practical value of true ideas is thus primarily derived from the practical importance of their objects to us.[18] Modern philosophy employed a model whose center is the static thinker in search of pure knowledge, untainted by the corrupting forces of the external and changing world. In contrast, the pragmatists saw the inquirer as fully engaged in her environment. The pragmatism developed by Peirce, James, and Dewey required an acceptance of the material world as the sole available and verifiable basis for thought. But it also led toward the assertion of the inseparability of thought and action, raising experience in the physical world and the specific experiences of each human being to a new and remarkable eminence.

This depiction of the individual as an agent of action immersed within the universe also generates an undercurrent of optimism regarding the individual's potential for self-determination. The source for this optimism is not difficult to locate. Peirce, James, and Dewey constructed a philosophic outlook with an innate openness that welcomed divergent contributions. It is, as James routinely pointed out, an inherently pluralistic philosophy. It presents so many points of difference, both from the common sense and from the idealism that have made our philosophic language, that it is almost as difficult to state it as it is to think it out clearly, and if it is ever to grow into a respectable system, it will have to be built up by the contributions of many cooperating minds.[19]

As a result of the pluralistic nature of pragmatism, a playing field that allows thinkers who would otherwise be unwelcome to contribute has opened. To quote James once again on this aspect of pragmatism:

> it lies in the midst of our theories, like a corridor in a hotel. Innumerable chambers open out of it. In one you may find a man writing an atheistic volume; in the next some one on his knees praying for faith and strength; in the third a chemist investigating a body's properties. In a fourth a system of idealistic metaphysics is being excogitated; in a fifth the impossibility of metaphysics is being shown. But they all own the corridor, and all must pass through it if they want a practicable way of getting into or out of their respective rooms.[20]

While many consider pragmatism to be the American contribution to philosophy, it is difficult to describe with exactness what the movement itself stood for or how it is understood today. This ambiguity can probably be accredited to the variety of meanings its founders assigned to what are widely accepted to be the central tenets of pragmatism. Peirce, James, and Dewey each had somewhat different understandings of what the thrust of the new movement was to be. In a letter to F. C. S. Schiller, Peirce attempted to address the definitional confusion in the following way: "I would let it grow and then say it is what a certain group of thinkers who seem to understand one another think, and thus make it the name of a natural class in the Natural History fashion."[21] Within this natural class of pragmatism, several key themes can be identified that have particular relevance to sport. Three that will have significance for me are addressed in the next section. They are: faith in the experimental method, the acceptance of risk, and the power of the human will.

V. FAITH IN THE EXPERIMENTAL METHOD

One of the hallmarks of both the pragmatic school of philosophy and the radically empirical understanding of experience is a reliance on the experimental method for the production of workable truth. Within this philosophic system, beliefs and concepts are generated through our interactions with the universe. In keeping with the model of radical empiricism, these beliefs are then returned at a later time to the flow of experience where they will be tested by a new investigation. In his essay "The Bearings of Pragmatism Upon Education," Dewey describes this key characteristic of pragmatism:

> The *experimental* habit of mind, that which regards ideas and principles as tentative methods of solving problems and organizing data, is very recent. An education based upon the pragmatic conception would inevitably turn out persons who were alive to the necessity of continually testing their ideas and beliefs by putting them into practical application, and of revising their beliefs on the basis of the results of such application.[22]

When assessing the relationship between the experimental method, the radically empirical approach, and pragmatism, it is worth noting that James called his empiricism *radical* because he believed it corrected the mistakes made by traditional empiricism, which attempted to better understand reality by dividing experiences into a series of categories. This arbitrary division of experience, initially undertaken in an attempt to better comprehend human experience as a whole, eventually degenerated into skepticism regarding the validity of philosophic inquiry. In describing how radical empiricism corrected the mistake that led James's predecessors down the dead end road toward metaphysical skepticism, Ellen Kappy Suckiel points out that

> in thinking of experience in terms of discrete, atomistic units, the classical empiricists missed the most important fact about it, namely, that experience is the immediate flux of life. It is a continuous stream each part having no distinct boundaries, each leading to and compenetrating the next. . . . It is this postulation of the reality of relations which distinguishes James's empiricism as *radical,* and which, he maintains, enables him to succeed where other philosophies have failed.[23]

Through radical empiricism, James claims that truth is understandable when we view life as a flowing process rather than as a set of distinct events or units. As a result, the conjunctive moments of experience, which stand between more memorable events, are "as real as the terms united by them."[24] This appreciation for the totality of experience provides "the foundation for his claim that truth is understandable solely by reference to intra-experiential and ultimately pragmatic tests."[25]

It is important to note that radical empiricism does not reject the use of conceptual categories, only the assertion that they are fixed and complete. To reiterate, James believed that concepts were useful in distinguishing various elements within the flow of unified experience but were too narrow to capture the full thickness of experience. James does not deny that there are objective realities within experience that concepts help us to better understand and explain. However, he asserts that, "what it *means* for beliefs to be objective, and what it means for beliefs to correspond to reality, are concepts that are themselves explicable solely by reference to the flux of experience."[26]

In establishing the experimental method's importance within the pragmatic tradition, it is important to note that beginning with Peirce, and then continuing through James and Dewey, the testing of hypotheses through daily living served as the basis for the production of truth claims. It was Peirce who claimed, "a conception, that is, the rational purport of a word or other expression, lies exclusively in its conceivable bearing on the conduct of life."[27] By this he meant that the meaning and worth of an idea, expression, or object is manifested through the results that it produces in our lives. As a result, the truth of any idea is never known until it is tested under live fire to determine its consequences. A new theory remains only our best guess until it proves its worth through practice. Therefore, any hypothesis must be tested to determine its validity, and even then, if it proves efficacious, it can be said to represent only our best stab at the truth to that point.

Peirce's attempt to define "hard" helps demonstrate what the pragmatists had in mind. How is it, he asked, that humans know that an object is hard? After all, hardness or softness seem to be abstract descriptions grounded in nothing more than an individual's perception. While we all understand what the term "hard" means, how is it that we know an object has such a quality in the first place? According to Peirce, we will not find the answer at the end of a lengthy epistemological theorem or stipulation. We would be better served by relying on the observable outcome when the object is used. If the object scratches another object, it is said to be harder. If the object is scratched, we can feel safe in labeling it "softer." To quote Peirce directly, "there is absolutely no difference between a hard thing and a soft thing so long as they are not brought to the test."[28] It is therefore the testing that establishes the meaning and worth of the conception.

This crucial step is of central importance in the experimental method, and therefore, in pragmatism. A hypothesis is generated based on an investigator's current understanding of the situation, and then that hypothesis is tested to assess its accuracy. The ratification or rejection of the conception cannot take place without the testing. And the testing itself requires action—an exchange between investigator and environment—which, in turn, leads to an outcome that supports or fails to support the original hypothesis. Even when a hypothesis is ratified as noted, the possibility for future revision, or even outright rejection, exists.

John E. Smith, in commenting on the pragmatic reliance on the experimental method, refers to this phenomenon as the "dynamizing of predicates."[29] The hardness or softness of an object becomes more than a lifeless description of an inanimate object. These qualities can only be assigned when the object is set in motion within the flow of common experience. Once we are willing to expose our hypotheses to the harsh light of testing, we may earn a workable level of certainty in the outcome that is produced. To cite Dewey once again:

> A merely mental coherence without experimental verification does not enable us to get beyond the realm of hypothesis. If a notion or a theory makes pretense of corresponding to reality or to the facts, this pretense cannot be put to the test and confirmed or refuted except by causing it to pass over into the realm of action and by testing the results which it yields in the form of concrete observable facts to which this notion or theory leads. If, in acting upon this notion, we are brought to the fact which it implies or which it demands, then this notion is true.[30]

A fundamental element for the experimental method, and consequently pragmatism, is thus a life lived in action, when great weight is given to the choices we make in pursuit of an intended outcome. It is through these choices of action that the individual is able to test and verify her ideas and the ideas of others. Lived experience then becomes the catalyst for an ever-growing catalogue of knowledge.

For the reasons stated previously, the experimental method of pragmatism is doubly important for the project at hand. On the one hand, it is the method we employ. We will engage in a radically empirical look at the experiences of movement and sport. From these we will draw concepts, meanings, and beliefs concerning the importance of sport. The tests of our results will be found in how well our ideas fit the experiences of others—past, present, and future.

In my own chapter, I will look to see what others have already learned in their own experiments of self-cultivation by way of the practices of endurance sport. As Peirce often insisted, a full inquiry requires a community of inquirers who, over time, work together to build a tradition of meanings and beliefs. In "Grounds of Validity of the Laws of Logic" Peirce addresses this balanced relationship between the individual inquirer and the sanctioning community:

> For he who recognizes the logical necessity of complete self-identification of one's own interests with those of the community, and its potential existence in man, even if he has it not himself, will perceive that only the inferences of that man who has it are logical, and so views his own inferences as being valid only so far as they would be accepted by that man. But so far as he has this belief, he becomes identified with that man. And that ideal perfection of knowledge by which we have seen that reality is constituted must thus belong to a community in which this identification is complete.[31]

Dewey made the same point in arguing that human knowing required a focus on "shared experience" through which a community could develop shared meanings and beliefs. In taking both radical empiricism and the experimental method seriously, the pragmatists worked with the regulative hope that humans could act creatively as individual, free-willed agents. The whole notion of self-cultivation requires such a regulative hope.

On the other hand, the theme of pragmatism's experimentalism will play a constitutive role in the content of this book as a whole. That is to say, I believe that the practices of atheletics and sport are inherently experimental. These are practices in which participants establish aims, both specific and general, and employ methods for achieving them. Lived success and failure mark the *truth* and *falsity* of the methods and perhaps, occasionally, of the aims themselves. Thus it is that the initial pragmatic theme of experimentalism plays a dual role in what follows.

VI. THE ACCEPTANCE OF RISK

Along with focusing on the experimental method, the pragmatists emphasized the importance of individual conduct. As Dewey points out, "James calls . . . for human life to be a continual process of re-experimenting and re-creating."[32] Individuals were to be held responsible for their actions and the resultant outcomes. People were thought, at least in part, to be architects capable of shaping both their own high achievements and ignominious failures. This non-deterministic depiction requires the individual to "go at life wholeheartedly," actively engaging the universe in a wrestling match for improvement and momentary stability despite the risks such behavior creates. The original pragmatic attitude, though short of a return to Hellenic fate, is about the gambling nature of human endeavor. This means it is also about a willingness to countenance the possibility of failure, loss, and losing. Pragmatism is no doubt also about how to deal with such an environment, how to find ways of stacking the cultural deck in favor of stability.

The constant struggle to attain a sense of equilibrium in the face of an aggressive universe generates innumerable possible outcomes. The element of risk, which guarantees uncertainty for the individual, demands an energetic response. Within the pragmatic conception, ugliness, evil, failure, and destruction are as important to the overall functioning of the cosmos as happiness, safety, and success. The participant in the cosmic game must be constantly fortified against the forces that can intrude upon a hard-won, temporary peace. Pragmatism calls on us to engage the universe with wholehearted energy, fully committed to the undertaking, even if unsure of the outcome. To desire a more endowed relationship with the universe is to engage in wishful fantasy.

James knew that an artificial Chautauqua-like land o' plenty, where all threats to well-being have been eliminated, where risk is removed, where the possibility of failure is replaced by endless days of lukewarm serenity, will never hold our attention over the long haul. As a risk taker, man is a creature that needs from time to time to exist apart from guaranteed security and reinforcement. Occasionally, we need our hard work, fidelity, and best intentions to be met with undeserved failure. The gambler, the athlete, and the cultivated individual must be familiar with the acidity of the tough-luck loss. Without these experiences, future victories can never fully ripen.

James stresses the important cultivating power of risk while reflecting back on a week he spent at the Assembly Grounds on the shores of Lake Chautauqua.

> I went in curiosity for a day. I stayed for a week, held spell-bound by the charm and ease of everything, by the middle-class paradise, without a sin, without a victim, without a blot, without a tear. And yet what was my own astonishment, on emerging into the dark and wicked world again, to catch myself quite unexpectedly and involuntarily saying: "Ouf! What a relief! . . . Let me take my chances again in the big outside worldly wilderness with all its sins and sufferings. There are the heights and depths, the precipices and the steep ideals, the gleams of the awful and the infinite; and there is more hope and help a thousand times than in the dead level and quintessence of every mediocrity.[33]

Those scholars who claim that the pragmatists preferred formulaic cures over risky endeavors should be aware of the red herring of seeming instrumental pragmatism. If we read just a bit more widely, we can capture their recognition of lived instability and the gambling nature of belief. Both the athletic and pragmatic approaches to life can accept this state of affairs. "I find myself," James said, "willing to take the universe to be really dangerous and adventurous without therefore backing out and crying 'no play.'"[34] Insofar as sport aims to test an individual's limits, it seems to adopt something like this Jamesian attitude. The athlete finds herself in a world whose safety "is unwarranted. It is a real adventure, with real danger, yet, it may win through."[35] As a result, the admission of experiment reveals the necessity of loss; to experiment is to expect in some instances to lose—and for someone, perhaps not the experimenter, to learn from the losing.

With the acceptance of risk and a wholehearted approach to living comes the possibility for excellence. Despite the uncertainty generated, the pragmatic approach can fire the individual with a belief in the possibility of high achievement. As a result, if safe living is the breeding ground of mediocrity, risk-taking becomes fertile soil for both tragedy and glory. As James argued, "For practical life at any rate, the *chance* of salvation is enough. No fact in human nature is more characteristic than its willingness to live on a chance."[36]

It is clear that this stance is not for the faint of heart; it is a system of belief that offers no metaphysical guarantees or individual anonymity. In the words of Smith, "our willingness to act, and the assumption of some risk and responsibility for action in relation to a belief, represent essential indices of actual believing."[37]

VII. THE POWER OF THE WILL

Following after the belief in the experimental method and the acceptance of risk comes a third central tenet of pragmatism—the belief in the power of the will. If the experimental method is adopted, and risk is accepted, truth claims become working conceptions that then demonstrate their worth through application. However, one cannot guarantee that individuals will undertake the risky proposition of creating innovative hypotheses, for there is always room for the person who refuses to formulate hypotheses that challenge an existing set of beliefs. In these cases the third pragmatic element must be present if improvement is to continue.

James's biographer Edward Moore describes the role the will plays within pragmatism in this way: "In refusing to exercise our will, in refusing to believe, we avoid error, but we also lose the right ever to know the truth. For truth is only discovered by those who have the courage to act on their beliefs and to put them to the test."[38] The will to believe in our ability to generate valuable truth is closely tied to the pragmatic conception regarding the role habits play in our lives, as habit is a sustained willingness. Faith in humanity's ability to manage the complexities of existence is not bestowed without cost upon the individual. Like all worthwhile qualities within the pragmatic conception, faith is a habit that is tough to come by, one the individual must develop over the course of a lifetime. The pragmatists saw skepticism as an ever-present force that threatened to infect our soul should we fail to be persistent in our attempts to cultivate openness to possibility. If we agree with Dewey's assessment of habits—that they allow us to gain some measure of control over our travels through experience in the rough and tumble universe—it follows that we would monitor very carefully the habits that we develop. Additionally, if we see our habits as the living manifestations of our deepest beliefs, it becomes profoundly important to study how we develop, and live through, our habits. This has particular relevance for this project, as there is no doubt that will and habit are constitutive of the lives of athletes.

Faith in the power of the will to control certain aspects of existence is representative of the optimism that is a part of pragmatism. And while this belief in individual autonomy may appear at first blush to be romanticized, the original pragmatic conception avoids the pitfalls that many of its self-help offspring continue to make to this day. After all, within the pragmatic conception, the individual is equally free to act on behalf of either her improvement or destruction. We, as habit-grounded agents, have the freedom to exercise our will in the pursuit of a belief that we find worthy of our fidelity. The powerlessness that accompanies a more deterministic outlook is replaced with an empowering sense of control over future events. As a result, the possibility for a future constructed to meet our desires exists. In the words of James, "free will pragmatically means novelties in the world, the right to expect that in the deepest elements, as well as in the surface phenomena, the future may not identically repeat and imitate the past."[39] George Sheehan's description of his return to running in mid-life describes the same transforming power of the will James spoke of:

> At the age of reason, I was placed on a train, the shades drawn, my life's course and destination already determined. At the age of 45, I pulled the emergency cord and ran out into the world. It was a decision that meant no less than a new life, a new course, a new destination. I was born again in my 45th year. . . . And in that hour a day of perfecting my body, I began to find out who I was. . . . In the creative action of running, I became convinced of my own importance, certain that my life had significance.[40]

It follows then that an individual's fate does not rest solely either in the hands of God or in blind serendipity. With this orchestrative power of the will comes a large helping of responsibility. We are now accountable for the actions that will alter our future. Responsibility for a well-lived life can no longer be skirted or relinquished to an invisible puppeteer who manipulates the strings that cause our actions. As individuals within the pragmatic scheme, we are accountable for our own becoming, required to balance the equal forces of burden and opportunity. Seven-time Tour de France champion Lance Armstrong describes the role his will played during training for his attempt to return to professional cycling after recovering from testicular cancer.

> I continued upward, and the mountain grew steeper. I hammered down on the pedals, working hard, and felt a small bloom of sweat and satisfaction, a heat under my skin almost like a liquor blush. . . . As I rode upward, I reflected on my life, back to all points, my childhood, my early races, my illness, and how it changed me. . . . *Move*, I told myself. *If you can still move, you aren't sick.* . . . As I continued upward, I saw my life as a whole. I saw the pattern and the privilege of it, and the purpose of it, too. It was simply this: I was meant for a long, hard climb. [41]

VIII. CONCLUSION

The essays that follow take up these and other themes in the pragmatic tradition with a specific focus on sport and athletic practices. The authors draw on the themes and ideas presented by Peirce, James, and Dewey to make sense of what we do when we engage in sporting practices. Some of the essays lean more toward Jamesian phenomenological description, others take a more traditional analytical approach to the questions with which they deal. Our hope is that these essays will show the usefulness of pragmatic thought and method for the philosophy of sport, and that they will engender response to and further exploration of the relating of pragmatism and sport.

NOTES

1. Christopher Hookway. *Truth Rationality and Pragmatism* (Oxford: Oxford University Press, 2002), 4.

2. See John J. McDermott's introduction to *Essays in Radical Empiricism: The Works of William James.* Eds. F. Burkhardt and F. Bowers (Cambridge: Harvard University Press, 1976).

3. William James. *Some Problems of Philosophy.* (Cambridge: Harvard University Press, 1979), 78.

4. William James. *Essays in Radical Empiricism.* (Lincoln: Bison Printing, 1996), 166.

5. John Dewey. *The Middle Works, 1899-1924.* (Carbondale: Southern Illinois University Press, 1899-24), 188.

6. . John Dewey. *Democracy and Education.* (New York: Macmillan and Company, 1916), 7.

7. William James. *Pragmatism.* (Indianapolis: Hackett Publishing, 1981). 61.

8. William James. *The Varieties of Religious Experience.* (New York: Mentor, 1958), 24.

9. Ibid. 39.

10. Henry Bugbee. *The Inward Morning.* (Athens: University of Georgia Press, 1999), 36.

11. Ibid. 37.

12. Ibid. 40.

13. See Mooney's introduction to *The Inward Morning.*

14. Quoted in Giovanna Barradori, *The American Philosopher* (Chicago: University of Chicago Press, 1994), 126.

15. In Henry Bugbee. *The Inward Morning.* (Athens: University of Georgia Press, 1999), xiv.

16. Ibid. 35.

17. William James. *Pragmatism.* (Indianapolis: Hackett Publishing, 1981), 92.

18. Ibid. 93.

19. William James. *Essays in Radical Empiricism.* (Lincoln: Bison Printing, 1996), 90-91.

20. William James. *Pragmatism.* (Indianapolis: Hackett Publishing, 1981), 29.

21. Peirce cited in Cheryl Misak. *Cambridge Companion to Peirce* (Cambridge: Cambridge University Press, 2004), 175.

22. John Dewey. *The Middle Works, 1899-1924.* (Carbondale: Southern Illinois University Press, 1899-24), 188.

23. Introduction to William James. *Essays in Radical Empiricism.* (Lincoln: Bison Printing, 1996), viii-ix.

24. Ibid. 107.

25. Ibid. xii.

26. Ibid.

27. Charles Peirce. *The Essential Peirce.* vol. 1. (Indianapolis: The Peirce Edition Project, 1998), 332.

28. Ibid. 403.

29. John Smith. *The Spirit of American Philosophy.* (Albany: State University of New York Press, 1983), 15.

30. John Dewey. *Philosophy and Civilization.* (New York: Capricorn, 1963), 23-24.

31. Charles Pierce. *The Essential Pierce.* Vol. 1 (Indianapolis: The Pierce Edition Project, 1998), 221.

32. Ibid.

33. William James. *Essays in Radical Empiricism.* (Lincoln: Bison Printing, 1996), 288.

34. William James. *Pragmatism.* (Indianapolis: Hackett Publishing, 1981), 296.

35. Ibid. 290.

36. William James. *The Varieties of Religious Experience.* (New York: Mentor, 1958), 408.

37. John Smith. *The Spirit of American Philosophy.* (Albany: State University of New York Press, 1983), 24.

38. Edward Moore. *William James.* (New York: Washington Square Press, 1965), 99.

39. William James. *Pragmatism.* (Indianapolis: Hackett Publishing, 1981), 118-119.

40. George Sheehan. *Dr. Sheehan on Fitness.* (New York: Simon & Schuster, 1983), 15.

41. Lance Armstrong. *It's Not about the Bike: My Journey Back to Life.* (New York: Putnam, 2000), 202.

ONE

Process and the Sport Experience

Douglas R. Hochstetler, Penn State University, Lehigh Valley

INTRODUCTION

In his article "Recovering Humanity: Movement, Sport, and Nature," Doug Anderson describes opportunities for humans to become re-created through the medium of movement and sport. Using the transcendentalists, and in particular Thoreau, to make his case, Anderson argues for the re-creative potential of movement. Participation in physical activity such as sport, particularly in nature, gets us away from what Anderson calls the "closure of civilization."[1]

Sport is not always viewed in this transformative light, however. The broader population in North America remains steadfastly focused on the product of competition. The largest concern is the end result, indicated primarily by numbers on the scoreboard. Gibson observed that "it is the blindness to internal goods in sport that leads to the valuation of results over performance. There is a quality of experience that can only be obtained through the practice of specific sports."[2] Yet many individuals miss the transformative power of sport as a practice. As Novak noted:

> There are priests who mumble through the Mass, lovers who read letters over a naked shoulder in love's embrace, teachers who detest students, pedants who shrink from original ideas. So also, there are athletes, fans, and sportswriters who never grasp the beauty or the treasure entrusted them.[3]

The purpose of this chapter is to suggest that process is an essential and often overlooked element in competition and sport. The process experi-

ence is fundamental in a logical sense, for *arriving at* ends such as winning or losing (products) entails many steps of *moving towards* (process).
In order to highlight the assets of process, I will focus on the nature of
struggle in sport. This is not a claim for competition without any concern
for winning. However, with today's excessive focus on the product, I
suggest we examine the process of sport. By emphasizing the process
element we may find many overlooked benefits for sport. I will also
suggest possibilities for developing process-sensitive sport.

Most of my experience as an athlete and coach has been at interscho-
lastic and intercollegiate levels. This is the type of competitive situation I
have in mind when I refer to sport. I recognize there are other venues for
competition, from informal backyard volleyball to the professional ranks.
Process certainly relates to these levels as well, albeit in different ways. It
is high school and college sport, however, that garner the focus of this
chapter.[4]

I. THE MEANING OF PROCESS

By process I mean the journey of sport experience—not only those end
points in sport (e.g., completing a period, crossing the finish line, besting
an archrival) but also those elements of sport that happen in-between, the
stages or phases of the competitive project. Each sport has its own competitive seasons, from pre-season to in-season to post-season to off-season. Process involves occurrences that happen during these time periods,
the changes of individual and team attitudes, values, and hopes. Process
also includes experiences—with other athletes, with coaches, with officials, opponents, and fans. These in-between periods and events are crucial for understanding and appreciating sport.

Athletes change over time. Their histories develop as they come in
contact with people, events, and ideas that impact their lives. Not all of
these occasions are major ones; some changes occur in relatively small
ways. As Novak contends, "most of an athletic career is prose, not poetry:
boredom and discipline, not drama."[5] Part of understanding sport then is
paying attention to the prose, the everyday, the arduous and repetitive,
the discipline. Sport understood in this manner focuses on *processes* rather than on *states of affairs*. The emphasis is on change, evolving experience, and striving rather than on the quiescence of achievement.

Philosopher Alfred Whitehead wrote at length about the importance
of process in human experience. In his book *Process and Reality*, Whitehead defined process as "the flux of things."[6] Later, Whitehead argued
that "the very essence of real actuality—that is, of the completely real—is
process. Thus each actual thing is only to be understood in terms of its
becoming and perishing."[7] Nancy Frankenberry compared the process
paradigm to cooking. She said, "Wherever one studies the production of

novel togetherness—whether in the physical, the biological, or the cultural dimensions of the universe—one finds the becoming of patterned process. To understand the Raw and the Cooked, one must theorize the Cooking as well."[8] Shifting to the sport arena, one could argue that in order to understand the untrained human being and the veteran athlete, it becomes important to theorize the training as well.

Process involves viewing products or end results such as winning and losing, home runs and strikeouts as part of the process as well. In one sense process is focused on the details of experiences. The runner focuses throughout an individual training run, cognizant of the tension in her hands, the sound of shoes treading upon a wood chip trail, split times at set intervals, and even her own thoughts and ruminations. Runners are conscious of every aspect of the running experience. In another sense, process involves a more 'distant lens' perspective, placing discrete experiences within the context of time and change. For example, the college pitcher is able to reflect on his athletic career, recognizing changes or shifts in his attitude toward baseball, the level of commitment to coaches, teammates, and the game, and also the development of both speed and accuracy of delivery. Experience allows this player to evaluate and reflect on individual moments against a backdrop of personal history.

In order to fully understand and evaluate process in sport, athletes must experience, recognize, and reflect on every aspect of sport. Wrong turns, traffic jams, and driving rain is just as much a part of the journey as interstate driving, air conditioning, and of course, getting there. All moments and discrete experiences are valuable in terms of understanding and appreciating the fullness of sport.

Relationship between Process and Product

Process and product, of course, are inherently related. If the process of sport is a journey, this implies that sport is shaped by one or more destinations. In turn, these end-products help to give direction and meaning to the journey itself. We value sport in part because we strive to win each contest or achieve a personal best. End points such as winning and losing are often described in terms of product, but are certainly part of the process as well. Athletes and coaches experience achievement and failure repeatedly throughout their competitive careers. These end points take on new meaning when viewed reflectively as part of the overall sport process. In this sense then, there is a distinct link between the process and product of sport.

Product (the end result) is also shaped in part by the process. I remember playing Little League baseball and our team winning a local championship. My memory of this result is tainted however because of the inappropriate behavior on the part of some of our fans. Parents routinely yelled both at umpires and at opposing players and coaches, at times even causing game stoppages. My teammates and I just wanted to play the game. The parents influenced the experience and ultimately the process, and we were left with a product (league championship) that was somewhat tarnished as a result.

On the other hand, if we have enjoyed or found meaning in the process, we are more likely to feel at peace with the outcome—regardless of the result. Our best experiences in sport—such as the "good sports contest"[9] described by Fraleigh—are times when we achieve excellence that is rich with aspects of the process. Even after winning a championship, or experiencing a successful season, we reflect on, and perhaps value most the process-aspects of sport. We remember teammates, discussions on bus trips, struggling through pre-season conditioning, brilliant performances, anticipation of the first day of practice, and of course the challenge and excitement of competition.

Exemplars of Process

Philosopher Henry David Thoreau provides an exemplar of the process-sensitive life. Writing in *Walden*, Thoreau said he wanted to:

> live deep and suck out all the marrow of life, to live so sturdily and Spartan-like as to put to rout all that was not life, to cut a broad swath and shave close, to drive life into a corner, and reduce it to its lowest terms, and, if it proved to be mean, why then to get the whole and genuine meanness of it, and publish its meanness to the world; or if it were sublime, to know it by experience.[10]

Thoreau focused on discrete moments of life around him. He had a broad appreciation for life, a deep understanding of the practice of living. He paid full attention to the detail of a variety of practices—surveying, making pencils, working as a handyman, and writing. As he walked throughout the woods he came in contact with various animals, plants, and other individuals as well. He was determined to experience as much of life as possible, both the good and the bad. Thoreau could be viewed as the consummate participant in the sense that he was not content to sit on the sidelines of life but was determined to play the entire game. He was also focused in a broader sense as well, placing the individual moments in the context of both his own experience and the world around him.

Thoreau spoke of experiencing life, partly through the process of change. He described the seasons—the warmth and light of summer, and of the harsh conditions of winter. Thoreau described winter not as a time of avoidance or neglect, but rather part of the natural process. His essay "Wild Apples" is a testament to this belief that harsh conditions generate an apple with a richer quality and, ultimately, a more unique taste. Thoreau admired the wild apples for they "have hung in the wind and frost and rain till they have absorbed the qualities of the weather or season, and thus are highly seasoned, and they pierce and sting and permeate us with their spirit."[11] Perhaps those athletes and coaches who fully experience the 'winter' of competition are wild and seasoned in a similar way.

There are, of course, sport practitioners who exemplify the process-sensitive life as well. One example is British miler Roger Bannister, the first human to break the four-minute mile barrier. After running the mile at White City Stadium, Bannister noted that running "expressed something of my attitude to life in the only way it could be expressed, and it was this that gave me the thrill. It was intensity of living, joy in struggle, freedom in toil, satisfaction at the mental and physical cost."[12] Bannister, even as a relatively young athlete, evidenced a deep appreciation and understanding of running as a practice and process.

There is no doubt that Bannister focused on the product, in the sense of seeking to win each contest. He took training seriously, dedicating himself to breaking the four minute mark, in addition to winning each race he entered. The product or end result did not consume him however. Bannister became keenly aware of, through his time as an athlete, much of the richness of movement. He wrote, "we run, not because we think it is doing us good, but because we enjoy it and cannot help ourselves . . . the urge to struggle lies latent in everyone."[13] Bannister realized the importance for humans to find a practice in which to participate.

Relationship between Process of Sport and 'Process Orientation'

Other professionals refer to sport and process as well. Sport psychologists frequently categorize athletes as either 'product oriented' or 'process oriented.' The product-oriented athlete values and finds meaning in the end result—usually winning. Along with winning, these individuals participate because of the tangible rewards and adulation, and view their competitors as obstacles. The process-oriented individual tends to place value on a broader scale, finding meaning in the activity itself. They emphasize aspects such as participation, striving for team or personal excellence, aesthetic sensitivity, and rapport with competitors.[14]

This psychological understanding of process orientation, however, falls short of what I term the process of sport. While it captures a greater share of the sport experience than does the product focus, and while process allows the athlete or coach to see the larger picture and importance of competition, it typically leaves out or undervalues some aspects of the sport experience, such as struggle, pain, boredom, grinding repetition, which are important in understanding the human significance of competition.

II. COMPETITION

Drew Hyland defined competition by looking at its root—'com-petitio' meaning "to question together, to strive together."[15] His aim was to reduce the element of alienation within competition, replacing it with the possibility and need for friendship. Alienation from opponents takes on a variety of modes ranging from mild irritation to all-out fights between competitors. Friendship, as Hyland describes it, involves pushing each other to achieve new heights and possibilities, the demand "that each be the best that he or she can be."[16] Hyland focused on the *together* part of competition. By way of contrast, my aim is to look at the *striving* part. Through this striving, expressed in terms of change over time, I want to suggest another possible approach to competition in order to realize the fullness and richness that is available. I want to examine the process aspect of sport—and in particular the part of the process of sport where struggle is most likely to occur.

As noted already, the process element is often overlooked. The majority of North American society focuses on scores, records, and statistics. Athletes and coaches direct energy to immediate tasks, setting short-term goals and aiming toward larger ones. Fans scan the sport pages to find how their favorite athlete or team performed. Fantasy football and baseball leagues derive meaning from individual player statistics and records.

Process, in this society, may be too abstract, too monotonous, or too slow for many people to recognize. Attention to this kind of detail, as Thoreau demonstrated by chronicling the tedious process of ice melting, takes great patience and powers of observation. Change is often subtle, with minor shifts and currents rather than cataclysmic events. Noticing the process of a single game is complex enough. It is much more difficult to examine the process of sport over the lifetime of an individual. The element of struggle, in particular, is overlooked and undervalued as well.

We value the struggle aspect of competition, as long as this struggle ends with victory. The media portrays stories of athletes who rise to athletic greatness from dismal conditions or unfortunate tragedy. But they rarely record the athletes and teams who struggle and do not succeed (Chicago Cubs notwithstanding), or even those who come close, like the Buffalo Bills or Boston Red Sox of the past.

It is not possible to completely delineate the entire range of process aspects of sport. These aspects are unique to individual sports, histories, and seasons. But it is important to outline a few of these aspects to begin. Sport is, after all, richly textured. Sport holds both the exciting and the drab—the brilliant touchdown completion and constant grinding in the trenches. Sport involves striving towards and achieving excellence[17] and also dwelling in the mediocre. Sport involves gaining knowledge[18] and also living with uncertainty and ambiguity. Sport involves developing friendships,[19] but at times it may also be a backdrop for isolation, distrust, and even alienation.

In sport we interact with people, with both the promise and uncertainty that such interactions bring. In sport we develop tenacity and perseverance. We learn to cope with injury and disappointment, and deal with success, failures, and events that are difficult to identify as either one. Sport provides, in many ways, the opportunity for conversation—during travel time, while on a training run, or even in the midst of competition. We may anticipate an upcoming event, wallow in a lost match, or relish the feeling of a well-placed shot. At times our legs may feel sluggish, weighted to the ground. At other times we may feel in control of our breathing, floating across the terrain. Sport holds too much to be reduced to the final outcome of competition alone. We attain only the breadcrumbs of sport's potential if we approach sport in this short-sighted way. It is reductionistic to place all of our attention on the product of competition. Our intent is to achieve excellence, gain knowledge, and develop friendships. But when we do not, the richness of sport may still entice us to participate. Through reflection we may realize this breadth of experience and place individual moments of struggle against a larger backdrop.

One aspect of the sport process, one noticeably absent from much attention, is struggle. By struggle I mean those moments of sport that are difficult, unpleasant—those times that are tough to endure. Struggle is one part of the becoming and perishing that practitioners experience. Through sport we become engaged with a variety of problems and undertakings. During competition we experience the mundane, boring, repetitive, tough, unpleasant, anxious, the inconsequential outcomes, and the defeats. When facing difficult situations and moments we change in the way we perceive teammates, opponents, the sport, and ourselves. By noting the importance of struggle, then, we may better understand the nature of competitive sport. Morford suggested three decades ago that sport had lost some of the agonistic qualities embraced by the Greeks. He argued that "we have made sport a place where I will prove myself rather than know myself—therefore, I must win, which is the outcome, not merely fight the good fight, which is the process."[20] This sense of proving oneself is evidenced in the verbal taunting, often referred to as "smack," which at times escalates into physical violence and bench-clearing brawls.

Individual attitudes vary with respect to struggle. Some view difficult times as an opportunity or challenge. The upstart Anaheim Angels faced the New York Yankees as clear underdogs in the 2002 American League Championship series, yet the Angels saw this problem as a tremendous opportunity. Others faced with struggle may view it as toil or despair (especially when the struggle happens over an extended period of time). When there is little joy in the doing, when the practice may even become unbearable, the practitioner may discontinue rather than persist in the struggle.

Struggle can also involve how one deals with an aspect of product, the winning and losing, achievement and failure. For instance, athletes at highly successful institutions may find it difficult to deal with the media pressure related to achievement. Coaches in these programs may be inundated with requests for speaking engagements and charity appearances. Struggle relates to the product in the sense of losing as well. In fact, struggle and losing seem to be more closely aligned. We think of teams that are going through a losing season as "struggling." Losing or even facing mediocrity is difficult and hard to endure as part of the sport process. As Roth wrote,

> Losing is tedious. Losing is exhausting. Losing is uninteresting. Losing is depressing. Losing is boring. Losing is debilitating. Losing is compromising. Losing is shameful. . . . The sooner we get rid of losing the happier everyone will be.[21]

Yet, competition logically entails the possibility of losing. Without this, after all, there would be no possibility of winning or of experiencing competitive sport.

The pursuit of excellence is a crucial approach to sport. Athletes in competitive sport, at all levels and in both individual and team competition, strive to perform to their best capabilities. Achieving excellence regularly may not always occur however. There may be times when, while aiming at excellence, we experience struggle through mediocre performance or even stinging defeat. How do we view those occasions when we do not attain excellence? Having a bad day on the golf course is not somehow less of a sporting experience than a bogey-free round. We may experience considerably less pleasure on these sub-par occasions, and might even be tempted to wrap our clubs around the nearest tree, but these times are not somehow non-sport or anti-sport. For a great majority of individuals, these are very much part of our sport experience. We do not have, nor should we expect, transcendent rounds every time we tee off. Yet when they do occur we relish the moment. While striving for excellence, we know that it is not possible to attain this level of perfection regularly. This is the nature of sport and life. Yet through these moments of struggle or mediocrity, the attentive and reflective practitioner may experience insight in ways previously unknown.

Consider a farming analogy, speaking to the value of struggle in our practices. Aldous Hawthorn wrote, "The struggle I have chosen is the undertaking of agriculture. This is no bleak prognosis. Farming is a molten thing, something that happens under extreme conditions. I like that my life is hewn. I like that what I have is earned. I like thickness and substance, both physical and spiritual, and that is what I have."[22] Sport too is molten, changing from practice to game to post-game, pre-season to in-season to post-season. Thickness and substance, and those individuals who represent these elements, are invaluable aspects of sport. We devote ourselves to a given sporting practice, and as a result we experience many things, including struggle as part of the sport process. This commitment to the practice helps us persevere when training sessions are repetitive, parents abusive, or injuries persistent.

At times struggle may appear especially barren. End results such as losing or experiencing mediocrity are not pleasant at all, and we certainly do not strive for these outcomes. Yet we experience defeat (as a product) and it becomes part of the sport process. Losing is, for the majority of practitioners, only too familiar, and certainly part of sport. Apart from competitions where ties are accepted, half of all teams experience defeat on any given day. For those in sports such as cross-country or bike racing, the percentage is even higher. Several hundred athletes may toe the start line, but only one crosses the finish line in first place.

By examining the struggle and in particular defeat in sport, I certainly am not recommending we try to look for ways to lose, in order to somehow struggle and experience more of life. Those players and coaches who always win are not somehow deficient in character. Yet these same individuals are missing an aspect of life that others, those that have experienced defeat, understand and even sometimes come to accept. There is a certain amount of knowledge available through the medium of struggle in sport. Through adversity athletes and coaches may learn about perseverance, team unity, or individual drive. In fact, these individuals may even find they learn more about themselves through struggle than through times of success. Novak, for example, recommended that one enter into rather than avoid defeat, to learn from defeat, not only to get better and win the next time but to know more as well. He wanted to soak in the experience of losing rather than quickly dismiss it. Novak, like Thoreau, realized that struggle is a part of living. This said, we do not have to like defeat in order to learn from it and learn more about the thickness and substance of sport. By the same token, those individuals who never experience a taste of success are missing a key ingredient in the sport experience. Those who have only experienced the struggle of losing are incomplete without experiencing the 'struggle' of victory as well.

We certainly need not abandon or ignore sport that constitutes some aspect of struggle, for it is part of sport. After all, the very nature of competition necessitates struggle against an opponent. Not all of our training runs can be transcendent or even pleasurable. Certainly we hope to experience, at least on occasion, some of the sublime, but this may not occur every day. There may be seasons of struggle, when practices are long and experiences of victory almost non-existent. These periods, like the winter described by Thoreau, are full of "dark and sluggish hours." But the winter season, of life and sport, is part of our experience nonetheless. Struggle also provides avenues for hope and opportunity to surface as well. Individuals who persist in times of trial inspire others to remain steadfast, committed to each other and their sport.

III. DEVELOPMENT OF PROCESS-FOCUSED COMPETITION

If the process element of sport is to be valued, then there must be tangible ways to encourage and develop this type of mind-set. One possibility is for practitioners to cultivate relationships with their practice.[23] In this way athletes focus on their sport as a craft, and upon reflection understand and appreciate the process. For runners, this involves learning about running—from training principles to nutrition guidelines to race strategies. These individuals strive to excel in their activity, setting goals and creating plans to achieve them. Through time, and over years of involvement with a particular sport, athletes can then experience a deeper appreciation for their practice and the experiential process. This may not happen with all athletes of course. Some remain chained to a focus on the results. Others however, through time, may develop the same kind of detailed focus that Bannister achieved with his running. Once this sense of perception is developed, the athlete is in a much better position to both realize and value sport as a process.

The deeper the relationship with the practice and movement subculture,[24] the more likely that practitioners will appreciate the intricacies and finer points of the practice. Phil Jackson, former coach of the Los Angeles Lakers and the Chicago Bulls, exemplifies how coaches might foster this kind of appreciation with their athletes. Jackson recognizes the importance of attentiveness in this attitude. He writes that in "basketball—as in life—true joy comes from being fully present in each and every moment, not just when things are going your way."[25] Jackson also realizes that in order for his players to realize the process, they need to become attentive to the practice. Unlike many coaches, Jackson limits his comments to players during games. During these times he wants them to disconnect from him so they can connect with their teammates and basketball. Jackson constantly emphasizes the process aspect of sport with his players, creating training sessions with the intention of having his players become reacquainted with the spirit of play. He is not afraid of using unorthodox coaching methods in order to get this point across. At times, to promote the concept of mindfulness, his teams have conducted practice sessions in silence, in order to promote concentration and nonverbal communication. For Jackson, the primary concern is with the practice of basketball. His love affair is with the activity rather than the result or winning. Jackson has been extremely successful in terms of product; he, unlike many coaches, however, sees past the narrow-minded product-only focus.

Of course in order for coaches to emphasize the process aspect of sport, they must have administrators (i.e., athletic directors, principals) who value the process as well. The administrator must place confidence in the coach and allow him/her the freedom to coach. These individuals need to provide job security for the coach, long enough for the coach to develop his/her own program. Short-term contracts may encourage coaches to take shortcuts in achieving excellence, quick fixes to win rather than a sustained effort towards a goal within a process-sensitive environment. Of course a coach needs to make progress with the team, be working towards and at times experiencing excellence as well in order for many of the process elements to come about.

Another method of promoting the process element of sport is for athletes to reflect on the process as they play. Cyclists might recognize the thrill of sprinting to catch the lead pack during a race or team practice or the smells of a newly mown field of hay. The golfer might notice the feel of a solid hit or attend to a deer skirting across the fairway at dusk. Coaches can teach not only strategy, skills, and so forth but also the aesthetic element of sport. Athletes can tune into these feelings, taking in as much as they can from their sport experience.

There are several possibilities for teaching athletes to appreciate the process of sport. On the individual level, coaches and experienced athletes can share their own journey in their respective sport. Doing so inspires others to think of personal experiences as well. In terms of institutional levels, teaching a process-sensitive approach to sport would best be done at the youth sport levels. At this age athletes are still likely to be enamored by the activity itself, perhaps not as apt to be engrained with the 'winning-is-everything' mentality. If these children are able to appreciate the process aspect of sport, hopefully their experience will transfer to the high school and college levels as well, and on throughout their lives.

Reflection is certainly a key element in recognizing the process element in sport. One way for athletes to notice the process elements of sport—both the discrete moments and also the subtle changes—is through keeping a journal. This log may take on many forms, from a diary of events to thoughts on sport and life. Regardless of the style, the journal allows athletes to reflect on their sport experiences. This act of writing and thinking about the experience may enable the individual to realize aspects of sport that may have otherwise remained latent.

A final method of promoting process in sport is through narrative (i.e., biography or autobiography). In this way the journey of individual athletes, coaches, or teams can be ascertained, with the focus being on the gamut of sport experience. Many fans enjoy reading about their favorite athlete or coach in order to find out their secret for success, or just to get a behind-the-scenes look into their lives. Those athletes or coaches who struggle in terms of achieving excellence rarely have their experience chronicled. To accurately represent the range of sport experiences, and the process therein, there must be an avenue for telling the stories of these individuals. A recent example of this type of story is told by Phil Conroy in his book *My Losing Season*.[26] Conroy, author of *The Lords of Discipline* and *The Prince of Tides,* writes about his experience as a basketball player for the Citadel during the 1960s. During this season, Conroy learns about himself, his teammates, the game of basketball, and competitive sport in general.

Developing experience with anything—people, career, and sport—happens over an extended period of time. Smith wrote that "no item reveals itself fully and completely in an instant or in one encounter; repeated encounter is necessary, and this means that experience requires time and is involved in change."[27] Some only realize the process of sport once their playing days are over. Tex Sample provides an example, reflecting on his experience as a baseball player:

> I played too much with my will, whatever in hell that is. I was so determined to win, to do it right, that I missed too many opportunities to play out of my desire or, when I did so, I played out of a distorted desire. I tried too hard to prove too much and missed the chance to play. I channeled too much of my passion into determination and overwhelmed the aesthetic flows of the game. I am making no claim that I would have played better, though it is hard to believe that I could not have played a little better since I was as bad as I was. But I would have played differently. My love of the game would not have been so consumed in extrinsic efforts to prove my manhood or to be a winner. Winning would not be eliminated, but had I enjoyed the dance more, the end of the ball would have taken a different turn.[28]

Sport viewed in this light becomes a dance whereby intricate moves, the companionship of a partner, and feelings of exhaustion and exhilaration are appreciated as much as the outcome of a dance competition.

IV. THE UPSHOT OF PROCESS FOR SPORT

It seems to me that appreciating or emphasizing process in sport has several tangible benefits. First, process gives credence to the variety of sport experiences available, a testimony to the richness of sport. It acknowledges the journey rather than only the result. As Scott Kretchmar notes, "Athletes look forward to having won, yet do not want this condition to come too easily or quickly. The end of a contest, though it brings with it some knowledge, is also frequently experienced with a sense of loss."[29]

Participants do find meaning in the process of sport. They realize that competition includes many aspects and moments, but these experiences often appear dim when placed against the final result. Writer and runner

Amby Burfoot writes about process in his running journals: "They [running journals] accept all workouts equally, the low key and boring as well as the sensational. Ninety-nine percent of the runs in my life have been unexceptional, and that's just fine with me. Looking back over them, they feel familiar, like a well-worn flannel shirt."[30] There is a sense that acknowledging the process in sport encourages us to continue our participation, even when the results may not be pleasant or desirable. Through commitment to the sport we begin to see the gamut of available sport experiences.

By viewing sport in terms of process, we begin to view the continuum of experience as an integral part of sport rather than relegated to tangential status. We recognize the variety of experiences in sport, rather than repressing those aspects that may be nondescript or unpleasant. Like Thoreau, we pay attention to every season, attuned to the subtleties of change in winter as well as summer. In this way, the sport experience increases its richness in ways similar to Thoreau's wild apples. It may be difficult to appreciate the boring, the tedious, and the strenuous. These aspects are, however, part of the sport experience just the same. To paraphrase Whitehead, sport is only to be understood in terms of its becoming and perishing. When we realize the subtleties of the sport process we gain a deeper appreciation for the activity.

Viewing competition through the lens of process also provides meaning for the difficult moments. This enables athletes who experience injury, defeat, or arguments with teammates to place these situations in a larger context. Frankl uses the analogy of a movie to explain this phenomenon. A movie "consists of thousands upon thousands of individual pictures, and each of them makes sense and carries a meaning, yet the meaning of the whole film cannot be seen before its last sequence is shown. However, we cannot understand the whole film without having first understood each of its components, each of the individual pictures."[31] It is when we view sport experience as a process that we can understand the meaning of individual frames or moments. By acknowledging the process aspect, we can experience sport in its entirety rather than avoid the unpleasant. This is not to say we seek out sporting moments of struggle any more than one might seek out an illness or serious injury. When we do experience these times of struggle, however, we realize that these moments are part of sport—and life—and we proceed with a deeper understanding of our humanity.

Finally, through the aspect of process, we have a deeper value of sport and respect for rules and the craft. If winning, the end product, is the only aspect of sport worth seeking or appreciating, then it becomes tempting to take short cuts in the pursuit of victory. This 'win-at-all-costs' mentality is certainly prevalent today, with many ethical consequences. If, however, we view process as central to the sport experience, then we may agree with Fraleigh, that someone who appreciates the process of

competition may be able to acknowledge the "good sports contest"—
perhaps the process focus even encourages or creates room for the good
sports contest. Those who respect the process will take intentional steps
to uphold their respective sport. They will work diligently to preserve
both the tests and contests[32] of their respective sports.

In conclusion, if the process of competition (the journey of various
sport experiences) is inherently linked to the product of competition
(achievement and failure), then it is important to further examine the
product in light of the process. Perhaps there is greater complexity and
richness in the end result of sport, just as is the case with the process of
sport. This examination might place the experience of product in a different light.

NOTES

1. Douglas Anderson, "Recovering Humanity: Movement, Sport, and Nature," *Journal of the Philosophy of Sport* 28, (2001): 140-150.
2. John Gibson, *Performance versus Results: A Critique of Values in Contemporary Sport* (Albany: State University of New York Press, 1993), 72.
3. Michael Novak, *The Joy of Sports: End Zones, Bases, Baskets, Balls, and the Conse-cration of the American Spirit* (New York: Basic Books, 1976), 121.
4. There are also different types of intercollegiate athletic programs as well, from the Division III model to what some refer to as the "Big-Time" athletic model of Division I—where football and men's basketball reign supreme.
5. Novak, 159.
6. Alfred Whitehead, *Process and Reality: An Essay in Cosmology* (New York: Free Press, 1969), 240.
7. Alfred Whitehead, *Adventure in Ideas* (New York: Free Press, 1961), 274.
8. Nancy Frankenberry, "The Process Paradigm, Rites of Passage, and Spiritual Quests," *Process Studies* 29, (2000): 352-353.
9. Fraleigh describes a badminton contest between two individuals as an example of what he terms a "good sports contest." The game is exemplary in terms of the level of play, competitiveness of opponents, and the display of sportsmanship. Having described this contest, Fraleigh goes on to develop a normative theory for sport in the book *Right Actions in Sport*.
10. Henry Thoreau, *The Portable Thoreau* (New York: Penguin, 1982), 344.
11. Henry Thoreau, "Wild Apples," *The Writings of Henry David Thoreau (Vol. 10)* (Boston: Houghton, Mifflin & Co., 1854), 382-383.
12. Roger Bannister, *The Four Minute Mile* (New York: Dodd, Mead & Company, 1955), 59.
13. Bannister, 248-249.
14. Arnold LeUnes & Jack Nation, *Sport Psychology: An Introduction* (Pacific Grove, CA: Wadsworth, 2002).
15. Drew Hyland, "Competition and Friendship," in William Morgan & Klaus Meier (Eds.), *Philosophic Inquiry in Sport* (Champaign, IL: Human Kinetics, 1988), 231-239.
16. Hyland, 236.
17. Robert Simon, *Fair Play: Sports, Values & Society* (Boulder, CO: Westview Press, 1991).
18. Warren Fraleigh, *Right Actions in Sport: Ethics for Contestants* (Champaign, IL: Human Kinetics, 1984).
19. Hyland.

20. W. R. Morford, "Is Sport the Struggle or the Triumph?" *Quest* 19, (1973): 83-87.

21. Philip Roth, *The Great American Novel* (New York: Holt, Rinehart & Winston, 1973), 287-288.

22. A. Hawthorn, "Viewfinder," *Farm and Ranch Living,* (June/July 2002), 33-34.

23. Alasdair MacIntyre, *After Virtue* (Notre Dame, IN: University of Notre Dame Press, 1981).

24. R. Scott Kretchmar, "Movement Sub-cultures: Sites for Meaning," *Journal of Physical Education, Recreation & Dance,* 71, no. 5 (2000).

25. Phil Jackson, *Sacred Hoops: Spiritual Lessons of a Hardwood Warrior* (New York: Hyperion, 1995), 4.

26. Phil Conroy, *My Losing Season* (New York: Nan A. Talese/Doubleday, 2002).

27. John Smith, *Experience and God* (New York: Oxford University Press, 1968), 30.

28. Tex Sample, "Baseball: A Spiritual Reminiscence," in Christopher Evans & William Herzog (Eds.) *The Faith of Fifty Million: Baseball, Religion, and American Culture* (Louisville, KY: Westminster John Knox Press, 2002), 211-212.

29. R. Scott Kretchmar, "The Strange Supremacy of Knowledge in Sport from the Moral Point of View: A Response to Fraleigh," *Journal of the Philosophy of Sport* 8, (1986): 85.

30. Amby Burfoot, "A Runner's Best Friend," *Runner's World Magazine* 37, no. 10 (2002): 75.

31. Viktor Frankl, *Man's Search for Meaning* (New York: Washington Square Press, 1984), 168.

32. R. Scott Kretchmar, "From Test to Contest: An Analysis of Two Kinds of Counterpoint in Sport," *Journal of the Philosophy of Sport* 2 (1975): 23-30.

TWO

Peircean Reflections on the Personality of a *Fútbol Club*

Daniel G. Campos, Brooklyn College of The City University of New York

The fortunes and misfortunes of sporting clubs forcibly and ostensibly affect the sentiments of players and fans. We know the experience of exhilaration or heartbreak that results from the successes and failures of our teams. In remembering a *fútbol* defeat of his Peruvian club, *Universitario de Deportes*, against Brazilian club São Paulo, Julio Ramón Ribeyro writes: "*Quien no conoce las tristezas deportivas no conoce nada de la tristeza.*"[1] The experience of anguish and sadness is especially acute when one's club is under danger of disappearing or in fact ceases to be. Alfredo Bryce Echenique's Peruvian club, *Ciclista Lima Association*, was demoted from First to Third division; eventually it disappeared. Years later, when *Ciclista Lima* has been forgotten everywhere but in the hearts and minds of its former fans, Bryce Echenique takes much offense when his friend, Abelardo Sánchez, affirms that Bryce's allegiance is to some other Peruvian club, "*como si el Ciclista Lima Association y yo jamás hubiésemos existido uno para el otro . . . ¡Qué grave error, mi querido Abelardo! Desaparecieron el estadio nacional aquel y tantas cosas más. Pero . . . ¿El Ciclista Lima Association desaparecer del fútbol peruano y de mi corazón . . . ?*"[2] Bryce Echenique's club could never disappear from his heart. It is this experience of a real, heartfelt connection between players, fans, and their clubs that motivates and underlies the following reflections.

I propose to examine here a *live* question that, as an *ex-jugador* and *aficionado* of a *fútbol club*, I believe concerns players and fans of sports clubs in general. My question regards the evolution in institutional personality of sports clubs and the crises of allegiance that, for players and fans, might ensue when the institutional identity of their club is threatened in some way. In this case, I propose to inquire philosophically into the evolving personality of my *fútbol club*—the club for which I played as a minor leaguer, which I followed while growing up in Costa Rica and even after I emigrated, and which I continue to love. More generally, however, the case study I undertake here concerns the effective ontological status of sports clubs, that is, their nature as entities that have effective practical bearings in the world. It examines the reasons why players and fans experience real affective relationships with such clubs, and the reasons why such relationships might be severed, leaving fans and players heartbroken. And so my question today goes to the heart of one of the *living* matters that a pragmatist philosophy of sport might address.

The *Club Deportivo Saprissa* was founded in 1935 in a shoe-repair shop in San José, Costa Rica, by a group of young players under the direction of Roberto Fernández, a minor league coach devoted to the formation of young players in the practice of good *fútbol*.[3] Meeting at the shop on July 16, the players decided to name the club after Ricardo Saprissa Aymá, a former international player of tennis, hockey, and *fútbol*, and former captain of the *Real Club Deportivo Espanyol* from Barcelona, Spain. *Don Ricardo*, as he is still fondly remembered by all *saprissistas* even today, showed great love and devotion for the club immediately, and he fostered the upbringing of several generations of minor league players and presided over many seasons of good *fútbol* and competitive success, including several national and international titles at all levels, from the minor to the major leagues. He presided over the club's rise to Costa Rica's first division in 1949, the club's playing tour around the world in 1959, and the construction of the *Estadio Ricardo Saprissa*, inaugurated in 1972. The last years of his presidency witnessed the progressive change from amateurism to professionalism in the upper divisions of the club. After *don Ricardo*'s retirement from the presidency in 1981, the club began to lose its emphasis on forming and providing opportunities for young players, increasingly opting to buy players from other clubs to play in its first division. An institutional crisis ensued—the sporting results were poor as the club played the worst *fútbol* of its history while acquiring burdensome debt. The crisis was longstanding: the club continued to accumulate debt, even if it continued to be popular and even if in the 1990s it won some national and international titles with many players bought from other teams and some players promoted from the minor leagues.

To resolve the financial crisis, in 2002 the club changed its legal status from an *asociación deportiva*, in which the club had *asociados* with one vote and players could be members of the *asociación*, to a *sociedad anónima deportiva*, in which *socios* have as many votes as the shares they own and players are not part of the *sociedad* unless they buy shares. In 2003, a Mexican multinational company bought 51 percent of the shares. The purchase saved the club from bankruptcy. The corporate president has promised to respect the identity and history of the club while turning it into a profitable enterprise, but journalists, players, and fans debate the club's new identity. A Mexican journalist puts the poignant question to all *saprissistas*: are you fans of a *fútbol club* or of a brand?[4] This question is a lively issue in Costa Rican football. I approach it as a metaphysical question by asking whether in changing from an *asociación* into a *sociedad anónima*, with all the related social and sporting changes, the club has become an entirely different entity, severed from its vital history. In so doing, as a former minor league player and as a fan I ponder whether the club *continues* to be that club to which I have experienced a real affective relationship or whether it is a different entity to which I no longer have any real connections. At stake for me, as for any player or fan, is whether there is any real connection grounding a relationship of allegiance to the club, or whether the real connections that used to underlie that allegiance have been severed so that the only remaining reason to remain allied is brand preference in a sports market.

Following the metaphysics of C. S. Peirce, articulated in his series of essays known as the *Monist* series of the 1890s, I propose that a *fútbol club* has a real personality, that is, a real "coordination or connection of ideas" that are continuous with each other and that develop toward a *telos*.[5] The question, therefore, is whether, in spite of the institutional changes, in the *Club Deportivo Saprissa* there is a continuity of personality, in the Peircean sense of a *real* connection of ideas that evolve toward general ends. Let us first clarify the Peircean conception of personality and then evaluate the case of the *Deportivo Saprissa*, before drawing some general conclusions about sympathy and affinity between players, fans, and their sports clubs.

I. THE PEIRCEAN CONCEPTION OF PERSONALITY

For C. S. Peirce, "there is but one law of mind, namely, that ideas tend to spread continuously and to affect certain others which stand to them in a peculiar relation of affectibility. In this spreading they . . . gain generality and become welded with other ideas."[6] According to this law, the continuity and mutual affectibility of ideas is *real* and *effective* in the world. Particular ideas, in their interrelation, really do become integrated into general ideas that have practical bearings and concrete effects in the world. According to Peirce, an idea is made up of three elements. The first element is the idea's intrinsic quality as a feeling—immediate, intense, and spontaneous. The second is its energy to affect other ideas—in other words, its element of relation and reaction. The third is the tendency to bring other ideas along with it—that is, its tendency to become general by way of continuity and integration with other ideas.[7] Recognizing, either logically or phenomenologically, that these are the three constitutive elements of an idea allows us to perceive that "instantaneous feelings flow together into a continuum of feeling, which has in a modified degree the peculiar vivacity of feeling and has gained generality."[8] Peirce emphasizes that a nominalist, individualist account of ideas makes the simplest facts of mind, such as a continuum of feeling across space and time or the influence of one idea upon another, meaningless, since it provides no reason for the relatedness and connectedness of discrete ideas even in an individual mind. Under a nominalist account of ideas, that is, there is no explanation for the integration of discrete ideas into a continuum of sensual and reasoning experience across space and time that individual persons do undergo. Thus, insisting on the reality of general ideas, Peirce writes: "These general ideas are not mere words . . . but they are just as much, or rather far more, living realities than the feelings themselves out of which they are concreted."[9] A general idea is a "living idea, a conscious continuum of feeling."[10] It is more real and vital than an immediate feeling because a general idea is continuous across space and time.

It is precisely from the continuity of a general idea that Peirce's conception of personality follows:

> [P]ersonality is some kind of coordination or connection of ideas . . . .[W]hen we consider that . . . a connection between ideas is itself a general idea, and that a general idea is a living feeling, it is plain that we have at least taken an appreciable step toward the understanding of personality. This personality, like any general idea, is not a thing to be apprehended in an instant. It has to be lived in time; nor can any finite time embrace it in all its fullness. Yet in each infinitesimal interval, it is present and living, though especially colored by the immediate feelings of that moment. Personality, so far as it is apprehended in a moment, is immediate self-consciousness.[11]

For our present purposes, I wish to emphasize two aspects of the foregoing Peircean conception of personality. First, that a personality is a general idea means that it is a general kind that needs to be specified. The development of personality is the continuous evolution of the general idea as it progresses from one particular specification into another. The key to the continuity of personality is that each successive specification continuously grows out of each preceding specification. When a personality evolves into a new particular expression, the change is not a rupture but a vital development. Living practice brings progressive clarity and specificity to the personality. Second, the personality as a general idea has to be lived in time. At any given infinitesimal interval of time, a personality is a living idea apprehended as the immediate feeling of that very instant. However, a personality is not merely the immediacy of feeling but also the relatedness and continuity of ideas. Otherwise, the conscious apprehension of personality would arise and vanish at every instant. Thus Peirce continues:

> But the word coordination implies somewhat more than this [immediate self-consciousness]; it implies a teleological harmony in ideas, and in the case of personality this teleology is more than a mere purposive pursuit of a predeterminate end; it is a developmental teleology. This is personal character. A general idea, living and conscious now, it is already determinative of acts in the future to an extent to which it is not now conscious . . . .This reference to the future is an essential element of personality. Were the ends of a person already explicit, there would be no room for development, for growth, for life; and consequently there would be no personality. The mere carrying out of predeterminate purposes is mechanical. [12]

The evolution of personality is not fortuitous variation but developmental teleology. Directionality is inherent in personality. The *telos* is constitutive of personality; that is, the ends and aims towards which a personality evolves inhere in the very vital constitution of that personality. For Peirce, however, the ends are not predetermined, but rather develop as the personality develops. A personality has a *telos* that is antecedently operative but not antecedently fixed. [13] That is, a *telos* provides order and directionality to the evolution of personality, but constrains neither growth nor creativity in giving new expression to personality. If this were not the case, the living practices of the person would be merely the mechanical fulfillment of predeterminate purposes. Even the very ends of a living personality expand as living practices creatively evolve, develop, and grow. This conception of personality, then, accords with Peirce's "thorough-going evolutionism"—not only the specifications of organic entities evolve, but also their general ends, and indeed the very laws and ends of nature.

In the case of human individuals it is clear, I think, how personality may be conceived as developmental teleology—as directional, creative evolution. At the very least, it seems safe to hold this conception of personality as a live hypothesis. Our personhood consists in the continuous, temporal specification of our individual personalities as each of us evolves towards his or her general ends; and as we live our lives, the very aims that provide directionality to our living evolve as well. For Peirce, however, a personality is a continuity of coordinated ideas that may extend beyond an individual into a 'corporation.' [14] From the hypothesis that "[a]ll that is necessary . . . to the existence of a person is that the feelings out of which he is constructed should be in close connection to influence one another," he draws "a consequence which it may be possible to submit to experimental test." [15] He elaborates on the consequence:

> Namely, if this [hypothesis] be the case, there should be something like personal consciousness in bodies of men who are in intimate and in-

tensely sympathetic communion. It is true that when the generalisation of feeling has been carried so far as to include all within a person, a stopping-place, in a certain sense, has been attained; and further generalisation will have a less lively character. But we must not think it will cease. *Esprit de corps* . . . sym-pathy, are no mere metaphors. None of us can fully realize what the minds of corporations are, any more than one of my brain-cells can know what the whole brain is thinking. But the law of mind clearly points to the existence of such personalities, and there are many ordinary observations which, if they were critically examined and supplemented by special experiments, might, as first appearances promise, give evidence of the influence of such greater persons upon individuals. [16]

In short, if personality is a teleological coordination of ideas, and if ideas can really and effectively influence each other among human individuals with common feelings and ends, it is conceivable that corporate personalities—understood as the teleological, evolving coördination of ideas of a community—are real. It is this hypothetical conception of a corporate personality that I wish to take seriously in examining the case of the personality of the *Club Deportivo Saprissa*.

II. THE PERSONALITY OF THE *CLUB DEPORTIVO SAPRISSA*

Let us turn, then, to an examination of this case. In Peircean terms, the fundamental question becomes whether the change from an *asociación deportiva* into a *sociedad anónima deportiva* is a change in specification of the club's personality that is part of its continuous evolution towards its dynamic *telos*. The following considerations incline me to think that this continuity in personality is in fact the case.

In my estimation, the personality of the club consists in the unity of players, coaches, executives, and fans in endeavors at all levels, from minor to professional leagues, that aim towards sporting excellence. This holds even if the particular institutional shape of this unified endeavor may change over time. The founding coach and players aimed at creating a club that would play competitive *fútbol* with grace and commitment. This sporting purpose, I submit, is the *telos* that provides directionality and continuity to the personality of the club. Prior to the foundation of the club, Coach "Beto" Fernández scouted players in *La Sabana*—a public, metropolitan park for the practice of various sports in San José. The best players that he could recruit united to found the club in 1935, and they immediately began to compete in the *campeonatos infantiles*, or under-17 tournaments. Ricardo Saprissa, the distinguished athlete after whom the club was named, fostered their practice of a graceful, offensive-styled *fútbol*. By 1937, the club competed in under-17 and under-19 tournaments. In 1940 and 1941, directed by *don Ricardo* and coached by Fernández, the club played and won its first international youth tournament in El Salvador. Between 1935 and 1947, *Deportivo Saprissa* won eleven *infantil* and nine *juvenil* championships in Costa Rica and three international tournaments.

I recount these historical facts to argue that, from its origins, the unified purpose of the coaches and players is to play graceful, offensive *fútbol* and to compete well. In embracing the club, Ricardo Saprissa embraced this general idea and felt a real *affinity*, or community of ends, with the players. In order to pursue the club's end, the initial specification of the club was at the level of minor leagues, first *infantiles* and then *juveniles*. At this stage, the *telos* of the club was already operative, even though it was not fixed; just as the club's specific personality was not fixed. In 1947, the club began to compete in Costa Rica's Third Division, that is, in the lowest tier of the major divisions. The club won all twenty-two games and ascended to Second Division. In 1948, *Deportivo Saprissa* lost the decisive game against *Gimnástica Española*, and did not win the promotion to First Division. The *Federación Costarricense de Fútbol*, however, considering that the club's increasing popularity in San José and Ricardo Saprissa's name would make the first division tournament more competitive and attractive, promoted the team anyway, and in 1949 *Deportivo Saprissa* played its debut season in the First Division. Since then, the club has competed every year, at all minor levels and in First Division. The 1947 affiliation of the *Club Deportivo Saprissa* to the *Federación Costarricense de Fútbol* at the level of major divisions constituted a new specification of the club's personality, but in no way altered the general *telos* of the club.

By reviewing the initial specifications of the club's personality, I want to emphasize that the club's unified purpose, the general idea that functions as its *telos* from its very origins, consists in fostering the excellent practice of *fútbol* in competition at all levels. Now, I suggest that there is preliminary evidence that this end continues to guide the growth of the club even under its most recent specification as a *sociedad anónima deportiva*. In fact, it may be that the under the new specification, there is a stronger emphasis on the formation of players from the minor divisions. As I already mentioned, in the 1980s the club began to hire more players brought up to first division by other teams and to provide fewer opportunities for its own youth players. I will appeal to my own experience as a pragmatic test. When I played in the minor divisions in the 1980s, I had good opportunities to play, including some international tournaments, and I had coaches, including former first-division players, who helped us to play *fútbol* with good technique and tactics. However, the pervasive feeling among players was that the club provided very few opportunities in the major divisions. I knew I was not skilled enough to aim at playing at that level, but some of my teammates were, and the prospect of few opportunities was discouraging. Setting aside my experience, one just needed to look at the starting first-division squad every Sunday to realize that most players were not from the minor leagues. The consequences were evident—*Deportivo Saprissa* was often at the middle of the pack and playing graceless *fútbol* from one season to the next. This leads me to hypothesize, though only in passing here, that the corporate personality of a *fútbol club* is actualized in the way it plays on the football field, and that, when the club is an example of the dis-coordination of ideas among directors, coaches, and players, that very dis-coordination is actualized in team play. As with the Saprissa of the '80s, the lack of real, effective 'sympathy' or 'feeling-with' was expressed in the team's play on the pitch.

In contrast to the foregoing situation, there now seems to be renewed emphasis on forming and promoting players from the lower divisions. In the club's first season under the new institutional arrangement, there was a directive not to hire foreign players in order to provide opportunities to young players from the club, many of whom have played for Costa Rica in recent FIFA Youth World Cups. Moreover, the new president, Jorge Vergara, declared that the aim of the club is to become a more comprehensive sports club for the promotion of Olympic-level excellence in gymnastics, track and field, and other sports. It remains to be seen whether this idea becomes actualized. But to the extent that this idea is effective, that is, to the extent that it already causes and directs present practices in the club, such as the planning of comprehensive sports facilities and the continuing support of the non-traditional women's *fútbol* at the minor league level, I can say from a Peircean standpoint that the idea is real and that it constitutes an evolutionary development of the *telos* of the club. There is reason to suggest that this *telos* is growing and evolving toward the fostering of sporting excellence of its athletes at all levels and in a variety of sports. The corresponding personality of the club becomes the coordination of ideas of directors, coaches, and athletes that effectively directs the club's practices towards this evolved end.

Moreover, any athletes who genuinely embrace this *telos* as the guiding principle of their sporting practices may genuinely become a part of the club and may authentically become an effective part of the club's personality. This possibility of embracing the club's aims allows for the possibility that players from other clubs could in all honesty and earnestly be attracted to *Deportivo Saprissa*. The club need not be a completely hermetic entity, closed off to any players who have not been brought up within its minor leagues. It is natural and desirable that any club should be open and flexible so as to incorporate players who 'feel-with' it. In the case of *Deportivo Saprissa*, my foregoing argument suggests that the primary reason for the incorporation of other players be a real commitment to playing graceful, offensive-minded *fútbol*, and not merely or primarily the promise of a high salary. This may sound naïve, but this "naiveté" or belief may be required in maintaining the integrity of the club's personality.

There are reasons, however, to consider whether the change from an *asociación deportiva* into a *sociedad anónima deportiva* in reality constitutes a rupture in the continuous evolution of the club's personality so that the new institution is an entirely different entity with an entirely different, discontinuous personality. The most salient issue is whether the *telos* of the club as a private, capital-based enterprise is severed from the club's constitutive ends. As Peirce himself points out repeatedly, the question of ends is both an aesthetic and ethical question for it is always a question of what is *the good* and how we ought to pursue this *good* deliberately; in this case, the question is what is *the good* of a *fútbol club* and how ought the club pursue its *good*. As owners of shares of a *sociedad anónima deportiva*, the *socios* of the club stand to gain profit from it. It is one of their explicit aims to turn the *Deportivo Saprissa* into a profitable business, given its enormous popularity in Costa Rica. Is it the case, then, that the constitutive ends of the club have been disrupted and that the aims of the new institution are not in harmony with the *good* ends of a *fútbol club*? Paraphrasing the provoking question of Mexican journalist Francisco San José, are the *good* ends of a *fútbol club* compatible with the ends of a business that sells a brand?

In my estimation, if profit-making were to become the dominating, overriding *telos* so as to subjugate the *telos* of practicing sporting excellence, then the new aims would be incompatible with the former ends and there would result a disharmony of ideas among directors, coaches, and players. Young players, especially, would become merely prospective products—they would be formed or discarded according to their prospects of becoming a marketable product. As a fan, I would merely be following whether the particular brand that I happen to buy through tickets, media audience, or replica jerseys, is the most successful brand available in the market. If this were so, my sporting heart would break, because then I would no longer 'sym-pathize' or 'feel-with' a club but purchase a brand. Stated most forcefully, a club that was founded in a shoe-repair shop in a humble San José neighborhood and that is followed most widely by the working class, would have become primarily a capitalist money-making scheme.

Nonetheless, I think there is no *necessary* incompatibility and disharmony of ends in the *Deportivo Saprissa* as a *sociedad anónima deportiva*. The club may continue to aim at practicing sporting excellence even as it generates financial resources as a business. The key to preserve the integrity of the club will be for *socios*, coaches, players, and even fans to keep alive an affective bond to the history of the club and a vital connection to the original *telos* that has guided and encouraged its evolution. The key will be for the profit-making aim to be ancillary to the *good* sporting aims.

There is, however, one more problem to raise regarding the constitutive *good* of the club. The origins of the *Club Deportivo Saprissa* are democratic in the sense that the club's plans and practices were determined in accordance to the articulated, expressed, and interrelated ideas of players, coaches, and directors. It was the players, meeting at a working-class shop, who decided to found the club and to seek the direction of Ricardo Saprissa. Even when the club had become an *asociación deportiva*, the club's *asociados* had opportunities for democratic participation in executive matters. But as a *sociedad anónima deportiva*, the club is effectively directed by Jorge Vergara, whose Mexico-based multinational company Omnilife owns 51 percent of the shares. As a matter of institutional structure, the ends and practices of the club now depend largely on the directives that the club owner may dictate. In this undemocratic dependence on the ideas of an owner, more than in the capitalist financial structure of the club, I find the primary threat of rupture and discontinuity in the club's personality. The former specification of the club as an *asociación deportiva* may have been more democratic, since that organizational structure facilitated the exchange of articulated ideas. So far, the ends and actual practices that the owner has dictated for the club accord with a continuous development of its evolving personality. Structurally, however, it is possible for the club owner to impose practices and aims in complete discord with the club's evolution thus far. The owner may, for example, resort to hiring expensive players from other teams if the club fails to win championships, the fans turn away from it, and *Deportivo Saprissa* becomes an unprofitable brand. It is in this undemocratic power of the club owner where the most latent danger for the club's continuous evolution lies.

Nevertheless, I believe that even in this situation, players and fans can have an effect on the club's development. If players truly aim at sporting excellence and if fans truly love the club's originating *telos* and its evolving historical specifications, they will effectively seek to be part, in the field or in the stands, of a *fútbol club* that aims at practicing good *fútbol*, rather than accepting to be the property or the consumers, respectively, of a brand. As a former player and enduring fan, I *feel* a real affinity, or community of ends, with *Deportivo Saprissa* when the team plays with grace and commitment, at all levels, fielding players that the club has cared to develop. When this is not the case, I feel disconnected from the club and if the disconnection were to become a severance, a real part of my own evolving personality would be missing. Likewise, if the players and the fans are disconnected from the guiding ideas of the club, the club's personality loses a real part of itself. Here lies my hope that the effects of players' and fans' ideas on the club are real.

III. ON SPORTING SYMPATHY AND AFFINITY

Let us now articulate, in general, the reasons why, from a Peircean standpoint, sports players and fans may experience an affective rupture in their allegiance to a sports club. Based on the foregoing argument and case study, I put forth that the reasons for the rupture are a discontinuation of both 'sym-pathy' and 'affinity' with the club, understood in the Peircean sense of 'feeling-with' and of 'community of ends' respectively.[17]

First, I have emphasized what it means to experience 'sympathy' for the club. Recapping, three inextricable constitutive elements of any idea are its quality as an immediate and spontaneous feeling, its energy to affect other ideas, and its tendency to become general. Thus a sports club, as a general coordination of ideas, has energy to affect the spontaneous, immediate, and energetic ideas of any member of the club that has a real relationship of allegiance with it. In other words, the club affects a real part of a player's or fan's own personality. Sports players, for instance, develop relationships with their clubs while learning to play in the club's facilities, being directed by coaches that often become mentors, and growing to respect the history of the club when they meet and are coached by former players. Players identify part of their own personalities as athletes of their particular club, making their club's sporting goals their own goals. All of these feelings, skills, and aims become a real part of the player's personality; they are real in as much as they affect who they are and how they live their lives. So it is for fans who grow up supporting their neighborhood's or city's club, going to the stadium to support the team, feeling the sporting fortunes and misfortunes of the club as their own, and analyzing games in their neighborhood's cafes and bars or at their work place. In my case, for instance, my 'feeling-with' the club, as an affective, energetic sentiment, is a real, experienced part of my own personality. It has been a part of me during my entire life: while attending my first games at the *Estadio Ricardo Saprissa* with my father, while learning to play in the training fields next to the *Estadio Ricardo Saprissa*, while being coached by former players such as Rigoberto "Feo" Rojas (*Ugly* Rojas), who played left-wing for Saprissa in its tour around the world in 1959. This part of my personality grew as the team's personality slowly evolved. The confluence of individual personality and club personality was reflected in my meeting *don Ricardo Saprissa*, while playing my first game for the club, in my competing nationally and internationally for the club, and in my traveling with fellow players. The life of the club and the life that I call my own converge when I go to the stadium to support the team, while feeling the happiness and sadness of the club's competitive successes and failures.

Thus, when something threatens to sever this relationship of 'feeling-with' the club, this threat implies that a real part of the player's or fan's personality is in danger of being disrupted. I now put forth, second, that the rupture of 'sympathy' is due to a disruption of real, effective 'affinity' with the club. When a player or fan ceases to experience a real 'community of ends,' the effective interconnection of corporate and individual personalities dies. In other words, the player or fan no longer feels and identifies the club's ends and directionality as her own. In my case, for instance, this would occur if Deportivo Saprissa's effective *telos* becomes successful profit-making by selling a sports brand instead of continuing to be the fostering and practicing of sporting excellence at all levels of athletic competition. When my 'affinity' breaks, my 'sympathy' becomes heartbreak. This account based on the loss of 'affinity' can be generalized to explain why players and fans may, at times, no longer experience a real connection with their former clubs. Whether consciously or unconsciously, whether explicitly or implicitly, the club's ends and their own are no longer related.

The discontinuation of 'affinity' may occur either when the club's *telos* changes so dramatically so as to be in fact discontinuous with the club's former constitutive *telos*, or when the player's or fan's individual sporting aims evolve in discord with the club's ends. In the first situation, what in fact happens is that the club is no longer the same entity, even though it may have the same name, portray the same emblems, and even claim the same history as its own. For example, this is what many *saprissistas* implicitly fear today, even though I have tried to argue that this disruption in the evolutionary development of the club need not be the case. In general, the question that players and fans should address in pondering whether, after a drastic institutional change, their club is in fact the same entity is whether the club's ends are continuous with its former constitutive *telos*. The answer to this question requires time to be elucidated since, according to Peirce, a personality has to be lived in and across time.

In the second situation, what in fact happens is that the player or fan no longer experiences her sporting aims as being connected with the club's. A player, for example, may come to identify his preferred style of play with the style of another club. Or he may learn to pursue his sporting aims in earnest sympathy and affinity with a variety of clubs. It may also be, for instance, that an athlete feels an affinity to the sport and not to a particular club. Likewise, a fan may develop an affinity for the excellent practice of a sport, and not for the good or poor practice of a particular club. Uruguayan Eduardo Galeano, for instance, in writing about his allegiances as a *fútbol* fan, confesses that in his youth he supported club *Nacional* from Montevideo, but that even then he could not help but admire and even applaud the style of Juan Alberto "Pepe" Schiaffino and Julio César "Pardo" Abbadie, players of *Nacional's* archrival club, *Peñarol*. Eventually he came to realize that his allegiance was to the practice of good *fútbol*, regardless of the club. Thus Galeano comes to take up his true identity as an *aficionado* of good *fútbol*: "*Han pasado los años, y a la larga he terminado por asumir mi identidad: yo no soy más que un mendigo de buen fútbol. Voy por el mundo sombrero en mano, y en los estadios suplico: —Una Linda jugadita, por amor de Dios. Y cuando el buen fútbol occurre, agradezco el milagro sin que me importe un rábano cuál es el club o el país que me lo ofrece.*[18] In Peircean terms, what Galeano explicitly realizes is that the *fútbol* ends that are a constitutive part of his personality are not linked to a particular club or national team, but to a specific style, to a certain dashing gracefulness, in the practice of *fútbol*.

In general then, the foregoing Peircean reflections explain why and how players and fans may experience and also explicitly resolve crises of allegiance with their sports clubs. As for my part, I have tried to illustrate how I have reasoned that my continuing allegiance to Deportivo Saprissa is the expression of genuine sympathy and affinity. It may be objected, however, that as a matter of philosophical analysis I have allowed my sentiment to overcome my reasoning—that I am simply searching for reasons to justify my feeling of allegiance at all costs. But I take care not to condemn philosophically my sentimentalism, for along with Peirce, I believe that "sentimentalism is the doctrine that great respect should be paid to the natural judgments of the sensible heart."[19] In this case, it is my *sensible* heart—a heart that makes sense, reasonably sensing heart—that inclines me to judge that there is continuity in the evolution of *mi querida S morada*, my beloved club, and that there remains a vigorous, vital bond that really links me with *my* club. In general, then, the foregoing Peircean reflections imply that heartfelt sports allegiances can be reasonably explained and sensibly defended, that sympathy and affinity in sporting matters are reasonably and sensibly constitutive of a sporting personality, of a sporting life.[20]

NOTES

1. Julio Ramón Ribeyro, "Atiguibas," in *Cuentos de Fútbol*, Ed. Jorge Valdano (Madrid, España: Alfaguara, 1995) 273. "Whoever does not know sporting sadness, knows nothing about sadness."

2. Alfredo Bryce Echenique, "Pasalacqua y la libertad," in *Cuentos de Fútbol*, Ed. Jorge Valdano (Madrid, España: Alfaguara, 1995) 98. "As if Ciclista Lima Association and I had never existed the one for the other…What a grave mistake, my dear Abelardo! That national stadium and so many other things disappeared. But…[how could] Ciclista Lima Association disappear from Peruvian *fútbol* and from my heart?"

3. See José Antonio Pastor Pacheco, *Historia del Deportivo Saprissa* (San José, Costa Rica: Fotorama de Centroamérica, 1988). All the details of the history of the club that I recount here are taken from this source.

4. Francisco San José, "Llegó el fútbol S.A.," *La Nación* (San José, Costa Rica), Saturday, March 8, 2003.

5. See C. S. Peirce, "The Law of Mind," in *The Essential Peirce: Selected Philosophical Writings*, Vol. 1 (Bloomington, Indiana: Indiana University Press, 1992) 312-333.

6. Ibid. 313.
7. Ibid. 325.
8. Ibid. 330.
9. Ibid.
10. Ibid.
11. Ibid. 331.
12. Ibid.

13. This way of putting the issue is due to a lecture by Professor Vincent Colapietro at the Pennsylvania State University on 8 October 2002. His account of the notion of the self in Peirce influences my discussion of personality in various ways. For his view see Vincent Colapietro, *Peirce's Approach to the Self: A Semiotic Perspective on Human Subjectivity* (Albany: State University of New York Press, 1989).

14. See C. S. Peirce, "Man's Glassy Essence," in *The Essential Peirce: Selected Philosophical Writings*, Vol. 1 (Bloomington, Indiana: Indiana University Press, 1992), p. 334-351.

15. Ibid. 350.

16. Ibid. 350.

17. Strictly speaking, Peirce does use the term 'sympathy' in this precise sense of 'feeling-with,' while I propose the term 'affinity' to capture an important aspect of Peirce's philosophical conception of personality, i.e., 'community of ends,' for which he does not offer a term.

18. Eduardo Galeano, *El fútbol a sol y sombra*, 5th Edition. (Montevideo, Uruguay: Ediciones del Chanchito, 2002) 1. "The years have passed, and in the end I have come to accept my identity: I am nothing but a beggar for good *fútbol*. I go around the world with my hat on my hand, and in the stadiums I implore: 'Give me a beautiful play, for the love of God.' And when good *fútbol* happens, I give thanks for the miracle without giving a damn which club or country offers it to me."

19. See C. S. Peirce, "Evolutionary Love," in *The Essential Peirce: Selected Philosophical Writings*, Vol. 1 (Bloomington, Indiana: Indiana University Press, 1992) 356.

20. Postscript: On 14 April 2011, the Mexican corporation presided by Jorge Vergara sold its shares of Deportivo Saprissa *Sociedad Anónima Deportiva* to a Costa Rican entrepreneurial group known as *Horizonte Morado*. Over the eight years of Mexican majority ownership, the club accumulated a series of sporting successes at the national and international level, including the 2005 CONCACAF *Copa de Campeones* (Club Champions Cup) and the resulting participation in the 2005 FIFA Club World Cup, where it finished in third place. The club in effect continued to foster sporting excellence in *fútbol*, mainly through the cultivation of young players from its minor leagues. However, several attempts to compete in other sports, including professional cycling and basketball, failed, thus trumping the goal to foster the excellent practice of sport more generally. Moreover, when the club began to sell its best young players to European clubs and the sporting results began to falter, there was a perception (perhaps justified) among fans that the Mexican ownership was only, or at least mainly, interested in economic profit. This exacerbated some troubling signs of nationalist resistance against foreign ownership among a sector of fans and former executives. Eventually, the group *Horizonte Morado* bought the majority of shares, claiming legitimacy before the fans because all the entrepreneurs are Costa Ricans and long-standing *saprissistas*. I find the signs of nationalism among fans and executives very troubling, but that problem is beyond the scope of this essay. In so far as the new group has promised to continue to foster the practice of excellent football among local youth, the signs point towards a continuation of the personality of the club as defined by its guiding *telos*. The central question for players, executives, and fans in defining the personality of the *Club Deportivo Saprissa* continues to be: What ends are we pursuing?

THREE

Paddling in the Stream of Consciousness: Describing the Movement of Jamesian Inquiry [1]

John Kaag, University of Massachusetts, Lowell

I. THE MORNING OF PAINFUL HYPOTHESES

"Five, you're late!"

A racing shell seats eight oarsmen front-to-back. In the flurry of practice, the names of the crewmen are lost and replaced by their respective seat numbers—one through eight. The coxswain, the navigator of the boat, shouts direction not by name, but by number. The terms "early" and "late" refer to the tempo and timing of the rowers' sweep. "Early" means that you are ahead of the collective stroke. "Late" means that you are falling behind. I was a novice crewman. I was fifth-seat. I did not know it yet, but I was "late."

"Five, you're late!"

Four-seat's oar handle struck my spine with a solid thump and quickly gave meaning to the coxswain's direction: I was really behind the stroke and needed to pick it up. I came to know my rowing self as I have come to know most things—through a painful process of trial and error.

No amount of yelling or explaining could have imparted the lesson of tempo and pacing. My back had to *feel* the lesson *in practice*. Athletics are only, and always, learned by heart, by the muscles. Coaches and coxswains seem to recognize this fact. They unstiffen our bodies, limber them up, and set them to work. It is in the bodily work of sport that we learn the technique and jargon of the game: I have never forgotten the meaning of being "late."

William James asserts that experience is situated at the heart of any higher forms of understanding. The challenge of explaining *how* experience is situated in relation to human understanding is, in many respects, the principal challenge of American pragmatism. This fact is reflected in "The Present Dilemma in Philosophy," when James notes that the dilemma that pragmatism faces is the task of reconciling two hitherto incompatible mindsets. The first "mental make-up" he describes is the "tough-minded," defined by its commitment to empiricism, sensationalism (referring to the bodily senses), experientialism, and pluralism. The second he describes is the "tender-minded," characterized by its rationalism, idealism, intellectualism, and monism. According to James, "most of us have a hankering for the good things on both sides of the line."[2] Unlike "most of us," however, the pragmatists "are more than mere laymen in philosophy" and refuse to *randomly* attend to the best of both worlds.[3] Instead, a cohesive philosophy is sought to unify aspects of the empiricist and rationalist tendencies. James is not careless in his word choice on this topic: "We are worthy of the name of *amateur athletes,* and are vexed by too much inconsistency and vacillation in our creed. We cannot preserve good intellectual conscience so long as we keep mixing incompatibilities from opposite sides of the line."[4] The project of pragmatism is to illustrate how these tendencies or temperaments are not necessarily "incompatible," and indeed, how they co-emerge in the process of human inquiry.

James maintains that inquiry must begin on the ground of human sensation, with a personal intimacy with the "facts" of the world. He parts company with the traditional empiricist, however, in his insistence that the experience of these facts is, *in some way,* continuous. James does not simply dismiss the notion of cohesive principles, but rather proposes a kind of principled process that is both driven and contained by experience. According to James, "The world of concrete personal experiences . . . is multitudinous beyond imagination, tangled, muddy, painful and perplexed," and, just like the first painful day of practice, is inseparable from a more cohesive understanding or athletic mastery.[5] He would agree with the sportsman that a youngster cannot learn the principles of rowing, throwing, or jumping without rowing, throwing, or jumping — without a sore back, shoulder, or leg.

Pragmatism assumes the sportsman's common sense by insisting that the truths of philosophy be "world-ready." Truth, like the physical body through which it is enacted, is exposed to the elements of nature, put through the practice of the real world, and bumped and bruised into adaptation. As James writes in "What Pragmatism Means," "Pragmatism unstiffens all our theories, limbers them up and sets each one to work."[6] One can "unstiffen" theories and "limber them up" insofar as the theory takes some living, breathing form in the organic world. In the real labor of the everyday, in all of its discontinuities and obstacles, we come to see from what sort of stuff our theories are made.

James' comment that the ideas are in the muscle is usually regarded as another of his anti-intellectualist jabs, as a demand for ideas that have experiential cash value. Here, I hope to take this interpretation a bit further, or at the very least, a bit more literally. A description of rowing musculature, muscular development in the activity of sport, will at once be a description of the pragmatic theory of ideas. Learning to row is simply learning: a mode of inquiry. Indeed, the rower's experience of muscular fitness, with its initial ache and subsequent growth, exemplifies a moment of James' epistemological approach. For American pragmatists, such as Peirce, James, and Dewey, the connection between the physical construction of the human organism and the structure of human reasoning goes far deeper than simple analogy.

This philosophical story is another pragmatic attempt to describe the physical habits of thought, the reforming embodiment of ideas. It has been intimated that a Jamesian approach to knowledge, and to philosophy itself, must, at points, embrace the coach's timeworn motto: "No pain, no gain." This being said, it seems reasonable to open with a reflection on the suffering and adaptation required in sport, highlighting the family resemblance it shares with philosophic tough-mindedness. Suffering and sacrifice, however, are only one side of inquiry. The painful lessons that perception teaches give rise at precious moments to a cohesive understanding of this experience, give rise to a passing sense of oneness with the world. Inquiry is not always characterized by brutal lessons imparted by the facts of experience; at times, habits of thought seem to coincide with empirical evidence. An intellectual, personal, and bodily flow is experienced—at least for the time being. It seems right to close with a description of these flow states, often mythologized and misconstrued in rowing literature, and do my best to return them to the experiential aches and pains that mark a novice season. In truth, the "hard knocks" of the experienced world engender habits of thought.

Endurance athletes are quick to identify the inextricable connection between the pain of trial and error, the habits of action and thought, and the almost mystical flow that can accompany physical activity. This reconnection seems in line with the work of James, but challenges at least a section of secondary scholarship. The synthesis of the tough- and tender-minded tendencies flies in the face of commentators who insist that James maintained alternative and contrary theories of truth—according to these scholars, James is *either* tough *or* tender, but not both. In recent years, this odd either-or has been construed in many ways: the Promethean or the mystical, the individual or the communal, the active or the passive.[7] In the end, however, these dueling couplets reveal themselves as iterations of the tough *and* tender, empirical *and* rationalistic, experiential *and* idealistic, pairings. With a hand from the experience of rowing, I hope to flesh out this pairing as being complementary rather than disjunctive. Henry Bugbee, a pragmatist and rower, addresses the odd communion between experience and transcendence in the tradition of American thought; he too employs the experience of the early morning sport to illustrate this connection. I will occasionally use certain comments made in his *Inward Morning* to supplement the discussion at hand.[8]

II. NOVICE SEASONS AND NOVEL IDEAS

A very early riser might catch a glimpse of a fall-time rowing ritual: the first day of novice practice. In the inky blue of pre-dawn, a ragtag band of underclassmen can be seen sitting on a row of benches on a hill just south of campus.

> "Where is the river?"
> "Are we going to practice *here?*"
> "Do we get to row today?"

The murmured questions swirl and expose the collective character of the group—confused and a bit naive. These are novices. They have rallied themselves and come to practice at the suggestion of others and, despite the chill of early morning, still believe that "this *might* be fun." They have the idea that "this *might* still work out." In this respect, a novice stands as a type of walking hypothesis, not yet validated, not yet disproved. The band of young rowers is sent for a thirty-minute jog, a preamble of things to come. The sun meets them on their return to the hill and exposes another common trait. What the murky darkness once masked now becomes painfully apparent: all novices are, by definition, scrawny. In some cases scrawny can mean thin and agile. Let me assure you, in this case, it is just another word for bony and awkward. A physiologist would insist that these youngsters do have muscles, but their young tissues have, to this point, been inactive and neither function as, nor appear to be, muscle as such.

The first day of practice is also known as "weed out day." The next hour-and-a-half separates the novices who will "make it" from those who may not; it remains the most jarring period of an oarsman's athletic career. Forty-five minutes of wind sprints—now they understand the reason for the hill. Forty-five minutes of step-ups—now they understand the reason for the row of benches that line the hill. Young muscles scream with this understanding, and drown out the idea of heroic oarsmen that brought them to practice. Exposure to the experiential trials and tribulations weed out the less fit, or more accurately, the less determined. The hypotheses that these novices embody, the ideas of rowing grandeur, are slowly adjusted under the pressures of bodily practice. Adaptation to these strenuous conditions takes time, too much time for the muscles of many first-year rowers. The number of drop-outs after the first day often outnumbers the returning novices.

In the introduction to *The Will to Believe,* James suggests: "Let us give the name of *hypothesis* to anything that may be proposed to our belief; and just as the electricians speak of live and dead wires, let us speak of any hypothesis as either live or dead. A live possibility is one which appeals as a real possibility to him to whom it is proposed"[9] For James, inquiry begins as a "good guess," as the idea that "this might work out." Such initial hypotheses emerge from the darkness of confusion somewhat randomly—they simply show up. The life of some hypotheses, however, like the tenure of some rowers, is relatively short. Neither the idealistic thoughts of shells and oars nor the muscles that personify these naive thoughts have been tested out. In "What Pragmatism Means," James re-states Charles Peirce's initial explanation of ideas as rules for action, re-flecting a belief that these "rules" are en-*acted* by organisms that face the real-world consequences of these hypotheses: "Ideas, which are them-selves but parts of our experience, become true just in so far as they help us get into satisfactory relation with other parts of our experience."[10] Rather than bringing us into "satisfactory relations" with other parts of our experience, many hypotheses lead us astray, alienating us from the experiential world and, in some cases, harming our physical bodies. These "rules for action" are found to be misguided, out of synch with the preexisting body of experience.[11] Indeed, these unfortunate casualties of the philosophic weed-out day may simply disappear, never to be seen again on the field of ideas.

It is true that a few ideas remain on this field despite their inability to cut the experiential muster. These chronically weak ideas, unable to "pull their own weight" in the demanding real world, are typically relegated to the upper echelons of the academy, the proverbial "junk boat" of thoughts. It is also true that these rarified ideas may reemerge on the practical scene, just as the muscles of the junk boat might be promoted to the B boat or even to the A shell. This promotion, however, occurs only after a great amount of time and after an even greater amount of adapta-tion.

III. THE GROWTH OF HABITS OF THOUGHT

This brings us to the crux of the Jamesian theory of ideas: adaptation. Just because an idea survives its initial trial by fire does not mean that it has acquired the needed muscle and coordination for the task at hand; no hypothesis comes fully equipped to deal with the problems of the every-day. According to the pragmatist and the coach, the young ideas of young muscles have a long way to go and may still prove unfit for the challenges of life and the more particular challenge of rowing. In *The*

Principles of Psychology, James sheds light on certain forms of muscular evolution that mesh nicely with the experience of those sore oarsmen who return from weed-out day and endure their novice season. He uses the section entitled "Habit" to explain how tissue, the embodied form of ideas, is transformed in active practice. James writes:

> The habits of an elementary particle of matter cannot change. . . . Because the particle is itself an unchangeable thing; but those of a compound mass of matter can change . . . either outward forces or inward tensions can, from one hour to another, turn that structure into something different from what it was. That is, they can do so if the body be plastic enough to maintain its integrity. . . . All these changes are rather slow; the material in question opposes a certain resistance to the modifying cause, which it takes time to overcome, but the gradual yielding whereof often saves the material from being disintegrated altogether.[12]

The "structure" in this particular case is the muscle of the athlete. In this sense, the rigorous demands of practice, the variable and unforeseen obstacles of the empirical world, might be considered the "modifying effects." The "resistance" to which James refers is embodied in the tightness of the unused muscle and is immediately reflected in the pain felt by all novices as their tissues stretch and work for the first time. The novice hypothesis must be "weak enough to yield to an influence, but strong enough not to yield all at once."[13] The investigation of rowing, the search for the principles of a complex process, will be cut short if the empirical facts reject rather than reform the body of inquiry.

James exposes a basic understanding of physiology by noting that repeated bodily activity leaves an "organic impression" on the structure and arrangement of tissue. For example, "our nervous system grows to the modes in which it has been exercised."[14] It physically adjusts to novel impulses; over time, such readjustments streamline these impulses and create a new set of nerve-nets. The stress of a novice season leaves its impression on the bony awkwardness of the novice and by mid-March, or in some unfortunate cases, by mid-May, a kind of muscular and ideological transformation occurs. Their ideas of rowing shift with their muscles; "this *might* work" becomes "this *is* work." They slowly develop an understanding of rowing as a mode of work best executed in compliance with certain rules and principles. James describes the experience of exercise: "Thus we notice after exercising our muscles or our brain in a new way, that we can do so no longer at that time; but a day or two of rest, when we resume the discipline, our increase in skill not seldom surprises us." He characterizes the body as "regenerative," "reproductive," "rebuilding," and "reparative," emphasizing an organism's capacity to recover from trauma.[15]

The fate of a live hypothesis is a grueling one. The pragmatic method insists that our "theories become instruments, not answers to enigmas, in which we can rest."[16] A well-equipped hypothesis, like a natural-born athlete, "appears less a solution, then, than as a program for more work."[17] Certain hypotheses will warrant lengthier examinations than others, but eventually every good guess shows its Achilles' heel; it is at this particular weak spot or pressure point that revision takes place. The good coach is slow to praise his players for fear of instilling a sense of complacency. He has been around the experiential block and knows just how hard to push on certain athletes, challenging their skills without breaking their spirit. The good pragmatist, playing with all of his empirical equipment, is slow to praise his "truths" for fear that they will fail to shoulder the complexity of the living world. James comments that "conceptual knowledge is forever inadequate to the fullness of the reality to be known."[18] He has been around the experiential block and knows that the twists and turns of experience inevitably cast doubt on working concepts. Accordingly, most ideas are behind the experiential times. They are horribly "late." These thoughts, however, are never seated in the "boat" of experience and have yet to receive a solid "thump" to instill the lesson of their lateness. In "The Notion of Truth," James criticizes the rationalistic tendency to view truth as an "inert static relation." According to the Absolutist, "when you've got your true idea of anything, there's an end of the matter".[19]

As opposed to this static vision of traditional epistemology, James comments that "Truth *happens* to an idea. It *becomes* true, it is *made* true by events. Its verity is in fact an event, a process: the process namely of verifying itself, its veri-*fication*."[20] This "verification" is never finished; it outlines truth, it delimits by recognizing what is *not* possible and what is not in synch with the situation at hand. Sometimes concepts are used quite effectively. On other occasions, it is precisely these concepts that lead some-*body* astray in the midst of unforeseen events.

IV. UNFORESEEN EVENTS AND CONCEPTUAL DISASTERS

Henry Bugbee rightly comments, "You might have thought that races were the moments of definitive rowing, and there is no doubt that we used to enter upon them with a special sense of being called upon."[21] There are times in this life when such a call remains unanswered or simply drowned out in the quiet sinking of a capsized boat. I cannot remember if it took place in Pittsburgh or in Boston; in truth, I have done my best to forget the event. I do remember that it was my first race.

"Ready all, row."

A head-race begins in a moving start. The shells are taken one-by-one in time trial form. The stopwatch starts as the shells round the first bend in the river and, at least in most cases, stops six kilometers later.

"Thunk."

One—two—three.
"Thunk."
One—two—three.

A *"thunk"* and a *"thump"* mean two very different things. A *"thump"* is the sound of being speared in the back with another rower's oar. A solid *"thunk,"* on the other hand, is the *sound of unison,* the sound of eight oars flipping into place at the same time. I *knew* we were together—it *sounded* good and *felt* alright. In retrospect, one might say that I let the concept of timing and pacing, the three-count that kept me on the stroke, guide my movements. This concept maintained my position, my pace, my state in the boat—at least for a time. James notes in "Stream of Thought" that, "If a new state comes, the inertia of the old state will still be there and modify the result accordingly. Of course we cannot tell, in our ignorance, what in each instance the modification ought to be."[22] In other words, one does not know when the wind is going to pick up, when the percepts of the empirical world are going to impinge on the habits of thought, on the concepts that habitually guide our action.

The six-kilometer race is a long one. The opening thousand and the closing thousand demand complete attention; the middle four kilometers, however, can be rowed in a kind of cruise-control. Partly seasoned rowers have practiced for several months and, with considerable pain and frustration, have developed a habit, a concept, of rowing. They employ this concept whenever they step into the boat and often employ it without regard to unexpected circumstances. James writes:

> Habit diminishes the conscious attention with which our acts are performed . . . our lower (thought) centres know the order of these movements, and show their knowledge by their "surprise" if the objects are altered so as to oblige the movement to be made in a different way. But our higher thought-centres know hardly anything about the matter.[23]

Indeed, our "higher thought-centres" may attend, not to rowing itself, but to the riverfront shops, the birds on the shore, the crowd on the bank, the wind in the trees.

And those trees were *blowing.* In hindsight, I am sure my oar had been catching water for some time. Three of my fellow oarsmen had been sharing in my inattention and were equally surprised when we caught simultaneous "crabs." A rower "catches a crab" when the back sweep of the stroke never clears the water and the blade pitches further under the surface. As the oarsman attempts to regain control of the submerged blade and elevated handle, he invariably shifts his weight in the shell, which in most cases temporarily "throws the balance" of the boat. In this instance, the balance was thrown, and so were we—into the water. It is hard to swamp an eight-man shell. It is even harder to live it down when you do.

The example at hand seems to reflect James' suspicion that these habits of thought, these principles for action, are brought to bear on perception as a way of making sense of the jumbling, buzzing confusion of experience.[24] Habits of thought arise from, and are molded by, experiential situations. James writes, "you can see the little lines of cleavage running through the character, the tricks of thought, the prejudices, the ways of the 'shop,' in a word, from which the man can by-and-by no more escape than his coat sleeve can suddenly fall into a new set of folds."[25] These cleavages of thought, the remnants of its experiential origins, are *system*-atically overlooked in the treatment of concepts as things rather than as instruments to be used. According to James, despite their *apparent* seamlessness, even the pure forms of mathematics and logic are all "abstracted and generalized from long forgotten perceptual instances."[26]

In the pragmatic use of concepts, these generalized forms return to the particulars of the world as tentative ways of understanding the experiential state of affairs. The pragmatic use of ideas is tentative insofar as the seasoned pragmatist, unlike the second-year oarsman, is attentive to the way in which conceptual schemas might fall short in making sense of the flux of life. The partly seasoned rower applies concepts *as if* these abstractions could *double* for the continuity of experience. This mistake may eventually "tip the boat" of intellectual life such that it reveals itself as incongruous with the purposes of the present moment. James describes the inability of the conceptual realm to take account of the superfluity of the empirical world. He writes that "Since the relations of a concept are of static comparison only, it is impossible to substitute them for the dynamic relations with which the perceptual flux is filled . . . [concepts] can only cover the perceptual flux in spots and incompletely."[27]

Inasmuch as habits of thought or concepts can mislead one in the midst of novel conditions, James suggests that concepts be employed "only when they help." One ought to "drop them when they hinder understanding; and take reality bodily and integrally up into philosophy in exactly the perceptual shape in which it comes."[28] Notice the move to take up reality in "the perceptual shape in which it comes" does not herald the death of philosophy, but rather encourages its enlivenment, or—more accurately—its *enlivening*. This openness to felt experience does not compromise the value of abstract knowledge; indeed, it is this openness that grants the very possibility of a falsifiable thought.

The evolution of concepts, the life and death and rejuvenation of thoughts and the individuals who embody them, is taken up in Bugbee's description of "immersion." He writes, "There is a continuing passage from thing to thing in which a kind of sameness or continuity of meaning deepens—ever confirming and ever relevant."[29] This "sameness" of the perceptual world, however, cannot be unified and expressed in its unbroken continuity as conceptual knowledge. The moments of the perceptual flux are the "same," but are the *same* only insofar as each arises in relation to our concepts independently, unexpected, *differently* from the previous moment. *Any* reflection on the moments of experience falls short of perfect description, and, in turn, begs its own revision. We may, at any moment, find ourselves radically out of place. As James highlights in "Stream of Thought," during certain intervals, concepts *seem* to find rest in the experiential world; they are stirred only so slightly by the "truth" of the felt moment.[30] However, these brief intervals in which static generalization seemingly holds sway are just that: brief. Bugbee echoes this sentiment, noting that "it is not by generalization that omni-relevant, universal meaning dawns . . . there is this bathing in the fluent reality which resolves mental fixations and suggests that our manner of taking things has been staggeringly a matter of habituation."[31] The "dawning of things themselves" revises the habit and fixation of belief. Interestingly, it is also in this dawn when partly seasoned rowers return to the site of conceptual disaster, to the memory of capsized boats and overturned "habits of thought." They return to the water, to the sound, to the feeling, to the experience of practice, and begin to return to their concept of rowing again—for the first time.

V. ROWING, WITNESSING, AND THE RETURNING OF AN OARSMAN

What happens to an inquirer when inquiry is temporarily overturned by the world of experience? Certain students, like certain rowers, tend to repeat the process of conceptualization described above and, unfortunately, merely repeat the excruciating and drenching effects when this concept proves out of joint with novel environmental conditions. Their concepts may be expressed in a slightly different form, but their determined and unreflective character remains the same and produces similar disastrous consequences. For others, however, this process of conceptual decentering goes far deeper, and in these cases what appears again is not simply another determinate thought, concept, or meaning. What is decentered, in this case, is not inquiry per se, but rather, more significantly, the inquirer herself.

James often comments on the ways in which abstract knowing is alienated from the knower. It is overlooked—or *consciously forgotten*—that abstract concepts are embodied, developed, and expressed in the body of inquiry, that is to say, in the flesh and blood of the inquirer. *It is forgotten that we, as human beings, are questioning.* For these forgetful individuals, the revision of concepts rarely translates into the revision of lives. Insofar as concepts are always embodied, the possibility of this type of personal revision always underpins the transaction of inquiry. It is, however, only in rare cases that this possibility is actualized.

To this point in the discussion, the account of rowing has been a description of what James calls in the *Varieties of Religious Experience* the "negative and tragic principle" of life. It has been framed as the strenuous, and even brutal, play between perceptual realities and embodied conceptual life. From this play, concepts are ingrained in the body of thought. This thoughtful body temporarily serves as the effective mediator between raw facticity and the situation of rowing. At unexpected moments, however, this embodied mediation falls short of its task and is, itself, laid low by the bare fact of reality. In my framing of the subject, I have also attempted to highlight the attitudinal shifts that can accompany the undergoing and doing of pragmatic investigation.

The novice, by definition, knows nothing of rowing and feels the aching immanence of experience, the uncomfortable disjunction between initial hypothesis and empirical fact. During this first movement, the novice is painfully aware of his body in the undergoing of experience. The partly seasoned athlete uses the painful lessons of empirical testing to reconstruct the idea of his rowing situation. Through this process of undergoing, of *being affected,* habits are ingrained by experience and, ever so slowly, begin to "talk back" to the perceptual world. For the first time, the rower attends to the "doing" rather than the simple undergoing of the situation. Ever more abstract in their conceptualization and increasingly unconscious in their utilization, these habits interpret experience haphazardly and arrogantly, leading the knower astray at the most inopportune of moments. While the perceptual pain of the novice season is continual and chronic, the trauma of the conceptual disaster is acute and wholly unexpected. Bugbee describes this process of inquiry: "One moment we understand, the next we may be lost. One moment we are lifted gratefully along with the gentle stream, another we are stranded, gasping and writhing, estranged from the element in which it is given to us to live."[32]

The third metamorphosis of the knower arises slowly and in parts— that is to say, if it arises at all. Many a rower, like many a knower, simply ignores this conceptual capsizing and preserves her abstract knowledge of the world. In other cases, however, a novel way of understanding begins to unfold. Just as habits of thought were molded from the bumps and bruises of the empirical world, this new understanding, according to the pragmatists such as James and Bugbee, grows from the painful inadequacy of objective conceptualization.

Experience creates habits of thought in the rower who, in turn, uses the concepts to readdress experience. It might be said that experience tries to talk about itself through this conceptualization. In a concept's attempt to reinterpret experience, a space opens between perception and abstraction. In certain cases, a proverbial chasm separates the two; the rower finds herself radically out of time, out of synch, out of place. She is encouraged to revise not only the working concept of rowing, but the very way in which conceptualization is approached.

The third moment is a shift in disposition and outlook—a shift in personal attitude. What changes is not simply the way in which the rower approaches the water on any *given* morning, but also the way in which the person approaches morn*ing,* dawn*ing,* row*ing,* itself. This shift in the nature of inquiry does not only yield new and more suited answers, but issues in a mode of inquiry that has been hitherto overlooked. For some rowers, the space exposed *between* the empirical and the rational, *between* the passive and the active, *between* the "undergone" and the "done," *between* the interrogative and the assertive, is discovered as a space to be quietly occupied.

It is worth noting that this shift in understanding is rarely accompanied by the fanfare or braggadocio of partly seasoned rowers. Indeed, it is almost always a quiet shift preceded by some first-race "crab" or other conceptual mishap in which habitual understanding is unreflectively applied to the novel flux of experience. Indeed, the athlete may seem sullen, despondent, reclusive—embarrassed by the unsuited idea that he once embodied. In most cases, however, this attitudinal shift is not *simply* a shift to despondence, but rather the assuming of a quiet attentiveness that characterizes a new *way* of thought. Note, that this assumption is *not* a thought but rather a *way* of thought.

There is a way in which the second-year rower flaunts her habits of thought and drives them noisily into the river of experience. Her bold manipulations drown out the directions of the perceptual world, the conditions of the moment. This oarsman and her concepts will eventually be overturned, but, with any luck, will emerge from the water and the accident with quieter concepts. In quieting the absoluteness of her rowing ideas, she is able to *hear* the wind pick up, *feel* the waves hit the boat, *think,* and *act* accordingly. This oarsman rows between the first two moments of her sport and, in so doing, embodies a third that continually mediates between the dejected undergoing of the novice and the arrogant manipulating of the partly seasoned athlete.

Bugbee emphasizes that *what* the knower knows is not some objective *thing;* one never *possesses* experience in its rawness as one might possess a specific thing. Instead, Bugbee writes that "a philosophic interest in knowing, in action, and in reality might be served by thinking of these matters we wish to understand, as matters about which our position is less akin to that of knowers and more akin to that of testifiers, witnesses."[33] Bugbee's notion of witnessing speaks to the foundation of pragmatic understanding, for it is the witness who stands at that precarious junction between perceptual appearance and conceptual articulation. It is the witness who stands open to the wonder of experience. It is the witness who may, *for the time being,* provide articulation of this endless stream. Witnessing is open to, and an opening for, the way meaning unfolds. The witness is aware, in a certain sense, of the way experience flows in its flowing. Less cryptically put, the witness not only experiences

the "tragedy" of life, but comes to embrace its tragic play, comes to anticipate the overcoming of certain concepts.

This open anticipation is a far cry from traditional and determinate
modes of knowing. Bugbee concludes: "We must learn to bear witness to
the meanings that dawn on us with respect to them, and this may be
quite different from advancing propositions which we can claim to demonstrate." Beneath the poeticism of Bugbee's comment lies the kernel of
pragmatic inquiry. James reframes the point in slightly different language, writing, "Experience is remolding us every moment, and our
mental reaction on every given thing is really a resultant of our experience of the whole world up to that date."[34] This sentiment seems appropriate in the description of the novice and in the description of the second-year oarsman. The younger oarsmen, however, fail to recognize the
import and bearing of this statement on their own experience.

It seems patently obvious to say that a rower rows, yet it seems odd to
suggest that the rower is *also rowed*. The seasoned oarsman is precisely
the conscious embodiment of this odd contradiction. Just as the witness *is*
and *is not* what is witnessed, the mature oarsman rows only to the extent
that he is *rowed* by the stream of experience. The traditional notions of self
and other, of activity and receptivity are compressed, and dilate, and co-
terminate in those quiet mornings of experience.

In the midst of sport, in an investigation of physical embodiment and
practice, we sweep, and have been swept, into a rather unexpected crosscurrent. We maintain our course and maintain the attention paid to embodied inquiry, yet another aspect of this course has emerged—another
current, so to speak. In our reading of James' physiological approach, we
have been led to his metaphysics, or, at the very least, to a description
remarkably akin to James' account of mysticism. This crosscurrent is unexpected, but not entirely surprising. James explains in *Varieties of Religious Experience* that the enchantment of the mystic can be described by the
theologian as "a gift of God's grace," but can simultaneously be explained by the physiologist as "a gift of our organism."[35]

It is a statement that is often glossed or simply attributed to "the
sentimental James," but here, in the midst of the physical, biological, and
experiential, a mystical suggestion rings true: "There is a state of mind,
known to religious men, but to no others, in which the will to assert
ourselves and hold our own has been displaced by a willingness to close
our mouths and be as nothing in the floods and water-spouts of God."[36]

I have often heard—and sometimes said—that rowing is a religion.
This "willingness" to "be as nothing" is perhaps the stance of the seasoned rower. In his notes on mysticism, James observes that most mystical experiences are brought on by going through "certain bodily performances," but when a certain consciousness sets in, "the mystic feels as if
his own will were in abeyance, and indeed sometimes as if he were
grasped and held by a superior power."[37] The passivity that claims the

mystic, however, is always of the active variety, always strangely attentive, always oddly purposive. Bugbee, in his quiet account of rowing,
underscores this understated mysticism. After a session in the boat, the
kind of session that "rounds out in an incorruptible song," the young
Bugbee returns to the dock. Upon his return, he passes his coach, John, in
the boathouse. John's remark is simple, almost koan-like: "You was moving."[38] In the dusk of a career, some athletes come to understand that
what moves—is moved. Its simplicity is rivaled only by its complexity:
one is simply moving. It is in this twilight when the "dawning of things
themselves" shows itself again, for the first time. Things are witnessed
not only as a particular immanence, but also as immanent repetition—a
sort of transcendence that never leaves the ground of experience.

NOTES

1. This article is reprinted by permission of *Journal of Speculative Philosophy*. Kaag, J.
"Paddling in the Stream of Consciousness: Describing the Movement of Jamesian Inquiry." The Journal of Speculative Philosophy 20.2 (2006): 132-145. Project MUSE.
Web. http://muse.jhu.edu/.
2. William James. "The Present Dilemma of Philosophy." In *Pragmatism*, 3-43 (New
York: Longmans, Green, and Co., 1907) 13.
3. Ibid. 14.
4. Ibid.
5. William James. *The Principles of Psychology*. (New York: Dover, 1907) 179.
6. William James. "What Pragmatism Means." In *Pragmatism*, 43–84. (New York:
Longmans, Green, and Co., 1907) 53.
7. Richard Gale. *The Divided Self of William James*. (Cambridge: Cambridge University Press, 1999).
8. Henry Bugbee. *The Inward Morning: A Philosophical Exploration in Journal Form*.
(Athens: University of Georgia Press, 1976).
9. William James. "The Will to Believe." In the *The Will to Believe*, 1–31. (New York:
Dover, 1956) 2.
10. William James. "What Pragmatism Means." In *Pragmatism*, 43–84. (New York:
Longmans, Green, and Co., 1907) 47.
11. Ibid. 56.
12. William James. *The Principles of Psychology*, vol. 1. (New York: Dover, 1950) 105.
13. Ibid.
14. Ibid. 110.
15. Ibid.
16. William James. "What Pragmatism Means." In *Pragmatism*, 43–84. (New York:
Longmans, Green, and Co., 1907) 53.
17. Ibid.
18. William James. "Percept and Concept—Some Corollaries." In *Some Problems in
Philosophy*, 68–101. (New York: Longmans, Green, and Co., 1921) 81.
19. William James. "The Notion of Truth." In *Pragmatism*, 197–238. (New York:
Longmans, Green, and Co., 1907) 200.
20. Ibid. 201.
21. Henry Bugbee *The Inward Morning: A Philosophical Exploration in Journal Form*.
(Athens: University of Georgia Press, 1976) 50.
22. William James. *The Principles of Psychology*, vol. 1. (New York: Dover, 1950) 242.
23. Ibid. 115.
24. Ibid. 179.

25. Ibid. 121.

26. William James. "Percept and Concept—Some Corollaries." In *Some Problems in Philosophy*, 68–101. (New York: Longmans, Green and Co, 1921) 72.

27. Ibid. 81.

28. Ibid. 101.

29. Henry Bugbee *The Inward Morning: A Philosophical Exploration in Journal Form.* (Athens: U of Georgia P. 1976) 52.

30. William James. *The Principles of Psychology*, vol. 1. (New York: Dover, 1950) 243.

31. Henry Bugbee *The Inward Morning: A Philosophical Exploration in Journal Form.* (Athens: University of Georgia Press, 1976) 83.

32. Ibid. 100.

33. Ibid.

34. William James. *The Principles of Psychology*, vol. 1. (New York: Dover, 1950) 234

35. William James. *The Varieties of Religious Experience.* In *The Essential William James.* Ed. B. Wilshire. (New York: State University of New York Press, 1984) 228.

36. Ibid.

37. Ibid. 403.

38. Henry Bugbee *The Inward Morning: A Philosophical Exploration in Journal Form.* (Athens: University of Georgia Press, 1976) 51.

FOUR

Running in Place: Significance on the Treadmill?

Doug Hochstetler, Penn State University, Lehigh Valley

I. COVERING MILES ON THE MILL

Several years ago my wife convinced me that we should purchase a treadmill, citing the numerous advantages this machine held in helping meet her fitness goals. Despite resisting for some time, I eventually consented and, as a result, have trudged down to our basement on many occasions to complete a multitude of miles on the treadmill. I began to wonder, however, to what extent movement on treadmills (in basements, fitness centers, and exercise physiology lab settings) allows one to experience significance.

My own treadmill use is obviously not uncommon. In recent years, cardiovascular equipment of all sorts—treadmills, elliptical machines, rowing machines, stair climbers, stationary bikes, and so forth—have become extremely popular forms of exercise for millions of people. These pieces of equipment, for some individuals, have replaced other more traditional forms of movement, such as running or walking outside as well as traditional team athletic pursuits.[1] Many people use cardiovascular equipment for reasons of convenience, safety, economics, and perhaps comfort. Indeed, there are some individuals who, if exercise equipment were not readily available, would not move at all—at least in an aerobic sense.

Despite their popularity, moving on treadmills does not offer the same experience as walking or running in natural surroundings. On one level, treadmill running appears to be innocuous—what is problematic about running on a treadmill once in awhile or even often? As a modern culture of increasingly sedentary individuals, perhaps we should rejoice that people are moving at all. This point I would concede, in that treadmills can be effective places to achieve physiological and health-related goals. For those individuals with singular expectations for movement, the treadmill may suffice. It seems to me, however, that treadmills are the sorts of places that discourage people from thinking about and experiencing movement in a richer sense.

I contend that movement holds the potential for shaping our lives in ways that go beyond the physiological. Our actions, even seemingly small ones, the things we do repeatedly, bring about significant changes in the way we operate and also perceive the world. Often the change we experience in life is gradual rather than dramatic. Many times the changes are so subtle that we fail to realize we are moving down a particular path. It is only when we reach a noticeable, perhaps troublesome, point that we realize how particular events or decisions have shaped us. The kind of activities we take up define our personhood. One who runs consistently begins to define him or herself as a "runner." What happens then if we begin to define ourselves as "treadmill runners"?

The purpose of this chapter is to examine the importance of place in movement, and its impact in terms of significance. Specifically, I contrast the experience between running on a treadmill and running outside. My claim is that treadmills tend to inhibit the running experience. My point is not that the treadmill logically precludes experiencing the significance of movement, but rather that treadmills are places where such possibilities are few and far between. To address these issues I turn to two American philosophers, Henry David Thoreau and William James, and their thoughts on meaning and significance. I suggest several ways we lose an aspect of the movement experience while running or walking on the treadmill.[2]

II. THINKING ABOUT THE MEANINGFUL LIFE

I want to begin this section by sketching a very brief notion of place in the context of a meaningful life. By place I mean a particular location[3] in time and space—a position from which one views and experiences the world in a particular way. Place is derivative from the Latin word *planta,* meaning sole of the foot. In this way our location literally grounds us in experience, providing an Emersonian angle of vision from which we face the world. We experience our embodied lives from a particular location in time. Where we choose to live shapes our experience in a certain sense, precluding us from being in other locations at the same time with the same experience. Thus, those in rural areas view life differently than others in urban settings. Sudanese refugees confront situations unknown to Western millionaires. A physical space impacts our experience and the way we interpret the world. Our location can impact the extent to which we can fulfill a significant life. It is possible to think of place as it relates to treadmills in two ways. First, there is the treadmill itself—the frame, belt, motor, and monitors. Second, there is the place where treadmills typically reside—in fitness centers, YMCAs, homes, and so forth.

As a way to explore the importance of place in movement, I want to examine the writings of Henry Thoreau and William James. These writers, known as key figures within the American philosophical tradition, were intent on finding meaning-ful ways to live. Moreover, both Thoreau and James argued that place matters in the success or failure of this quest. Thoreau magnified this importance by intentionally living beside Walden Pond for a two-year period. He recognized the centrality of location in experiencing a meaningful life, an actual physical space. In his *Walden* treatise, Thoreau wrote at length about significance in a section titled "Where I Lived, and What I Lived For." Thoreau realized that residing with family in Concord hindered his goals as a writer and poet. The house, abuzz with family and friends, afforded little of the quietness or reflective qualities that Thoreau desired and considered important. He felt confined and thus deliberated about a change of location. At the urging of mentor Ralph Waldo Emerson, Thoreau built a 10 x 15' cabin beside Walden Pond, spending $28.12 to complete his new home. Even though his abode was quite small, Thoreau remarked that he "did not feel crowded or confined in the least. There was pasture enough for my imagination."[4]

Thoreau went to Walden to experience a significant life, but it was not his intention that people read him literally. He realized that everyone should find *their own* place to live, rather than following the lead of others. For Thoreau, however, the woods provided a place with opportunities to experience nature. He found plenty to observe and as his needs were few, he had time to reflect on these experiences in his writing.

For Thoreau, this particular place included both simplicity and solitude. This modest abode provided Thoreau with the "necessaries of life," the simplicity he desired, as well as close proximity to nature. He found that he grew immensely during times of solitude, listening to the sounds of nature which prompted reflection on self and others. At one point he noted, "I love to be alone. I never found a companion that was so companionable as solitude."[5] Moving to Walden allowed Thoreau to simplify, in the sense of reducing his needs, which allowed him to focus on other concerns. Being restricted by a chosen form of poverty enabled him to be close and attentive to significant experiences in life.

Thoreau realized the centrality of place for movement as well. He advocated walking to locations that held promise. For him, this direction was generally to the south and west of Walden. Thoreau walked in those directions because "the future lies that way to me, and the earth seems more unexhausted and richer on that side."[6] The direction he chose held woods, farmlands, and ground not yet tamed by Massachusetts expansions. He described his walking at length, detailing everything he experienced—the sights, sounds, and smells. He took his walks in the woods, to what Anderson terms the "border world" between over-civilization and the uncivilized aspect of humanity.[7] Thoreau realized that finding the right place to live was a central aspect of a meaningful life, a quality similarly recognized by his contemporary, William James.

James wrote at length about the importance of place in his essay "What Makes a Life Significant?" He opens his talk by mentioning his time spent at Chautauqua Institute, an educational and retreat center in New York started in the late nineteenth century. While at Chautauqua, James and other attendees had the opportunity to take a wide range of educational courses and listen to engaging speakers and enthralling orchestral concerts.[8] At this pristine location, James wrote, "you have culture, you have kindness, you have cheapness, you have equality, you have the best fruits of what mankind has fought and bled and striven for."[9]

After some time, however, James found himself ready to leave this version of utopia, which bothered him. He could not understand why he would willingly leave this ideal location. James thought what he missed at Chautauqua was the element of precipitousness, of "strength and strenuousness, intensity and danger."[10] In this sense, he did not find Chautauqua a location conducive to the development of perseverance or determination. In this place of tranquility there was very little need for struggle, except, James noted, in the occasional ball game. "Sweat and effort," he wrote, "human nature strained to its uttermost and on the rack, yet getting through alive, and then turning its back on its success to pursue another more arduous still—this is the sort of thing the presence of which inspires us, and reality of which seems to be the function of all higher forms of literature and fine art to bring home to us."[11] For James, the meaningful life involved finding places that were primordial and savage. He desired a life that promoted heroes but was hard-pressed to find this in Chautauqua. What is the possibility of heroes, he wondered, without darkness, evil, or death?

Place, for James is important in the pursuit of a significant life. However, James acknowledged that even people in repetitive, dreary, manual labor jobs could find meaning in doing—if they were linked with some great vision or ideal. These individuals, in spite of their location and circumstances, are able to display the traits of heroism, courage, and strenuousness which James held so dear. It must be clear, however, that these individuals are rare. Often, monotonous activities are deterrents to the significant life. Those individuals in places where boredom and drudgery hold sway may therefore be relegated to endure their existence rather than experience meaning.

In sum, both Thoreau and James noted the centrality of place in the pursuit of the significant life. They realized and experienced firsthand the profound influence place had on one's experience and outlook. In addition, both writers realized the extent to which location impacted their quest for meaning. They wanted to witness and describe the kind of life that supported a meaningful life. Having examined the ideas of Thoreau and James, I want to focus on movement and place, in particular the phenomenological act of running on treadmills as a counterpoint. To do this I offer two journal entries from treadmill runs.

III. STRENUOUSNESS AND SOLITUDE—EXPERIENCE ON A TREADMILL

May 19 Journal:

I ran on one of the treadmills at school today. This was one of my longest runs on a treadmill so far—37 minutes total. I find it extremely hard to sustain interest for much longer because of the monotony. I warmed up slowly, gradually increasing my speed. At the 15 minute mark I began a series of five repeats, pushing hard for 2 minutes with 2 minutes recovery. The repeats started at a 6:40 per mile pace (for 3 times), moving to 6:35 and finally to 6:31 pace with a slight incline. This was an effective workout and it was nice to have the immediate pace feedback provided by the monitor.

In certain respects this workout represents the strenuousness advocated by James. I am able to exert tremendous energy on the treadmill just as I can outdoors. Exercise physiologists, in fact, utilize treadmills for research purposes, pushing runners to their ultimate limits. When on the treadmill I sweat, strain, persevere and finish my runs winded, tired, and, many times, sore. Yet it seems to me that something is missing. This kind of running does not contain the same degree of strenuousness as running outdoors.

March 12 Journal:

This afternoon I run on our treadmill at home, tucked in the corner of the basement playroom. While running I listen to music through headphones, providing motivation for my movement. Today I listen to the Alarm, a nice upbeat recording that mirrors my energy level on the treadmill. As I run, on the wall directly in front of me is a picture of my father. Dad, an Iowa farmer, was photographed for his 60th birthday in the turkey house, dressed in overalls with a red cap, surrounded by 6,500 toms (the male turkeys) that he raises. When running on the treadmill I often think of the irony that I, at times, find meaning and physical activity through running (even on treadmills) while Dad finds meaning, and plenty of physical activity too, through the normal day's farm work.

Down in the basement, removed from family and friends, tuned in to music on the headphones, I am alone and to a certain degree experience the solitude advocated by Thoreau. His experience of solitude, however, differs from my time on the treadmill. Thoreau valued the solitude of Walden, in part because he was able to experience nature and also self. This afforded Thoreau the opportunity for musement in a way that contrasted with his life in Concord. The treadmill run is certainly a much different experience than that of running near Walden Pond or any other outdoor setting. This is especially true when I wear headphones. My avenues to experience are restricted rather than opened, focused on the lyrics and music rather than any external stimuli such as nature provides. Running indoors, I find myself inclined to constantly look at the time remaining, but when I do so the time seems to stand still. I switch the display mode so I see an unchanging display—such as the incline—and attempt to forget about the time left in order to make it seem to go faster.

IV. TREADMILL RUNNING AND THE MEANINGFUL LIFE

Part of living a significant life hinges on the extent to which we find meaning in our daily activities. In the following section I outline several ways treadmills tend to be places that inhibit striving towards a signifi-cant life—one of meaning and experience. By meaning I refer to the cohe-rency and poignancy of life. I refer to experience in the thick sense, not as a mere acquiring of incoherent sensory data, but rather, borrowing from Dewey "when the material experienced runs its course to fulfillment." [12] I want to frame these comments by thinking about treadmills as potential playgrounds. Those individuals seeking a meaningful life value the im-portance of autotelic activities. In this sense, those in pursuit of play need to find locations conducive to the play experience and ones that promote what Hyland terms the "play stance." [13] Torres defines play as: "an auto-telic manner of approaching and unfolding in the world that necessarily includes a player and a playground." [14] He goes on to note the "funda-mental unity and reciprocity of player and playground." [15] In short, this autotelicity depends on this relationship between the individual and the environment—the basketball player and the gym/team/opponent; the swimmer and the pool/team/opponent; and the runner and the treadmill or the outdoors. I now turn to the player-playground relationship for examining treadmills as possible sites for meaning and significance. What follows is a look at the symbiotic relationship between the runner and place, in particular the treadmill runner and treadmill.

V. TREADMILL AS PLAYGROUND? SITES FOR DISCOVERY AND TRANSFORMATION

Torres writes, "Players and playgrounds are not static entities that come into contact with one another to produce play. Playgrounds change players and conversely, players affect playgrounds."[16] For the baseball player, the ball field can become a site of transformation. The individual may feel drawn to this place and, as a result, gradually enter into the baseball practice community. Likewise, the individual's willingness to strive, learn, and compete may invite others into the fold. Torres goes on to say that "Players' potentials to engage in playgrounds evolve constantly. The other side of the play coin is that playgrounds offer a multitude of changing opportunities. Imagine how diverse and promising the interpenetrations between these two always changing poles are."[17]

To what extent does a physical setting tend to promote or inhibit significance? Some places appear to be more conducive playgrounds—sites where significance, meaning, and/or play are likely to appear. These settings are, of course, myriad, but may include running along the shores of a tranquil lake at sunrise or competing in a closely contested baseball game before supportive fans. In terms of running, even traversing the same route day after day offers the promise of changing dynamics (i.e., weather, scenery, thoughts) that represent the interpenetrations Torres has in mind. On the other hand, there are certainly places where it may be extremely difficult to experience meaning or play. Treadmill running flirts with this danger as a location where the "latent possibilities" are squeezed from the experience. In general, those activities which encourage participants to view movement as something to "get through" may not promote significant experiences. That said, it is important to qualify that extremely strenuous activities, ones that participants just hope to finish, quite likely contribute to significance in ways vastly different from "getting through" a run on the treadmill.

Treadmills are certainly not likely candidates as potential playground sites. The repetition of the treadmill—running mile after mile with the same foot strike on the same surface in the same environment—appears to be in opposition to play. Repetition is not necessarily play-opposed however, as Torres rightly asserts: "Repetition is welcome as far as it permits acquaintance with the play environment so discovery and transformation is possible."[18] Skill development, often acquired through drill work and repetition, provides the backdrop against which play may flourish. In order to become a talented and creative athlete, one must continually work on and fine-tune fundamental skills. The treadmill fails not necessarily because of the repetition but for its inability to put the runner in a position to experience play and subsequently discover (both self and nature) and become transformed. I now want to offer four ways in which running on a treadmill, not once, but over an extended period of time, can be a detriment to a life of meaning.

My argument turns on the relation between running, the discovery of meaning, and the possibility of self-transformation. Part of the attraction of play is the extent to which the players experience discovery of both nature and the nature of the self. Plato famously noted that we discover more about people in an hour of play than a lifetime of conversation. Play, and other experiences of significance, also allow us to discover inroads to self as well. This discovery tends to be limited, however, when moving on treadmills.

VI. LOSING OUR MUSE—RUNNING AWAY FROM DISCOVERY

First, we might run on a treadmill at the expense of our own muse. Anderson, following Charles Peirce, defines musement as "a particular form of mental play. . . . In being a conversation with the universe of experience, musement begins as a phenomenological act; it involves an element of perception. It then, with continuity, proceeds to an interrogation of what is found phenomenologically or perceptually." [19]

Repetitive activities in general are pregnant sites for reflection and musement. Thoreau spent hours hoeing beans in the summer sun, and found that "labor of the hands, even when pursued to the verge of drudgery, is perhaps never the worst form of idleness. It has a constant and imperishable moral, and to the scholar it yields a classic result." [20] My summer jobs as a college student and educator have been of the repetitive sort as well—carpentry, cement work, painting, and roofing. As such, these times provided me with the opportunity to converse with experience. These self-conversations, or musements, arose with phenomenological acts such as measuring, nailing, and brushing. To a great degree these forms of repetitive activities all moved towards an end product and were creative in this sense. Whether this appeared in the form of a finished basement, driveway, or freshly painted barn, my summer occupations provided a way to perform a labor-intensive activity while prompting considerable time and space for reflection and contemplation. In another respect these experiences laid the groundwork for future reflection. In this sense, Bugbee explains that "experience must continue underground for some time before it can emerge as springwater, clear, pure, understood." [21]

Treadmills, like forms of manual, repetitive labor, would appear to hold the same potential for reflection and musement. Prison reformers instituted treadmills in nineteenth-century British penitentiaries. They hoped that prisoners would have plenty of time on the wheel to dwell on their transgressions and potentially repent. It is possible to experience insights while engaged in monotonous activities like treadmill running.

While on the treadmill we may find musement through paintings on the walls or people beside us on other machines. While this is possible, it is certainly not as likely as experiencing musement through other reflective experiences. It seems to me that outdoor settings provide substantially more inroads to the phenomenological act of experience. Unlike running on a treadmill, running outdoors presents an eternally changing environment—moment-by-moment, day-by-day.

Part of the difficulty with treadmills is that individuals seldom approach these places with the intent of seeking musement. Most are merely hoping to take their medicine as it were, cope with the boredom, and then move on to other more meaningful activities. Rather than movement as reflection or an enterprise and adventure of its own accord, treadmill running is often done just to "put in the time," a monotonous means to health and fitness ends.

Anderson contends that "It is only in hearing from ourselves that we may be *self*-defining and *self*-realizing; only in hearing do we come alive to the meaning of life."[22] In this sense the treadmill often shuts out any chance for reflection that often comes through running in the natural world (even if that means running through a downtown major metropolis). Treadmill runners often purposefully distract themselves from the experience at hand. Individuals on treadmills listen to iPods, watch television, or read magazines—all generally within their own bubble of individualism.[23]

The very notion of distancing oneself from experience is at the heart of Thoreau's critique of early-American culture, and the same holds true today. Why would we purposefully engage in activities, especially leisure activities, where our prime motivation is to distract self from the very experience? Of course, at times this form of disassociated thinking may have pragmatic benefits—trying to avoid thinking about pain at the end of a marathon, for example. Research indicates, however, that experienced, and successful athletes, rather than disassociate from pain, actually focus on the pain and then consciously work at ways to get through the experience.

Treadmills, in terms of their location, also tend to offer more possibilities for distraction rather than for musement. When I run on our treadmill at home, civilization is not far away. The children's toys surround me, scattered over the floor reminding me of my parental duties and responsibilities. The phone, behind me and to my left, is another constant reminder of society. When it rings I know my wife or children will answer it, but I realize that an unassuming caller may circumvent my run—if I choose to answer the call at least. Treadmills in health clubs, while removed from the home setting, still may distract the runner with blaring music, televisions, and casual conversations between gym members.

The treadmill also limits our capacity for discovery by restricting our vision. Treadmill running requires a focused gaze in order to maintain balance. When a running partner and I choose to run indoors on days of inclement weather, I am not able to casually look at him as we chat like we do when on our runs outdoors. I'm fearful that, while turning to look for more than a brief period, I will lose my balance. Or, I may steal a quick glance while holding onto one of the rails. The range of vision is limited and often changeless. The runner looks at the treadmill itself much of the time—the readouts with time, miles, distance, and calories. Again, while vision is restricted within certain parameters, the avenues of experience are restricted as well.

My gaze while running outside is typically 10-15 feet ahead. I may become locked into the pavement or path, picking a spot ahead and continuing to stare at that portion of the road or trail. But at other times I may look from side to side, admire fields of corn or soybeans, extend my step to avoid a puddle, or make eye contact with an approaching car or bicyclist. The horizons that running in natural settings provide are replete with possibility. Even a five-mile loop run every day throughout the year changes in terms of scenery, with variations throughout the seasons—providing an encouragement to observe. Quite often these deviations are subtle and slow, requiring a great deal of perceptive skills to notice.

This process of vision and discovery through running is an enhanced impetus for stories as well. When I think of places I've run, many come to mind—the golf course in State College, Pennsylvania; around the section near our farm in Iowa; on the trail in the Little Lehigh Parkway, and many more. I often think of memorable runs, conversations, sights, and experiences in conjunction with these particular places—running with Jeff and Tim in Cardiff, with Pam and Gabriella in Seattle. On the other hand, it is difficult to think of any memorable run on the treadmill. What would distinguish one as such? There is no change in scenery, no need (unless I so choose) to change the pace, the incline, the mileage, or effort. These runs are largely about finishing and getting on to something else, hardly the material for stories and memories.

VII. THE VALUE OF SPONTANEITY IN TRANSFORMATIVE RUNNING

In addition to playgrounds affording opportunities for discovery of self and nature, these places also hold the potential for transformation. Those that enter into play relationships develop into different human beings by virtue of these relationships. As an example, two consecutive summers spent bicycling across the United States changed me in both subtle and dramatic ways. I became adept at bike maintenance (especially changing flat tires), found I was a bit less patient than I previously thought, and came away from the trips with a desire to try my hand at bike racing. In short, I emerged from these 5-week, 3,000-plus-mile trips a different person. I continue to reflect on and appreciate the way they transformed my life in meaningful ways. The memories find their way into my classroom discussions as I recall these experiences in the context of ethical decision-making, or the good life, or compassion. Playgrounds have a way of bringing this about, particularly in terms of the spontaneity and risk involved.

Conversely, treadmills possess a certain degree of sterility, one example being the exercise environment itself. Most treadmills are in climate controlled fitness centers. Clients know that the temperature will be 65 degrees (give or take a few) every day. Some treadmill runners will even turn on a fan or possibly turn up the heater if the temperature is not to their liking, or if their treadmill is in the confines of their own home. Running outside provides no such control. The runner may deliberate between a long or short-sleeve T-shirt, wearing a hat, gloves, or not. Running outside without proper clothing can lead to dangerous consequences, namely heat stroke or hypothermia.

Running on a treadmill provides very objective feedback—miles run, calories burned, and current heart rate. In fact, the treadmill has become a benchmark for research equipment because of its ability to standardize the experience. Researchers place subjects on a treadmill and can control the location, speed, incline, workout length, temperature, and many other assorted variables. With these restrictions in place, the researchers are then able to look at differences across stride lengths, hip angles, heights, weights, genders, and so forth. It is much more difficult to standardize the running experience outdoors. Even the same 10-mile path, while consistent for distance, may vary according to past weather conditions, temperature, lighting, and, of course, speed. When one runs outdoors it is possible to take technology along—in the form of heart rate monitors, wristwatches, or other pieces of equipment—but we are not forced to subject our run to technological standards. We do not need the equipment in order to experience the run, as is the case on the treadmill.

The terrain on treadmills remains unchanged—the belt continues to move beneath the runner's feet, whirring along with the constant slap of shoes across the surface. This terrain is much different than found outdoors, unlike sidewalks, grass, trails, or macadam. These surfaces have a different sound, different feel, with even and uneven ground. The surface outdoors takes the runner to places with wildlife or even locations with considerable traffic. This movement puts the runner in a position to experience the spontaneity of the elements, of nature, and other humans as well. Running on a treadmill provides very few chance encounters. No dogs will chase us. No neighbors will greet us. We will not step in a pothole or come upon new terrain or unexplored territory. We select our program—hills, cardio, fat burning, or manual—enter our time, level and then begin to run. Depending on the day, the exercise routine may range from mildly interesting to bearable to numbingly boring. On treadmills we may lose a certain amount of transformation that arrives via spontaneity.

Finally, treadmill runners may encounter fewer risks than their outdoors counterparts. Because of the nature of running outside, there are more things that could and do go wrong. We develop safety measures to run outside. We carry mace, wear ID bracelets with medical information, tell people our route, choose safe places and times to run, vary our routes, and run in well-lit areas. Treadmills do include a certain amount of risk consistent with running outside. In both places the runner may experience fatigue, disappointment, muscle strain, or even serious physical injury. On the treadmill, however, a great deal of danger is reduced. Treadmills diminish the risk with warning labels and safety features. On the treadmill there is safety from inclement weather or other unwanted intrusions. Manufacturers attempt to reduce the chances of injury—and therein reduce their own chance of lawsuits—by providing warning labels. When we do hurt ourselves on a treadmill (i.e., develop shin splints or runner's knee) the cause of our injury is not risk per se but rather monotony and overuse.

The downside of reducing the majority of risk, however, is an impact on the overall experience. As James noted, there is also less chance of doing something heroic or of developing a meaningful story, for good or bad. It is hard to imagine a life-changing event taking place on the treadmill. This is not to say that the meaningful life necessitates an overabundance of risky behavior. We should certainly note the importance of seeking balance between reckless abandon (taking too many chances that may put self or others at extreme and unnecessary risk) and sterile safety.

In addition, running outside involves a certain degree of commitment that differs from the treadmill. To illustrate, a father and son once embarked on a hike together. They chose a gentle path around a lake, the father carrying his infant son in a backpack. As he walked the skies began to darken and when they had reached the point where the path was the farthest from their start point—almost exactly halfway around the lake— the skies opened up and it began to pour. Had the father and son been walking on a treadmill, they could have avoided this situation, but at this point on their walk they could not shut off a button. They simply had no easy way home but instead had to endure the elements and situation at hand. What resulted, however, was a powerful story of a father's love and protection. The point of the story was not to avoid walking through the woods, but rather how love and affection brings us through dire circumstances in a way that is not found when we sit on the sidelines of experience and life.

Running on a treadmill is certainly safer than running outdoors. In fact that is why many people choose to run indoors. Either in the gym or their home these individuals are able to exercise a great deal of control over their personal safety. They need not worry about someone hiding in the woods or about getting lost. Medical professionals, or at least a telephone, are close by, should they pull a muscle while running. The terrain is level the entire time, without potholes, tree roots, or sidewalk ridges. Finally, attached to a safety strap by the wrist, if they should fall the machine will automatically shut off, preventing further injury.

CONCLUSION

In conclusion, running (and movement in general) is more significant than a means to another end. It is possible to experience meaning in the doing itself. We, as a modern society, risk limiting this experience when we confine ourselves to running on treadmills. We risk experiencing movement as an instrumental mode of being rather than the kind of significant life of James or the meaningful life of Thoreau.

Let me suggest a few ways to combat the problem. First, we need to continue to think and write about the significance of movement forms. In so doing we must emphasize the place that often determines, or contributes to, the form of the movement. Second, we need to continue to reflect on the significance of movement as the telos of a meaningful life and especially in our lives as sport philosophers. We should think intentionally about the places we move, yet allow for spontaneity as well. Running on treadmills is certainly better than a sedentary life. However, if we value a life of meaning, where movement has possibilities to serve beyond a mere means to ends, then when we think intentionally about our places to move, we would do well to stay off the treadmill lest we move in place in our thinking as well as our moving.

Is it likely for people to experience significance on the treadmill? It is possible to find meaning, or perhaps create a meaningful life, out of the direst circumstances. But when we have the freedom to choose where we move, then it would seem prudent to choose the places that provide the most opportunity to experience meaning. Running outside puts me in a position to be the kind of person I want to be—unconstrained, free to roam and make decisions about direction and path (not just about speed or incline)—and that is a good place to be.

NOTES

1. Robert Putnam, *Bowling Alone: The Collapse and Revival of American Community*. (New York: Simon & Schuster, 2000).

2. While I acknowledge the multitude of exercise equipment available, I will only focus on treadmill use in this chapter, but would make broad comparisons with other cardiovascular machines as well.

3. Throughout this chapter I use the terms "place" and "location" interchangeably.

4. Passages from Thoreau come from Henry David Thoreau, *The Portable Thoreau*. Carl Bode, Ed. (New York: Penguin Press, 1964) 340.

5. Ibid. 386.

6. Ibid. 603.

7. Douglas Anderson. "Recovering Humanity: Movement, Sport and Nature," *Journal of the Philosophy of Sport*, 28, 4.

8. Chautauqua Institute is still in existence. A friend of mine spent this summer teaching writing courses at the institute. While there, he had the opportunity to listen to Jesse Jackson, take a course on Bob Dylan, and stay active with a golf membership at the Chautauqua golf course.

9. William James, *Talks to Teachers*. (New York: Dover, 2001) 132.

10. Ibid. 271.

11. Ibid. 272.

12. John Dewey, *Art as Experience*. (New York: Capricorn Books, 1934) 35.

13. Drew Hyland, *The Philosophy of Sport*. (New York: Paragon House Publishing, 1990).

14. Cesar Torres, Unpublished Dissertation. *Play as Expression*. (State College: Pennsylvania State University, 2002) 178.

15. Ibid. 141.

16. Ibid. 76.

17. Ibid. 77.

18. Ibid. 221.

19. Douglas Anderson, *Strands of System: The Philosophy of Charles Peirce*. (West Lafayette, IN: Purdue University Press, 1995) 146.

20. Thoreau. 406.

21. Henry Bugbee, *The Inward Morning*. (Athens, GA: The University of Georgia Press, 1999) 140.

22. Anderson. 145.

23. For more on a trend in the United States on the decline of civic and community involvement, see Putnam, *Bowling Alone*.

FIVE

Where Should LeBron's Loyalty Lie? Where Should Ours?

Mathew A. Foust, Lander University

INTRODUCTION

The American pragmatist engaged in this essay is Josiah Royce. Some readers may, owing to Royce's German idealist inheritance, not regard Royce as a pragmatist. But Royce's intellectual heritage, like the majority of philosophers, is vast and variegated, with the thought of Charles Peirce and William James among those informing his philosophy. Royce himself declares, "I assert that personally I am both a pragmatist and an absolutist," contending that not only are these philosophies reconcilable, but that they are "in truth reconciled."[1] Royce's pragmatism is especially prominent in his ethical and social thought, which emphasizes familiar pragmatist themes of meliorism and the centrality of community. Here, we will consider Royce's philosophy of loyalty in relation to sport.[2] Royce would appreciate such an application of his thought, as he frequently cites fair play in sport as a particularly influential model of loyalty.[3] Moreover, applying Royce's philosophy of loyalty to a contemporary situation in sport weds theory to practice, and is thus all the more to be regarded as a project in the pragmatist spirit.[4]

'Loyalty' is a term that arises with such frequency in sport that it must be considered one of its most cherished values. For instance, we tend to find it an admirable break from business as usual when a star player of a small- or mid-market Major League Baseball (MLB) team takes a 'hometown discount' to stick with—be loyal to—his team and its fans, when a more lucrative contract with a large-market team is likely available.[5]

Conversely, should this same player opt to sign with a rival of his present team, especially if for a nominal difference in contractual details we might describe the act as one of betrayal—disloyalty—to his team and its fans. Star pitcher C. C. Sabathia has served as an illustration of the first scenario and something like the second. In 2005, Sabathia signed a two-year, $17.75 million contract extension with the Cleveland Indians, when he could have become a free agent after the 2006 season. At that time, Sabathia was quoted as saying, "Over the winter, I was thinking about letting things play out and eventually seeing what I could get on the [free agent] market, but when I got to spring training and was around all the guys—who are more than just my teammates, they're my friends—I called my agent and said 'This is where I need to be.' I'm just so comfortable here. It is like my family."[6] In 2008, however, Sabathia's loyalty to his "friends" and "family" had apparently waned. Although it was widely reported that the Indians offered a four-year, $72 million dollar contract, the most lucrative contract that they had ever offered a player, Sabathia was reticent to enter contract negotiations. When the Indians fell out of contention, they were forced to trade Sabathia, in order to recoup something from what had become more and more clearly an imminent loss. Sabathia finished the season with the Milwaukee Brewers, another mid-market team, but entered free agency at season's end and signed a seven-year contract of $23 million per year with the New York Yankees, the most lucrative contract given to a pitcher in MLB history. While attending a home playoff game of the Cleveland Cavaliers of the National Basketball Association (NBA) in 2009, Sabathia was shown on the Jumbotron, eliciting a mixture of boos and cheers.[7] We may interpret this polarized reaction in terms of loyalty. Some fans, perhaps, were expressing appreciation of Sabathia's former loyal service to their hometown baseball team, while others, perhaps, were expressing resentment of Sabathia's disloyal abandonment of this same team. Judgments of Sabathia demonstrate the importance of loyalty in our estimations of the character of people in the world of sport. Many other examples are available, and not all pertain primarily to players of sport. We frequently speak of the loyalty of ownership, management, coaches, and fans.

Along with the premium that we place on loyalty in sport comes the perplexity of negotiating conflicting loyalties. It is true in sport, as much as in life generally, that there are times when one loyalty is at odds with another, or several loyalties cannot be honored at once. These times may very well count among the most difficult that we endure. It is times like these in which philosophy might impart its most useful wisdom. In *The Philosophy of Loyalty*, Royce describes what he believes being loyal requires and addresses the problem of conflicting loyalties. Royce very much intends for these theories to be utilized in daily life, as he seeks to "clarify and simplify our moral situation."[8] In this essay, we will do just this with respect to a salient situation in sport.

Before proceeding, I think it important to share that I was born and grew up in Cleveland. Although I am no longer a resident of Cleveland, I still think fondly of the city as home. When it comes to sport, my loyalty lies—and presumably always will—with teams from Cleveland. It is not easy to be a fan of Cleveland teams, as they do not typically enjoy success, and when they do, the success is often bittersweet. Our vignette about Sabathia is illustrative of this effect; just when it seems that the Indians might have the pieces in place to capture their first World Series championship since 1948, their ace pitcher reneges on his loyalty to the team, dominos seem to fall, and the team renews its perennial process of rebuilding. Remaining a fan of Cleveland teams in the face of the recurrence of such scenarios requires true loyalty. Remaining a fan of Cleveland players who leave us for apparently greener pastures also requires a good deal of loyalty, a loyalty that, as indicated by the mixed reactions to Sabathia's presence at the Cavs game, is more difficult to come by. My own experience of seeing him on television then was that I froze in bewilderment, caught between old but familiar feelings of affection and new but raw feelings of resentment. I can only imagine that had I been among those in attendance, this internal conflict would have been greatly intensified.

The situation to be addressed in this essay is that of LeBron James, formerly of the Cleveland Cavaliers. Like Sabathia, James stuck with Cleveland when first given an opportunity to go elsewhere. At the end of the 2005-2006 NBA season, James signed a contract extension, electing to stay with the Cavaliers through the 2009-2010 season. Like Sabathia, James faced the decision anew, as he became eligible for free agency following the 2009-2010 season. Just as Sabathia's loyalties clearly underwent revision between 2005 and 2008, James's loyalties underwent revision between 2006 and 2010. On July 8, 2010, James announced, in a much-hyped ESPN special dubbed "The Decision," that he was "going to take [his] talents to South Beach and join the Miami Heat."[9] The overwhelming sentiment shared by Clevelanders was that of having been betrayed. When asked how to explain his decision to the people in Cleveland, James mustered a somewhat incoherent string of remarks. Among these was James's initial response: "I mean, it's heartfelt for me. You know, it's hard to explain, but at the same time my heart, in the seven years I gave to that franchise, to that city, it was everything."[10] Are Cleveland fans right to believe that LeBron has betrayed them? Was LeBron, in fact, disloyal? With the help of Royce's philosophy of loyalty, we will ask: Where should LeBron's loyalties lie? Moreover, in light of where LeBron's loyalties now lie, where should that of his fans lie? While the latter question will reverberate most with Cleveland fans, our approach to it will be of service to any fan who develops a loyalty to a player that they think to in some way be reciprocated, only to see the player choose to switch uniforms and adopt a new loyalty.

ROYCE AND LOYALTY

The Philosophy of Loyalty is a collection of eight lectures throughout which Royce develops a concentrated account of his philosophy of loyalty. In the opening lecture, Royce offers "a merely preliminary and tentative view" of the topic, defining loyalty as: "*The willing and practical and thoroughgoing devotion of a person to a cause.*"[11] A very important aspect of Royce's philosophy of loyalty is not yet articulated. We will arrive there in due time, but first, this preliminary definition calls for elaboration.

First, loyalty is, according to this definition, the devotion to a cause. One might argue that this part of the definition is too narrow, for loyalty may be found in not only the devotion of a person to a cause, but in the devotion of a person to another person, to an institution, to an ideal, or to any number of things other than causes. Royce's notion of a cause, however, encapsulates each of these kinds of instances of loyalty. Royce first cites "the devotion of a patriot to his country" and "the devotion of a ship's captain to the requirements of his office"[12] as examples, but soon adds the loyalty of lovers to his list, noting that they "are loyal not merely to one another as separate individuals, but to their love, to their union, which is something more than either of them, or even than both of them viewed as distinct individuals."[13] In short, supposed loyalty to an object other than a cause really just is loyalty to a cause. A patriot's loyalty to his country can be understood, for instance, as loyalty to the cause of promoting the well-being and flourishing of his country. The loyalty of a ship's captain to the requirements of his office can be understood as loyalty to the cause of fulfilling the duties of ship's captain. The loyalty of a lover can be understood as loyalty to the cause of sustaining the strength of the bond uniting the lover to the beloved. We can add to these examples that the loyalty of a player to his team may be understood as loyalty to the well-being and flourishing of his team, which is typically understood in terms of winning. It is commonplace for players to claim that their ultimate goal is to win a championship. The same can be said for the loyalty of a player to his fans, as players frequently speak of their goal of bringing a championship to the area in which the team is based.

Second, loyalty is willed. One cannot be loyal if one does not choose to be. "The loyal man's cause," Royce asserts, "is his cause by virtue of the assent of his own will."[14] This explains why the notion of an involuntary "team player" would strike one as peculiar. One cannot authentically be a team player if one is not willingly devoted to one's team. The need for loyalty to be voluntary is brought into sharper relief by the supposition that loyalty requires devotion that is both practical and thoroughgoing.

By practical, Royce means that loyalty requires the loyal to act. Loyalty is not, therefore, merely a feeling or emotion. "Adoration and affection may go with loyalty," Royce explains, "but can never alone constitute loyalty, . . . The loyal man serves."[15] Thus, the loyalty of the player to his team is not simply his feeling of pride to be a player of his team; loyalty requires action expressive of that feeling. He does his part to help bring about the intended victory or, in the long term, the intended championship. Clearly, this involves putting forth a determined effort during any given contest against an opponent, but because one's ability to put forth such effort is affected by that put forth in practice and other types of training, loyalty demands such effort during practice and training, too. The player may go further than this, performing other loyal action that might be construed as conducive to his cause. For instance, if he believes that boosting the morale of his team will shake them out of a slump, he may instigate a social affair through which his team might bond or relax and perhaps play more effectively in subsequent contests.

In claiming that the willing and practical devotion of the loyal to his or her cause must be thoroughgoing, Royce means that the devotion must be sustained. If one is loyal to a cause, one does not waver in one's devotion to it. The loyal player gives, as the cliché quite popular in sport goes, 110 percent. This means that the loyal player is ready to serve the team at any moment, and in whatever capacity is most needed toward furthering the team's cause. This aspect of loyalty is captured by the willingness of a player to "take one for the team." The popularity of this phrase is indicative that a host of examples can be cited. The prevalence of the term 'sacrifice' in baseball (e.g., *sacrifice* fly, *sacrifice* bunt, *sacrifice* squeeze) is telling; the batter willingly passes up the possibility of raising his batting average in order to advance a teammate or teammates on base.[16] A player may demonstrate the thoroughgoing character of his devotion by performing an action that will likely harm his person, such as making the minimal expected effort to avoid being hit by a pitch, in order to make it to first base. A thoroughly devoted starting player may accept without complaint having his playing time reduced or being demoted to a bench role, if such an adjustment is deemed conducive to the team's cause.

Royce adds one other feature to his preliminary sketch of loyalty, namely, that loyalty is social. "If one is a loyal servant of a cause," Royce states, "one has at least possible fellow-servants."[17] For Royce, the cause to which a loyal person is devoted always concerns other persons. The player's loyalty to the requirements of his role clearly concerns other persons, among whom are, at the least, his teammates, coaches, and trainers. His teammates, for instance, share his cause of winning and cooperate with him toward this mutual end. It is common to speak of a star player's "supporting cast." The idea is that while a star player contributes a good deal toward his team's cause, he is not by himself sufficient. He needs fellow-servants to this cause, not just because several loyal players are better than one, but because loyal players augment each other's loyal activity. The star player's skillful service to the cause improves the abilities of his teammates to perform their service skillfully and vice versa.

Again, the language of sport is telling; in basketball, the number of *assists* a player or team records is regarded as an indicator of how well the player or team is synchronized and executing plays. The loyal player's coaches may counsel him as to how best to be loyal to the requirements of his role, or may perhaps simply show confidence in decisions that he has made in this regard. The loyal player's trainers will ensure that he is healthy enough to play as effectively as the cause requires, and work toward improving his health to this status when he is injured or ailing.

We have now articulated Royce's preliminary definition of loyalty. This definition contains several elements that Royce believes to be essential to loyalty. That is to say that without either willingness, practical action, thoroughgoing devotion, or a cause, there is no loyalty. We have illustrated each of these aspects of loyalty with examples in sport embodying these aspects. An important element must be added, however, and doing so is our next task.

ROYCE AND LOYALTY TO LOYALTY

We have seen that for Royce, loyalty is always directed at a cause, but we are presently unclear as to what constitutes a worthy cause. We are also unclear as to how to adjudicate between or among what appear to be conflicting worthy causes. Royce's responses to these questions come in the form of his notion of loyalty to loyalty. He states, ". . . a cause is good, not only for me, but for mankind, in so far as it is essentially a *loyalty to loyalty*, that is, is an aid and a furtherance of loyalty in my fellows. It is an evil cause in so far as, despite the loyalty that it arouses in me, it is destructive of loyalty in the world of my fellows."[18] In other words, service to worthy causes promotes loyalty in general while service to unworthy causes undermines loyalty in general. Serving the cause of fair play by becoming a referee and performing that vocation properly would seem an example of the former. The loyal referee increases loyalty in the world of his fellows by demanding loyalty to the rules of the sport and penalizing instances of disloyalty to those rules. Moreover, we might imagine other referees admiring his skillful loyal refereeing and following his example. Choosing the same vocation but serving the cause of personal advantage by accepting bribes in exchange for making calls favoring a player or team would seem an example of the latter. While this referee might indeed be loyal to his cause, he undermines loyalty in the world of his fellows. He is complicit in the disloyalty to the rules perpetrated by whoever has offered him the bribe. Moreover, we might imagine other referees admiring his skillful disloyal refereeing and following his example.

The loyal referee may be used to illustrate how loyalty to loyalty assists when faced with a conflict of causes. A referee may be loyal to the cause of refereeing, on one hand, and loyal to the cause of his family, on the other. At some point, he may be required to choose between being a loyal referee and being a loyal family member. For instance, at the same time that a contest he is supposed to officiate is to occur, a family member requires his help. In either case, he knows that he is the person best suited to the task and he knows that he cannot be in both places at once. He must choose one at the expense of the other. By what method shall he choose? For Royce, the referee must choose the loyalty that is most loyal to loyalty. "Look first at the whole situation," Royce advises, "Consider it carefully. See, if possible, whether you can predict the consequences to the general loyalty which your act will involve."[19] Perhaps the referee is able, upon such consideration, to see that one action is more loyal to loyalty than the other. He knows, for instance, that while not as skilled a referee as he is, the referee who would act as his substitute is competent. He also knows that no similarly effective substitute will be found in the case concerning his family member. Consideration of how others' loyalty might be affected by his decision also suggests that he should choose the cause of his family. His conflict is thus dissolved. But perhaps the case is not as clear as just presented. Then what?

"[I]f," states Royce, "at the critical moment, I cannot predict which of two modes of serving the cause of loyalty to loyalty will lead to the more complete success in such service, the general principle certainly cannot tell me which of these two modes of service to choose."[20] Nonetheless, loyalty to loyalty is a guide in the face of such ignorance, for "it now becomes the principle, *Have a cause; choose your cause; be decisive.*"[21] In other words, *"Decide, knowingly if you can, ignorantly if you must, but in any case decide, and have no fear."*[22] How is it that loyalty to loyalty *becomes* this new principle? Acknowledging influence from Harvard colleague William James's "The Will to Believe" essay, Royce instructs, *"As soon as further indecision would itself practically amount to a decision to do nothing, —* and so would mean a failure to be loyal to loyalty, *—then at once decide. This is the only right act."*[23] In other words, because the failure or refusal to choose any cause would fail to promote loyalty, when the question becomes "Choose a cause or do not," loyalty to loyalty always instructs, "Choose." As addled as the referee of our example might be, he must decide, as his lack of a decision produces no loyal service and may indeed produce the opposite; continued inactivity may harm either or both his profession and his family. "Henceforth," Royce states, "with all your mind and soul and strength belong, fearlessly and faithfully, to the chosen personal cause until the issue is decided, or until you positively know that this cause can no longer be served without disloyalty. So act and you are morally right."[24]

We have now described both Royce's preliminary definition of loyalty and the central addition that he makes to this conception, the principle of loyalty to loyalty. Much more could be said concerning Royce's philosophy of loyalty, but we would be taken beyond the scope of this chapter. Our concern is to think through a contemporary issue in sport, utilizing the basic tenets of Royce's philosophy of loyalty. We turn now to the apparently conflicting loyalties of LeBron James.

LEBRON'S LOYALTIES

Much has been made of LeBron's loyalties. The subject became particularly popular in 2007, when James attended an American League Division Series game in Cleveland, between the Indians and Yankees, wearing a Yankees cap. Although he grew up in Akron, Ohio—approximately forty miles south of Cleveland—James grew up a fan of the Yankees and has maintained this loyalty, despite becoming a Cleveland sports icon. As one journalist described the scene, "In a move that provides quite the dilemma for Cleveland fans, James not only sported enemy gear to Thursday's Game 1 against the Yankees at Jacobs Field, but he even playfully taunted fans by doffing his Yankees cap and raising it in front of a camera during an interview with TBS."[25] Cleveland fans were divided on the issue, some upset that James would flaunt his loyalty to the Yankees so brazenly, with others forgiving of James's loyalty to the Yankees on account of his loyal service to the Cavaliers. There was no shortage of fans and critics outside of Cleveland weighing in on the issue, as well. The subject of how a professional athlete ought to comport oneself when harboring multiple and conflicting loyalties attracted much discourse on the heels of James's actions.

James also grew up a fan of the National Football League's (NFL) Dallas Cowboys, and has maintained this loyalty, as well. Like his loyalty to the Yankees, James has manifested his loyalty to the Cowboys in the face of Cleveland athletes and fans. In 2008, James donned both his Yankees cap and a Cowboys t-shirt while consorting with Cowboys players and ownership on their sidelines before the Cleveland Browns' season opener in Cleveland. Again, fans and critics stood divided with respect to how to feel about James's actions. Cleveland Browns wide receiver, Braylon Edwards, was not among those disturbed by James's actions, however, stating, "I give him credit for being loyal."[26] The apparent implication of Edwards's comment is that James is to be credited for not reneging on his loyalty to the Cowboys, established well before he became a fixture in Cleveland sports, in order to become a fan of the Browns. Such a loyalty would be artificial, and thus not truly loyalty, and it is better for James to be truly loyal than not.

Of course, Edwards, while at the time a player on a Cleveland team, is not a lifelong Clevelander with thoroughgoing devotion to Cleveland sports teams. Many people of this description interpret James's unabashed displays of loyalty for teams other than and opposed to those of

Cleveland as suggestive that James's loyalty to the Cavaliers is not to be counted on. The suspicion is not that James would ever be disloyal to the Cavaliers while a Cavalier, but that despite his roots in the Cleveland area, James will have no qualms about becoming a member of another team in 2010. As one Cleveland journalist resignedly put it, "I guess we have no choice but to count our blessings and simply celebrate our Yankee-loving-Cowboy-hugging-global icon until he divorces us and takes his game somewhere else."[27]

This remark implied that James's leaving the Cavaliers was factually imminent. While this strong of a position was, at the time, not well supported, the worry that James would take his game somewhere else was not without grounding. One writer opined, "even if James is being a bit of a brat by flaunting his out-of-town allegiances smack dab in Cleveland venues, that is no excuse for the locals to react like rubes. It feeds the image of the city as having an inferiority complex, something to apologize for."[28] In fact, Cleveland does have an inferiority complex, perhaps particularly when it comes to sport, but this feeling is not that of rubes, but of people alert to their own history of disappointment. Consider first that none of the three major teams in Cleveland has claimed a championship since the 1964 Browns (before the NFL championship was referred to as the Super Bowl). Consider next that many star players have spurned contract renewals with Cleveland teams in order to pursue more lucrative contracts elsewhere. In addition to Sabathia, Manny Ramirez, Jim Thome (former Indians), and Carlos Boozer (former Cavalier) are among those in recent memory who have done so.

Perhaps the most crucial consideration, however, is James's own statements about his future. Asked explicitly what role loyalty will play into his decision, James responded, "You do what's best for you and your family and what's best for your career. Loyalty definitely has a big part to do with it, but the time you spend with that respective team, you give a lot of loyalty. Every night I go out, I play hard. That's loyalty."[29] James's implication seems to be that he saw himself as loyal insofar as he served the Cavaliers' cause while a Cavalier. Loyalty to the Cavaliers beyond the time during which he was contractually obligated, however, may not be compatible with what he perceived to be best for himself, his family, and for his career. In another, more recent interview, James distinguished his loyalty to Akron from his loyalty to the Cavaliers, stating, "My loyalty is to Akron. I'm looking forward to this upcoming season, but I'm looking forward to the summer of 2010, too, to see what may happen. . . . You know, I love this city and I'll always give back to this city no matter what my profession, if it takes me somewhere else."[30]

Still, Cleveland fans had reason to be optimistic. James stated, "When I decide to make the decision, it's going to basically put me in a position where I feel like I can win multiple championships. If it's staying here, I'll be here. If it's moving elsewhere, I'll have to look at my options."[31] Although many speculated that James would sign with the New York Knicks or New Jersey Nets, on account of both the lucrative possibilities that could come with playing in such a large market and James's friendship with part-owner of the Nets, rapper Jay-Z, the Cavaliers had built an appreciably better team around James than that which he would have found with either of those franchises. Few suspected that the Miami Heat would create the salary cap space to accommodate Dwyane Wade, Chris Bosh, *and* James.

Further, while James had undeniably pointed to the possibility of leaving the Cavaliers, he claimed to "have never given any indication that [he was] leaving Cleveland," saying in September 2009, "I've been happy with what the franchise has done for me and my family. It's been great. Hopefully everything goes right and hopefully I can sign a big contract to stay in Cleveland."[32] Cleveland fans had grounds for optimism.

Still, Cleveland fans have heard such hopeful words before and, as the case of James illustrates, they know that such words are no guarantee of continued loyalty. As we have seen, James values a number of loyalties, and these loyalties appear to have come into conflict, culminating in the decision to leave the Cleveland Cavaliers. What guidance would Royce's philosophy of loyalty have offered James in this situation? What guidance does it now offer to his fans?

CONCLUSION

James had negotiated conflicting loyalties before, as witnessed in his decision to publicly support the baseball and football teams to which he has been loyal since boyhood, even when these teams compete against Cleveland in Cleveland. But the decision that he made in the summer of 2010 caused a much greater impact. If James had employed Royce's philosophy of loyalty when making this decision, he would have needed first to recall that for Royce, loyalty is the willing, practical, and thoroughgoing devotion of a person to a cause. James would need to determine whether his apparently conflicting loyalties were, in fact, by this definition, loyalties. The loyalties in question would be, at the least, these: James's loyalty to Cleveland, to the Cavaliers, to his fans, to himself, to his family, to his career, to Akron, to winning multiple championships, and to his friend, Jay-Z. Determining which of these apparent loyalties are, in fact, loyalties in Royce's sense, is something that only James himself would be able to do. He would have done well to do so, however, for if Royce's conception of loyalty errs, it does so on the side of stringency. If any of James's loyalties were to meet Royce's description of loyalty, then James would have something(s) special, and all the more reason to exercise delicacy in his deliberation.

If James were to still have a true conflict of loyalties on his hands, he would need to determine what course of action is most loyal to loyalty. That is, James would need to determine, as far as he is able, which decision will most result in the increase of loyalty amongst humanity. We must not put this duty past James, as he has aspired to be, and has become, a global icon. Moreover, when asked whether he sees himself as a role model, James has replied, "Of course I'm a role model. Any pro athlete that plays basketball—plays any sport—is automatically a role model. I'm happy to be one, too." [33] Professing to value loyalty, accepting responsibility as a moral example, and recognizing that the world is watching, James's decision would have been made with intelligence and care if guided by Royce's principle of loyalty to loyalty.

Most fans of James would not have been greatly taxed, should he have remained a Cavalier. Because he has left, however, many fans have been left to sort out their feelings about him. Like the reactions to Sabathia described earlier, those feelings are in conflict. Caught between affection and resentment, fans, too, might implement Royce's philosophy of loyalty in order to come to terms with *The Decision*. At the least, they need to determine whether their loyalty should lie more with James or with the Cavaliers. Other loyalties, such as their loyalty to the NBA or to fellow fans siding with or against James, might also come into play. And while fans are not global icons and role models like James, their actions are often noticed and imitated by fellow fans. Thus, where the loyalty of we, the fans, lies is as significant a question as that of where LeBron's does. Royce's philosophy of loyalty offers a way of working through this question.

NOTES

1. Josiah Royce, *Lectures on Modern Idealism*. [1919] (New Haven, CT, and London: Yale University Press, 1964), 258.

2. Royce's philosophy of loyalty is most definitively presented in: Josiah Royce, *The Philosophy of Loyalty*. [1908] (Nashville, TN: Vanderbilt University Press, 1995).

3. In a striking expression of this sentiment, Royce claims, "The coach, or the other leader in college sports, to whom fair play is not a first concern, is simply a traitor to our youth and to our nation." See: Royce, *The Philosophy of Loyalty*, 124.

4. For a recent application of Royce's philosophy of loyalty to sport, see J. Brent Crouch, "Gender, Sports, and the Ethics of Teammates: Toward an Outline of a Philosophy of Sport in the American Grain," *Journal of Speculative Philosophy* 23(2) 2009: 118-127.

5. Such instances grow fewer in number, and the phenomenon of a star player remaining on the same small- or mid-market MLB team for the duration of his career may be extinct. In his book on loyalty, James Carville devotes a chapter to loyalty and sport wherein he praises the loyalty of Tony Gwynn, exemplified in Gwynn's having done just this despite plenty of reasons and opportunities to do otherwise. See: James Carville, *Stickin': The Case for Loyalty*. (New York: Simon & Schuster, 2000), 171-172.

6. Associated Press, "Sabathia to make $24.75 million next three years," April 27, 2005, http://sports.espn.go.com/mlb/news/story?id=2047624.

7. Chris Assenheimer, "Tribe notes: Sabathia still feels at home in Cleveland," May 30, 2009, http://chronicle.northcoastnow.com/2009/05/30/tribe-notes-sabathia-still-feels-at-home-in-cleveland/.

8. Royce, *The Philosophy of Loyalty*, 6.

9. For the transcript of "The Decision," see http://espn.go.com/blog/truehoop/post/_/id/17853/lebron-james-decision-the-transcript.

10. Ibid.

11. Royce, *The Philosophy of Loyalty*, 9 (emphasis in original).

12. Ibid., 9-10.

13. Ibid., 11.

14. Ibid., 10.

15. Ibid., 10.

16. The batter may be credited with one or more runs batted in (RBIs), however, and if this is his motivation, the sacrifice is not altogether sacrificial.

17. Josiah Royce, *The Philosophy of Loyalty*, 11.

18. Ibid., 56 (emphasis in original).

19. Ibid., 90.

20. Ibid., 88.

21. Ibid., 88 (emphasis in original).

22. Ibid., 89 (emphasis in original).

23. Ibid., 89 (emphasis in original). James's "The Will to Believe" (1896) pertains to the rationality of adoption of religious belief in the face of a lack of coercive evidence for or against the existence of God. James believes that all persons must believe in God or not, conceiving of agnosticism as amounting to deciding to not believe.

24. Ibid., 90.

25. David Briggs, "LeBron spurns Tribe, sports Yanks cap," October 5, 2007, http://mlb.mlb.com/news/article.jsp?ymd=20071004&content_id=2250946&vkey=ps2007news&fext=.jsp&c_id=mlb.

26. Quoted in: Associated Press, "LeBron's out-of-town loyalties rub some Cleveland fans wrong," September 9, 2008, http://sports.espn.go.com/nba/news/story?id=3578795.

27. Phillip Morris, "Sick of LeBron James not cheering for Cleveland," September 8, 2008, http://www.cleveland.com/morris/index.ssf/2008/09/sick_of_lebron_james_not_cheer. html.

28. Steve Aschburner, "LeBron's loyalties all in good cheer," September 12, 2008, http://sportsillustrated.cnn.com/2008/writers/steve_aschburner/09/12/lebron/index.html? eref=si_topstories.

29. Joe Zedalis, "James' decision will hinge on winning 'muliple (sic) championships'," November 19, 2008, http://sports.yahoo.com/nba/rumors/post/James-decision-will-hinge-on-winning-muliple-c?urn=nba,123320.

30. Quoted in: Starting Blocks, *The Plain Dealer*, "LeBron James tells ESPN: 'I'm looking forward to 2010, too, to see what may happen'," August 24, 2009, http://www.cleveland.com/ohio-sports-blog/index.ssf/2009/08/lebron_james_tells_espn_im_loo.html.

31. Quoted in: Joe Zedalis, "James' decision will hinge on winning 'muliple (sic) championships'," November 19, 2008, http://sports.yahoo.com/nba/rumors/post/James-decision-will-hinge-on-winning-muliple-c?urn=nba,123320.

32. Quoted in: Tom Withers, AP Sports Writer, "LeBron rides toward free agency," September 2, 2009, http://sports.yahoo.com/nba/news;_ylt=AhHoJpTIeKoE2TQ6.NXJVCi8vLYF?slug=ap-lebronathome&prov=ap&type=lgns.

33. Quoted in: Noah Wolf, "Humble James welcomes title of role model, plays his part flawlessly," *The Lantern*, March 3, 2004,http://media.www.thelantern.com/media/storage/paper333/news/2004/03/03/Sports/Humble.James.Welcomes.Title.Of.Role.Model.Plays.His.Part.Flawlessly-624443.shtml.

SIX

Agapastic Coaching: Charles Peirce, Coaching Philosophy, and Theories of Evolution

Tim Elcombe, Wilfrid Laurier University

The world of sport in all of its existential manifestations offers humans potential sources of deep and rich meanings. Those engaging in athletics can at once live sport for health and well-being, to celebrate or express, and/or to test and compete. Within the same marathon, for example, some run to improve their health, some run to celebrate the memory of a loved one, and others dress up in costumes as a form of expression while running. Some runners seek to achieve new personal bests in the marathon, while still others compete for prizes through victory and final placements relative to the other participants. Some runners will live the run in some or all of these different and dynamic ways throughout the 26.2 miles.

Participants of sport, particularly those focused on testing or contesting[1] in athletics, typically seek to improve their performance or achieve success in competition. In other words, athletes usually embrace objectives that frame their athletic participation, looking for ways to "evolve" as athletes. To help athletes meet their evolutionary aims, athletic coaches increasingly serve a valued role within the sporting world. Coaches work with athletes of all shapes and sizes, at all ages and levels, in virtually all sports. Coaches aid athletes with training and preparation, help construct strategies for success, and assist participants in their physical skill and conceptual development. Emerging as central figures in the worlds of sport, coaches often serve as the gatekeepers of experiences, the crafters of athletic identities, and the facilitators of new trends or techniques.

But what does it mean to be a good coach? How do successful coaches function? One way coaches approach these questions is through the development of coaching philosophies to guide their methods. However from a pragmatic view, such an understanding of 'coaching philosophies' as fixed and unwavering ideological commitments is shallow and narrow. Conceived not as a tool to gain certainty or knowledge for the sake of control but as a method for dealing with the worlds we live within, pragmatism changes the idea of coaching philosophy to assist coaches working with athletes in the ever-changing sport world.

Pragmatism can help make ideas about coaching and coaching philosophy clearer by making ideas about evolution clearer. Understanding different theories about evolution illuminates approaches coaches adopt while working with athletes. And knowing what one means by evolution can help illuminate what best serves coaches in their attempts to help athletes engage in their own development. Appropriating ideas from Charles Peirce's essay "Evolutionary Love,"[2] I draw two related conclusions regarding disparate theories of evolution and their influence on coaching practices. First, I argue that most coaches functionally fall into one of two categories related to polarized conceptions of evolution: tychastic and anancastic coaches. Second, I argue for the advantages of an agapastic approach to coaching based on Peirce's conception of evolution through creative love (agapasm) to tychastic and anancastic coaching. But first, it is important to consider the state of coaching and ideas about coaching philosophy in the twenty-first century.

I. COACHING AND COACHING PHILOSOPHY

Coaches in contemporary culture often occupy influential and revered positions in the sport world. Although not always the case,[3] athletics coaches are today as famous (or even more famous) than the athletes participating in sport. Historical names such as John Wooden (basketball), Alex Ferguson, Rinus Michels (soccer), Bela Karolyi (gymnastics), Vince Lombardi (American football), Victor Tikhonov, Scotty Bowman (hockey), and Bill Bowerman (track) reverberate through their respective sports and beyond. The omnipresence of coaches now makes their absence (as in the case of tennis star Roger Federer[4]) seem strange and unusual. In the United States, famous athletes changing coaches at the height of their careers, such as golfer Tiger Woods[5] or 2004 Olympic 400 meter track gold medalist Jeremy Wariner, face unrelenting media scrutiny. Along with this sense of "strangeness" or "uncertainty" there is an assumption that athletes with a "coaching void" lack a key ingredient for the successful attainment of their desired outcomes.

In athletic worlds with high (including economic and political) stakes associated with success, organizations turn to coaches to deliver desired outcomes. Athletes often seem like mere pawns carrying out the will of omnipotent coach-masters. Consequently, many coaches live in climates of high risk and high reward. American higher education institutions, for example, regularly pay football and men's basketball coaches yearly salaries totaling more than entire academic department budgets. But these same coaches often face the looming specter of public dismissal when institutional athletic success fails to "materialize." Even at youth and recreational levels, coaches often feel pressured to deliver success—pressure most often applied by parents and administrators with vested interests in the performance of individual athletes or teams as a whole.

These twenty-first-century coaches embody and embrace seemingly innumerable describable styles of coaching. Typically, observer categorial classifications focus on the disciplinary approaches, tactical commitments, and relational leanings to distinguish between coaching styles. Coaches are described as "democratic" or "autocratic," "free-wheeling" or "controlled," and "a player's coach" in either the affirmative or negative sense. However, the descriptive power and accuracy of these labels usually fall short, leaving us with empty descriptions of coaching styles.

Beyond descriptions, coaches themselves seek to construct a coaching philosophy filled with maxims and fixed principles that unwaveringly guide them in all coaching actions and decisions. The concept of "philosophy" in this context seems interchangeable with strategic and technical allegiances, motivational tactics, and external expectations. Coaching "how-to" manuals line the shelves of bookstores. Conference attendees typically flock to hear the latest techniques and "philosophies" presented by recently crowned championship coaches. Ask a basketball coach about her coaching philosophy and she is most likely to describe defensive commitments, disciplinary methods, or favorite motivational quotes. The *really* successful coaches extend their recipes for success into non-sport domains, including business and politics.

"Effective" coaching philosophies in the twenty-first century conceptualize "a philosophy" as a set of ideological absolutes—athletic "wisdom" in a certain narrow and final sense. Pragmatic scholar Thomas Alexander argues that such a conception of philosophy, or as he calls it "philepistemy," justifies projects of static belief fixing and knowledge accumulation.[6] Coaching philosophies in this view serve as a means for "controlling" the athletic world coaches find themselves functioning within.

Pragmatists instead view philosophy as something entirely different from collected ideologies and static wisdom. From the perspective of pragmatism's originators Peirce, William James, and John Dewey, philosophy serves as a *method* used to critically examine and subsequently reconstruct the beliefs, values, and ideas that fund our lives. In the same vein, pragmatism suggests coaching philosophy should be conceived as a method by which to critique and reconstruct the beliefs, values, and ideas employed when working with athletes.

Peirce's descriptions of different evolutionary theories make clear the difference between traditional ideas about philosophical method and a pragmatic approach. Not all ideas about how evolution happens (or happens best) converge. Different theories of evolution summarized by Peirce in his essay "Evolutionary Love" highlight the differences among three main ways theorists conceptualize evolution: tychasm, anancasm, and agapasm. Peirce did not see the demarcation of his own categories as "perfectly sharp," yet maintained that the differences were real: "There is in the nature of things no sharp line of demarcation between the three fundamental colors, red, green, and violet. But for all that they are really different. The main question is whether these three different evolutionary elements have been operative."[7]

The ideas related to "evolution" capture much of sport and its appeal to humanity. Younger athletes seek to evolve in order to function at their highest realized levels of physicality and performance. Aging athletes look for ways to evolve to offset diminishing physical capabilities. Underperforming teams search for means to transform their evolutionary trajectory. Championship teams consider ways and means to continue evolving in the face of new expectations and never-ending challengers. The coach, in essence, assists in these processes of change, adaptation, growth, compensation, survival, and success—to name a few elements that relate sport and evolutionary theories.

By using Peirce and his ideas about evolution to accurately categorize coaching styles, perhaps a new, more invigorated approach to the practice can be stimulated. Peirce's three theories of evolution seem to capture *real* coaching categories. Coaching is at bottom about evolution with teams and individuals striving for growth. It only seems appropriate, then, that theories of evolution might serve as the basis for a categorial classification of coaching styles.

II. TYCHASTIC AND ANANCASTIC EVOLUTIONARY COACHING THEORIES

The man most famous for bringing evolutionary theories into the public consciousness, Charles Darwin, published his seminal work *On the Origin of Species* in 1859. Darwin did not "invent" evolution; ideas related to evolutionary theories slowly took shape throughout the 1800s. Darwin's great contribution, Louis Menand contends, was the challenge his theory of natural selection provided to the assumptions guiding humankind's conception of how the world works.[8] Prior to *On the Origin of Species*, most theorists posited versions of Plato's world of essential forms to understand the structure and functions of the world. The only question to answer was the source of these essences or ideas that guided all life.

Conversely, rather than emphasizing the common properties or es- sences of the world, Darwin emphasized the central role of variation in *On the Origin of Species*. Darwin's proposals offered a radically different way to view the world's past, present, and future. Darwin's work also changed how the world thought, and drove a wedge between two polar- ized visions of evolution: evolution by way of deterministic laws and evolution by chance.

The same year Darwin published *On the Origin of Species*, Charles Sanders Peirce (1839-1914) graduated from Harvard. Peirce, the origina- tor of pragmatism, was greatly influenced by Darwin's method of critical scientific inquiry and theory of natural selection. Although Peirce did not accept Darwin's work as a finished and complete theory, his systematic philosophy emerged in no small part in response to the ideas presented in *On the Origin of Species*. Peirce's evolutionary cosmology exemplified this influence, as did his triadic approach to thinking. In "Evolutionary Love," Peirce set out to distinguish three theories of evolution—three theories applicable to the construction of coaching philosophies.

1. Tychasm and Tychastic Coaching

Peirce described a first mode of evolution, the one adopted by most of Darwin's ardent followers, as *tychasm*: "evolution by fortuitous varia- tion."[9] Following the lead of Darwin, proponents of tychastic evolution suggested chance and sheer spontaneity accounted for the changing world. No "working hypothesis" guided the adaptations and transforma- tions evident in nature. Those subscribing to tychasm discounted claims of evolution as purposeful, bounded, hierarchical, and controlled. In- stead, tychasm promoted a sense of pure individuation not constrained by any telos and emphasizing functions, transitions, sequence, and luck.[10] In sum, tychastic theories of evolution promoted pure, random purposelessness that eliminated the possibility of prediction.

Peirce's evolutionary account of tychasm describes one of the two approaches typically adopted by coaches. *Tychastic coaches* function with- out "working hypotheses," leaving athletic outcomes in the hands of a purposeless, disinterested athletic universe. No teleology is at work in this coaching environment; instead, pure spontaneity unbounded by any constraints propels the evolution of the athletes and team.

Tychastic coaches can function in different ways. Some tychastic coaches "stay out of the way" and allow the athletes and teams to explore the possibilities of sport without any coach-imposed constraints. For ex- ample, Guy Lewis, former head coach of the University of Houston bas- ketball program, seemingly allowed his high-flying Phi Slamma Jamma crew to play within a constraint-free environment. By adopting a "roll out the ball" laissez-faire approach, Lewis gave space for spectacular basketball talents, including Clyde Drexler and Hakeem Olajuwan, to flourish—taking Houston to the 1983 and 1984 National Collegiate Athletic Association (NCAA) championship finals.

Lewis' approach, rare in an athletic world that demands coaches publicly display a sense of control, relied on fortuitous natural selection to guide his athletes. Based on his actions, Lewis appeared to believe his athletes possessed qualities and characteristics necessary to survive and flourish in 1980s American intercollegiate basketball. Consequently, Lewis' role, or the role of other coaches adopting a "let it be" approach, emphasizes chance's role in flourishing. This methodology embodies Darwin's claims about the survival and flourishing of certain finches in the Galapagos Islands—the randomness of the environment creating accommodating conditions for some finches, hostile conditions for others.

Other coaches subscribing to a tychastic approach engage more regularly with the athletes than a "hands off" coach such as Guy Lewis. These tychastic coaches randomly introduce drills and skills to the athletes without the guidance of a "working hypothesis." One can imagine the coach arriving at each practice with some new activity conjured up or derived from a coaching manual or workshop. Activities and skills are not conceptualized relative to some guiding structure or set of principles. Tychastic coaches, in this context, seem to emphasize the pure "firstness"—a Peircean term for the immediate 'feltness' of an experience.[11] Coaches and athletes are encouraged to feel the sensuousness of physical exploration and expression. Each drill exists independently from other drills. No striving occurs for the attainment of some recognizable goal. Evolution in this instance occurs when disconnected variations "thrown out" by athletes or teams in an athletic struggle unintentionally leads to fortuitous survival or flourishing. Teleology yields to pure chance.[12]

2. Anancasm and Anancastic Coaching

Diametrically opposed to the evolutionary theory Peirce referred to as tychasm is *anancasm*. The anancastic theory of evolution concluded that mechanical necessity operated to alter the world. Proponents of anancasm (generally anti-Darwinists) argue that only one logical conclusion could emerge from a given set of premises. This evolutionary theory, in contrast to tychasm, emphasizes clearly defined and unchanging purposes, boundaries, and hierarchies. Anancastic thinkers believe antecedently fixed objectives, truths, and habits drive evolution: necessity driven towards a fixed teleology. Menand likens this approach to a billiard-ball theory as each singular event directs the future chain of events.[13] A necessarily leads to B which only leads to C ad infinitum. Chance, luck, and variance, from an anancastic view, exist only in appearance. Destiny and mechanical necessity drive the world forward.

Based on Peirce's conception of anancasm a second classification of coaching styles emerges. *Anancastic coaches* drive hard towards fixed teleologies through a mechanical style determined by necessity. Anancasm focuses on pure "secondness"—the Peircean category describing brute opposition in experience.[14] These coaches push and pull athletes in the direction of pre-established goals and expectations. Technical expertise and strategic certainty serve to propel athletes and teams toward narrow and fixed conceptions of "efficiency," "effectiveness," and ultimately "success." Anancastic coaches determine athletes and teams will use 'x' approach, in the framework 'y,' to achieve 'z' objective.

The majority of coaches in our modern sport environment exemplify the anancastic coaching style. Set recipes are available and consumed for every part of coaching, including motivation, technical and strategic operations, as well as team and athlete selection. Coaches subscribing to this style look to control every factor possible. Psychological, physiological, and technological manipulation is crucial for "success" as coaching becomes increasingly formalistic and reductive.

Coaches subscribing to an anancastic coaching style search for a finished map that makes clear the road to certain success for their teams and athletes. All of their actions must lead to some fixed end as variance along the way only leads to chaos and thus cannot be permitted. Consequently, the coach assumes an all-knowing, all-powerful role. Without such a figure to set the boundaries and enlighten athletes as to *the* way, fixed ends become unattainable.

Anancastic coaches are thus typically looked upon as experts. These coaches adopt methods "necessary" to bring about the "required" changes to "fix" the habits that "pilot" athletes to success. Less-experienced or less-successful coaches attend clinics, buy videos, and consume books in the hopes of being led to the optimum methodological advances—akin to paint-by-number artistry. In the Greek sophist tradition, anancastic coaches become technical masters. Questioning the ends, considering transformational methods, embracing variation merely wastes valuable time on the road to success. No room is given for the flourishing of an individual; instead, she must submit to the decisions, values, and expertise of the coach, team, or larger athletic community.

Peirce viewed these two poles of evolutionary theory—mechanical necessity at one end, absolute chance at the other—as insufficient doctrines. The two warring theories, Peirce argued, neglected the Gospel of Love.

III. AGAPASTIC EVOLUTIONARY THEORY

Peirce acknowledged in "Evolutionary Love" that he would be accused of *sentimentalism*. As he noted, sentimentalists since the French Revolution tended to be described as illogical and oblivious to the cold, hard facts of the world.[15] Peirce, a logician and phenomenologist, nevertheless relished the title of "sentimentalist. He described sentimentalism as "the doctrine that great respect should be paid to the natural judgments of the sensible heart."[16] Yet the changing times threatened to eliminate love, sympathy and strong feeling from political, scientific, and educational discourse.

Peirce argued that the Gospel of Greed had instead seduced the world. This resulted in a philosophical outlook wherein greed is "the great agent" in the evolution of humanity and the universe.[17] Too great an emphasis on "intelligent" economics, effective operations, and utilitarianism promoted the individual as the center of the universe. But for Peirce, self-love did not equal love. Love needs to be "other-directed" and requires reciprocal relationships. The Gospel of Love suggests progress takes place from the merging of each person's individuality "in sympathy with his neighbors."[18]

Conversely, Peirce described the Gospel of Greed's notion of progress as taking place "by virtue of every individual's striving for himself with all his might and trampling his neighbor under foot whenever he gets a chance to do so."[19] Peirce predicted the Gospel of Greed would destroy the modern world: "The twentieth century, in its latter half, shall surely see the deluge-tempest burst upon the social order,—to clear upon a world as deep in ruin as that greed—philosophy has long plunged it into guilt."[20] Neither intelligent greed nor utilitarian conceptions of the public good incorporated love, and thus for Peirce were inadequate doctrines for accounting for progress or growth. In contrast, Peirce believed love or agape should be at the "heart" of discussions of evolution and growth. Yet as Alexander's view of modernity suggests, Peirce's concerns for the future seem to have come to fruition: "Human life stands in need of liberation; most of our experience, if not totally anaesthetic, is far from meaningful or fulfilling. It falls toward either of two extremes, to simple, loose disorganization which neither commences nor completes anything or to rigid, lockstep mechanical routine which deadens the mind due to the absence of intrinsically fulfilling ends."[21]

But, is there a middle position between tychasm and anancasm? This is what Peirce aimed to provide for us employing the ideal of agapic love. For Peirce, love did real work in the universe; to talk effectively about evolution, politics, science, and philosophy, love had to be in the discussion. Peirce described love as "circular": love at once "projects creations into independency," while also drawing impulses into "harmony."[22] To emphasize his point, Peirce pointed to St. John's Golden Rule. Peirce believed this adage captured the true evolutionary philosophy: "growth comes only from love, from—I will not say self-*sacrifice*, but from the ardent impulse to fulfill another's highest impulse." Only love could stimulate and account for the evolution of the universe: "Love, recognizing germs of loveliness in the hateful, gradually warms it into life, and makes it lovely." [23]

Thus Peirce considered how a theory of evolution grounded in love and constituted by *both* the force of spontaneity and the force of habit might work. Habit forces new elements of form to "take practical shapes, compatible with the structures they affect, and in the form of heredity and otherwise, gradually replaces the spontaneous energy that sustains them." [24] Spontaneity breaks up the continuity of habits, creating the conditions for growth and intensifying feeling. [25] This lived transformation of habits, like love, serves a double role to "establish new features" and to "bring them into harmony." [26] Reconstructed habits, rather than pre-determined or purely instinctual habits, thus become tools for decision-making. [27]

Peirce's third evolutionary mode, agapasm or evolution by creative love, exhibits all of the general elements found in tychasm and anancasm. Through the transaction between spontaneity and constraint, agapastic evolution incorporates relationality, growth, and a developmental teleology. Functions *and* purposes, transitions *and* boundaries, sequence *and* hierarchies always at once play a role in Peirce's conception of agapasm. Peirce recognized that Darwin's main contribution to humanity was to promote the centrality of variation to evolution. But Peirce also recognized the need for starting points, for structure, for form. Peirce's agapastic theory of evolution thus incorporated elements of tychasm, but rejected pure randomness. His agapasm also adopted evolutionary ideas found in anancasm, but rejected undifferentiated oneness and the "authority of prior use." [28] Evolution occurred, from Peirce's agapastic perspective, subtly and continuously, rather than abruptly and sporadically. Growth, Peirce believed, came from growth:

> Growth by exercise . . . is what it is to learn. But the most perfect illustration is the development of a philosophical idea by being put into practice. The conception which appeared at first, as unitary, splits up into special cases; and into each of these new thought must enter to make a practicable idea. This new thought, however, follows pretty closely the model of the parent conception; and thus a homogeneous development takes place. [29]

Unlike tychasm (no teleology) and anancasm (fixed teleology), Peirce's conception of agapasm provided a pragmatic optimism—meliorism through what he called *developmental* teleology. Agapastic evolution also satisfied another of Peirce's central concepts, *fallibilism*, which he described as the "thesis that no inquirer can ever claim with full assurance to have reached the truth" since new evidence can arise and must be taken into account. [30] Thus Peirce believed experiences in the world should help shape our goals rather than succumb to an accepted, fixed telos. Teleologies, from a pragmatic view, do real work as "working" hypotheses to guide action—our aims or goals may thus develop over time. A developmental teleology, central to an agapastic theory of evolution, opens the possibility for inquiry, for growth, yet without guarantees greedily required by both tychastic and anancastic theories.

IV. AGAPASTIC COACHING

Peirce's conception of evolution through creative love when applied to coaching (agapastic coaching) creates a middle road between tychasm and anancasm, a road that incorporates some of the qualities of both these styles of coaching. The spontaneity of tychasm allows for creativity; the continuity of the anancasm offers order. Taken together, these elements open space for growth, for evolution. Thus coaching through "creative love" brings new features into play, while bringing them into harmony. Agapasm focuses on what Peirce called "thirdness"—relations of mediation and integration.[31] In its most developed form, thirdness involves reflexivity. As growth occurs, the principle of growth similarly grows—a premise Peirce developed in his description of agapastic evolution.

Moving beyond pure secondness provides the opportunity for sport to go beyond its increasingly anaesthetic nature. But moving from pure secondness to pure firstness is similarly insufficient. Athletes and teams without constraints can move aimlessly in meaningless environments; for them evolution is only possible by chance. Yet we cannot deny the need in sport and coaching for the spontaneity and lively affect firstness can have on our habits.

Agapastic coaches recognize the need to harmonize spontaneity and necessity. Teams and athletes have histories they carry forward. These histories create order and regular habits but do not negate the possibility for and the need for spontaneity. Further, spontaneity requires constraints for true creativity to occur; creativity depends on regularity and lawfulness in some respects. This dialectic of spontaneity and constraint pushes the boundaries of athletic participation in new and dynamic ways.

Thus, agapastic coaches subscribe to a developmental teleology. The goals, expectations, and purposes of the coach, athlete, and team, are given ongoing and careful attention. They are always in process and adaptable. Orientations toward the future are not fixed and are instead subject to growth—the specific ends are not given at the outset. Further, as growth occurs it turns upon itself and expands the principle of growth. Teams and players, when coached by an agapastic coach, engage in a form of inquiry into the possibilities and discipline of their athletic experience.

Phil Jackson, the recently retired ultra-successful former head basketball coach of the National Basketball Association's (NBA) Los Angeles Lakers, appears to fit the agapastic coaching style. Jackson's Lakers team won three consecutive NBA championships to start the twenty-first century and another two back-to-back in 2008-09 and 2009-10. Prior to his Los Angeles coaching tenure, Jackson won six NBA championships with the Chicago Bulls. Each of Jackson's championship teams has been stocked with exceptional talent. In Chicago, the Bulls' Michael Jordan and Scotty Pippen teamed to form one of the greatest duos in NBA history. His first Lakers' dynasty was driven by two of the top players in the league—Shaquille O'Neal and Kobe Bryant. Jackson's last two championship teams featured Bryant, as well as complementary stars Pau Gasol and Lamar Odom. Thus many question Jackson's true coaching worth because of the superior talents of the Bulls in the 1990s and the Lakers in the new millennium.

However, it is the uniqueness of Jackson's teams that embodies his apparently agapastic style and accounts for his successes. Jordan and Pippen formed a devastating perimeter combination; Kobe and Shaq were the most dominant inside-outside duo; Gasol and Odom functioned as highly skilled "big" players to support Kobe's perimeter talents.[32] Somehow Jackson achieved success with all three uniquely constructed teams. Jackson, when responding to questions about successes with different types of teams, states, "different teams call for different responses." His first Bulls team needed to "learn to trust" one another, while the first Lakers team "needed me to be patient."[33] Further, he understands each team is different from year-to-year. After his first championship with the Lakers, new problems, new opportunities, and new personalities emerged. However, these changes were not ahistorical—new habits developed spontaneously with new combinations of players and these slightly altered the team, the players themselves, and, ultimately, the league.

Beyond dealing with the personalities and talents of his teams, Jackson's tactical methodologies leave room for both spontaneity and continuity. "Practice," Jackson writes, "is a time for players to make the kind of mistakes that allow them to grow." Yet at the same time, he argues coaches must have standards and expectations: "I do want to feel free to do something interesting or offbeat to get my players' attention."[34] Jackson's allegiance to the "Triangle Offense" similarly exemplifies his commitment to agapasm. This offense depends upon movement and reflexivity. The players function as a single unit, assessing the defense and finding indeterminate opportunities to score. It is an offensive system designed to constrain the players, yet afford them opportunities for individual exploration and creativity. Habit provides order, directionality, structure, and limits. Spontaneity disrupts to creatively open space for growth, possibility, and new habits in an ever-changing athletic world.

Phil Jackson's coaching exemplifies the ideas of Peirce's agapastic theory of evolution. The construction of blueprints, for example, seems to serve as a process for Jackson rather than as an end. Athletic worlds constantly change, and therefore it is important to "never repeat[ing] with exactitude."[35] Yet we always start somewhere, in the middle of a moving history. Consequently, experiences within the athletic world should live with a dynamic and developmental teleology, rather than fit a fixed teleology.

Jackson also appears to embody the idea of 'love' as it relates to coaching. Love, in this context, is not about the display of emotion but is about the approach one takes in preparation, in presentation, and in dealing with others.[36] To coach through love requires a sense of vulnerability, the courage to risk, and the need to support athletes unconditionally. As Anderson and Ventimiglia argue, the certainty of a fixed telos is replaced by the certainty of love, no matter the outcome.[37] Consequently only the loving coach, the agapastic coach, provides athletes with the courage to risk, to accept the real possibility of failure. As Peirce writes,

> Suppose, for example, that I have an idea that interests me. It is my creation. It is my creature; I love it; and I will sink myself in perfecting it. It is not by dealing out cold justice to the circle of my ideas that I can make them grow, but by cherishing and tending them as I would the flowers in my garden.[38]

Only through risk can athletes grow. Limits must be probed and redefined; habits must be transformed and reconstructed; objectives must be sought and refined—all without guarantees. Consequently coaches must be 'prepared', must be knowledgeable, and must be willing to risk as well while providing unconditional love: agapasm.[39]

V. CONCLUSION: AGAPASTIC COACHING AS A SUPERIOR METHOD

The field of coaching, like many of our pursuits in modernity, embodies a rationalistic and scientistic ethos. Elite coaches often operate more like stimulus-response seeking laboratory scientists than the leaders of athletes and teams. We find scientific terminology being employed in the coaching world as in the building of "team chemistry." Coaches study the latest motivational techniques, perform psychological evaluations on athletes to determine their level of character, and employ team building procedures to "create" team chemistry. Two parts players, one part coach, and a pinch of character—or whatever the new recipe is for team cohesion.

Chemistry of course refers to chemical bonds necessary to maintain the fixed structure—they cannot be broken without changing the structure or destroying it all together. Attempts to create "team chemistry" through anancastic coaching methods are similarly fragile. When the coach adds the necessary "ingredients" to create a solid, fixed structure, he is never completely sure what the fixed substance will be (our chemical-coaching theories have yet to gain this level of predictability). If the coach is not happy with the product, he must either accept it or destroy it (or be removed from his position).

Too often coaches try to fit teams into their coaching mold. When new coaches begin with previously established teams, often the entire group of athletes must be replaced to fit the style of the coach. Is the fixed telos, the necessarily mechanistic approach of the acancastic style of the coach, appropriate for *this team*, at *this time*? Most coaches do not take these questions into account. They drive hard toward their fixed, final goals while taking no (or lots of) prisoners along the way.

These determinate and unwavering authoritarians who understand the game "better than anyone else" are the coaches we typically celebrate. When one achieves, others will flock to observe and apply the exact formula in different situations. We buy their books and videos, attend their conference presentations, and gain access to their innermost insights into coaching—or so we think. The field of coaching thus collectively embarks upon a quest for certainty to eliminate the chance and spontaneity that can only serve to reduce the predictability of athletic contests.

So if the traditional anancastic style is not the best approach, perhaps it is the anti-establishment tychastic coaching style. Interestingly, the success of Phil Jackson likely generated some curiosity about and interest in tychastic coaching. Jackson's renowned connection to Eastern philosophy piqued the interest of many. Often referred to as "Zen Master," Jackson's success and unique style pointed many to the use of Eastern philosophic methods for coaching. However, one needs to understand Jackson's "Zen" in context. The necessary elimination of ego in the Zen tradition does not truly capture Jackson's coaching style. Jackson remains committed to structure and winning, and is not opposed to confrontation. But the influence of Zen on Jackson is important. He recognizes the importance of firstness and encourages spontaneity and chance. These characteristics of firstness provide participants with exploratory and expressive opportunities.

But does tychasm hold participants? Pure firstness lacks meaning and the grounds for formation of habits. Without direction and structure, athletes and teams will most likely be set adrift. Their experience as athletes could be compared to the purposeless, meaningless, and sensually stimulating experience of riding a roller coaster. Certainly the phenomenological quality of roller coasters, and sport, can be intoxicating, but is it enough? Not likely.

Therefore, by taking the good qualities of anancasm and tychasm coaches can create an athletic environment of creativity, spontaneity, passion, discipline, meaning, and purpose—an agapastic approach. From tychasm, coaches appreciate the role spontaneity and existential exploration play in athletic development. As Peirce argued, "everybody knows that the long continuance of habit makes us lethargic, while a succession of surprises wonderfully brightens the ideas."[40] From anancasm, the constraints and recognition of continuity as operative in the world teaches coaches the central need to help athletes form habits—habits "destined to be broken up and so to render the mind lively."[41] A fixed telos does not allow the athlete and team to develop as constant revision is necessary. Athletes can commit to evolving as individuals and team members without being denied the phenomenological sensations and spirit of exploration available in sport. But in addition to the spontaneity, there are constraints under constant revision to allow for meaning and purpose.

If coaches truly are the gatekeepers to the athletic world and formulators of sport culture, they have been granted an esteemed position in culture. They hold the keys to experiences central to the lives of so many. Yet our sport world seems to be moving toward the two extremes forwarded by Alexander: mechanical lockstep routine, or loose and meaningless disorganization. Agapasm provides an opportunity to forge an attractive middle path. Our greatest cultural achievements—by artists, athletes, politicians, scientists—all developed when the creators loved their subject matter. These creators also undertook their work with a spirit of exploration and inquiry and adopted a developmental telos. These men and women also recognized the reality of human fallibility. Much of life involves trial and error in the ultimate quest is to make the world better.

The same holds true for sport. Sport should not be a mechanically scientific endeavor dictated by set recipes and technical manipulation. Nor should it be a meaningless and purposeless endeavor. Sport should be loved in a Peircean sense. Coaches, in many ways, hold the key to expanding sport's possibilities by loving their athletes and their sports. And in many ways, the field of coaching needs new ways of thinking—an agapastic revolution that opens space for risk built on foundations constantly passed forward.

NOTES

1. For a pragmatic discussion on tests and contests, see Scott Kretchmar and Tim Elcombe, "In Defense of Competition and Winning: Revisiting Athletic Tests and Contests," in William J. Morgan (Ed.) *Ethics in Sport* (2nd ed.) (Champaign, IL: Human Kinetics, 2007), pp. 181-194.

2. Charles S. Peirce, "Evolutionary Love," in Nathan House and Christian Kloesel (Eds.) *The Essential Peirce: Selected Philosophical Writings, Volume 1 (1867-1893)* [hereafter *EP1*] (Bloomington, IN: Indiana University Press, 1992), pp. 352-371.

3. Prior to the late 1850s, few athletes or teams utilized the services of coaches. As the competition between American intercollegiate athletic rivals Harvard and Yale

intensified the increasingly rational approach adopted within sports began to include coaches. Many abhorred the notion of coaches directing these gentleman amateur athletes in noble football, baseball, and crew contests. In fact, coaches remained off the "sidelines" until the turn of the century when football coaches, including John Heisman and Amos Alonzo Stagg, glamorized the profession. See Ronald A. Smith, *Sports and Freedom: The Rise of Big-Time College Athletics* (New York: Oxford University Press, 1988).

4. Federer, one of the greatest tennis players of all time, rarely uses a coach to assist in his preparations.

5. Woods changed coaches from Butch Harmon to Hank Haney in 2004 despite winning eight major titles while working with Harmon. After parting ways with Harmon to transform his swing, Woods failed to win a major in ten attempts, prompting the media to challenge the prudence of his decision.

6. Thomas M. Alexander, "Between Being and Emptiness: Toward an Eco-Ontology of Inhabitation," in William J. Gavin (Ed.) *In Dewey's Wake: Unfinished Work of Pragmatic Reconstruction* (Albany, NY: State University of New York Press, 2003), p. 129.

7. Peirce, "Evolutionary Love," p. 363.

8. Louis Menand, *The Metaphysical Club: A Story of Ideas in America* (New York: Farrar, Straus and Giroux, 2001), p. 121.

9. Peirce, "Evolutionary Love," p. 362.

10. Menand, *The Metaphysical Club*, p. 124.

11. Nathan Houser, "Introduction," in *EP1*, p. xxx.

12. Few coaches at the elite level or in high-profile positions, however, subscribe to a tychastic coaching style. The demands placed on coaches require a visible presence in fostering the evolution of teams and athletes. Anxious administrators, athletes, spectators, and parents, rarely acknowledge the promotion of pure spontaneity and fortuitous chance as adequate coaching. Coaches not actively participating in the development of skill or competitive situation risk being accused of not coaching at all. The rise in popularity of all-star team events (including Amateur Athletic Union [AAU] basketball) has increased the number of tychastic coaches at the grassroots level, however. Coaches in these scenarios are expected to not interfere with the natural and instinctive athletic abilities. They are merely expected to serve as coordinators and resource facilitators.

13. Menand, *The Metaphysical Club*, p. 196.

14. Houser, "Introduction," p. xxx.

15. Peirce, "Evolutionary Love," p. 356.

16. Ibid.

17. Ibid., p. 354.

18. Ibid., p. 357.

19. Ibid.

20. Ibid., p. 356.

21. Thomas M. Alexander, *John Dewey's Theory of Art, Experience, and Nature: The Horizons of Feeling* (Albany: State University of New York Press, 1987), p. 203.

22. Peirce, "Evolutionary Love," p. 353.

23. Ibid., p. 354.

24. Ibid., p. 360.

25. Douglas R. Anderson and Michael Ventimiglia, "Learning and Teaching: Gambling, Love, and Growth," in Douglas R. Anderson *Philosophy Americana: Making Philosophy Home in American Culture* (New York: Fordham University, 2006), p. 172.

26. Peirce, "Evolutionary Love," p.360.

27. Menand, *The Metaphysical Club*, p. 145.

28. Ibid., p. 88.

29. Peirce, "Evolutionary Love," p. 361.

30. Houser, "Introduction," p. xxii.

31. Ibid., p. xxx.

32. For non-basketball aficionados, the Jordan-Pippen strength came from their abilities as 6'6 and 6'8 athletes capable of scoring from the outer edges of the offensive zone, or by attacking the goal with quickness. Bryant, at 6'8, plays a game similar to Jordan and Pippen, however the presence of O'Neal (at 7'1 and over 330 pounds) presented new opportunities and challenges to score. Bryant emerged as the unquestioned Lakers star player with the support of the less physical but highly versatile big men Gasol (7'0) and Odom (6'10) in Jackson's last two championships.

33. Phil Jackson and Charley Rosen, *More Than a Game* (New York: Seven Stories Press, 2001), p. 281.

34. Ibid., p. 150.

35. Menand, *The Metaphysical Club*, p. 227.

36. Anderson and Ventimiglia, "Learning and Teaching, p. 183.

37. Ibid., p. 172.

38. Peirce, "Evolutionary Love," p. 354.

39. Anderson and Ventimiglia, "Learning and Teaching, pp. 172-173.

40. Peirce, "Evolutionary Love," p. 361.

41. Ibid.

SEVEN

Gender, Sports, and the Ethics of Teammates: Toward an Outline of a Philosophy of Sport in the American Grain

Brent Crouch, San Diego State University

In this essay, I argue that the ethics of teammates is an underdeveloped region of the philosophy of sport (and philosophy generally) and that there are resources within American philosophy to analyze and develop its phenomena. The teammate relation has been neglected because the dominant model of the internal structure of teams, a model that I develop via Josiah Royce's theory of loyalty and community, treats these relations as secondary to the relation of loyalty to a team's cause. The teammate relation should, however, be a central focus for philosophers because (1) interactions with teammates form the primary source of interaction in sports, and (2) because it appears, contra Royce, as primary for many athletes. To adequately theorize this relation and its ethics, the dominant Roycean model must therefore be seen as not universal, and an alternative model should be developed. I lay out a two-part program to do so that draws on Charles Peirce's logic of relations, and Jane Addam's version of care ethics.

In September, 2007, coach Greg Ryan of the USA Women's Soccer Team made a bold strategic decision. Instead of playing ace goalkeeper Hope Solo in the World Cup semifinal match against Brazil, Ryan elected to start veteran Briana Scurry. This decision was highly publicized by the sports media because it appeared to be such a radical and questionable decision. True, Scurry had played well against Brazil in the 2004 Olympic

Games and had helped secure the victory, but that was three years prior and Solo had since earned the starting role. It was a risk, a gamble. And in the end, it was a gamble that failed dramatically. Scurry gave up four goals, and the US team lost 4-0.

The events that followed made news outside of the sport's world. Solo criticized publicly her coach's decision, stating, "It was the wrong decision, and I think anybody that knows anything about the game knows that. There's no doubt in my mind I would have made those saves. And the fact of the matter is, it's not 2004 anymore." The reaction to Solo's comments by her team was dramatic. Solo was benched for the bronze-medal match, and then suspended from the team. In fact, she was not allowed to attend the match, nor attend the medal ceremony where her teammates received the bronze. At the end of the tournament, she was also prevented to return to the US on the same flight. After a few months, Solo rejoined the team. Yet, despite a public apology and a team meeting to clear the air, only one player visited her room, joined her for meals, or sat next to her on the bench.

Solo's teammates' reaction has been criticized by many and found, by many others, to be downright perplexing. Kasey Keller, a US Men's Soccer Team goalie and 18-year professional veteran in English pro leagues stated what most in the sporting world were thinking: "In England guys get in fights and arguments all the time, and usually within an hour or by the next day everything's fine. But to be completely ostracized? I've never heard of anything like that." Others have claimed, however, that women soccer players, and women teammates in general, inherently handle conflicts among themselves differently. Cat Whitehill, a teammate of Solo's, stated after the incident that male teammates "can punch somebody in the face and it's done with. For girls, we don't punch in the face. We hold it in, and when it comes out, it's fire, which is really awful. But as women we all understand that people are human, and I think everybody has truly forgiven Hope. We can still have a bond with her."[1]

Solo's situation is not a rare occurrence in competitive team athletics. In America, thousands of players and coaches negotiate ethical problems among teammates every day. In my own experience as a volleyball coach and player, I have witnessed and participated in similar events—though perhaps not as extreme!—on both men's and women's teams. But Solo's public situation, and also the attempts to understand its moral dimensions, does throw into relief three philosophically interesting facts. First, the ethical relations among teammates, that is, *intra-team* relations, are highly important, and extend beyond the bounds of competitive sports. Business and educational practices are replete with them. Second, these relations appear widely variable; Whitehill's statement above, for example, sorts them into masculine and feminine categories. Third, these relations have not been adequately addressed philosophically, nor have they been addressed clearly in popular culture. The evident groping about for explanations and answers in popular writings, and the facile solution proffered about inherent differences between the sexes indicates at once the lack and the need for real philosophical reflection on situations like Solo's and the ethics of teammates generally.

In this essay, I want to explore why I think the ethics of teammates is so important for philosophy to study, and then offer the following series of arguments. (1) The usual, and yet often unconscious, model of *team* and *intra-team* relations adopted by American competitive athletics (and philosophers of sport) may be represented with more clarity via Josiah Royce's theory of loyalty and community. (2) This model provides a coherent logic and ethic of intra-team relations, *but at the same time, reduces their value* by deriving them from an apparently deeper relation—that of the relation of each team member to the goal, or the *cause*, of the team. (3) Because of this reduction, relations of teammates to one another are *not* usually considered a topic for serious inquiry. (4) More importantly, however, the Roycean model fails to justly account for relations among teammates whose value and fecundity seemingly *exceed* that of the relation of team member to the cause of the team. This failure points to the need of an alternative model of *team* and *intra-team relations*. I conclude the essay with a program for future research in this direction.

ON THE IMPORTANCE OF AN ETHICS OF TEAMMATES

Although the literature on ethics and sports is voluminous, it is narrowly focused on the following issues: fair play and the development of moral virtue and character.[2] The issues surrounding fair play often concern the rules of competition and players' comportment with respect to these rules. Analyses of cheating, the use of performance enhancing drugs, and respect for one's opponent are typical topics. The inquiries into the relation of team sports and moral virtues, on the other hand, are more directly connected with the general theme of moral edification. There is a long history of discussion surrounding the benefits or harms of competitive athletic participation upon the character of both the players and the viewers of competitive athletic events. In general then, the focus, thus far, has been upon the ethics of *inter-team* interactions within the boundaries of competition, and upon the moral development of individual competitors.

This twin focus is important to highlight, for it reveals an important point: the prevailing model of the structure of athletic teams clearly deemphasizes *intra-team* relations among teammates. The lack of scholarship on these relations is an indication of this general orientation, as is the confusion with situations like Solo's.[3] Intra-team relations, however, are, in my view, more important to address than inter-team competitive relations, and more important than the study of the cultivation of moral virtues in these contexts.

The simple reason why arises from the following indisputable fact: by far the most interactions a player has in her playing career is with her teammates. These interactions occur prior to, during, and after training. They occur when traveling to and from competitions. And they occur in times of relaxation away the sport. To give just one example: a competitive Division I NCAA women's volleyball program will spend three to four weeks of two to three practices a day, six days a week *prior* to the actual competitive season beginning and, therefore, prior to competing in a formal match. This time does not include the time spent together at meals or in the weight room. During the season, practices run two to four almost every day that the team is not competing. After the season ends (it is 3-4 months long), off-season training begins. Since an average team plays in roughly thirty matches *a year*, a simple calculation and comparison confirms my point: teammate interaction is the primary type of interaction that occurs in competitive team sports. Youth team sports are not much different; competitive matches are infrequent and teammate interaction predominant.

The effects of such massive interaction on the lives of the participants are difficult to fathom. Plausibly, habits and moral conceptions cultivated in these interactions are transferred into broader social settings, and vice-versa. And, given the number of participants in team sports in America at all levels and age groups, the effect of these habits and conceptions in general social life, not to mention within teams themselves, is probably substantial. Philosophical reflection on the structure of teams and the norms that govern their internal interactions, and those norms that *should* govern them should be of paramount concern to philosophers.

Why, then, has the ethics of teammates not been addressed? There are two major reasons. First, much of the philosophical inquiry into sports has most likely come from observers of sport rather than active participants. To the observer, the experience of team sports is primarily confined to formal competitions, and so the philosophical problems that present themselves are sorted through that medium. Hence, it is not surprising that concern primarily for fair play and issues like sportsmanship should dominate the ethical literature on sports. The second reason is much more influential: the prevailing model (adopted by most athletes, viewers, and scholars) of the structure and internal relations of teams deemphasizes the ethical relations among teammates. This deemphasis occurs on a formal and axiological level. I turn now to an explication of this model.

THE PREVAILING MODEL OF THE STRUCTURE OF COMPETITIVE ATHLETIC TEAMS

In our classical American tradition, Josiah Royce's logic of community and his ethic of loyalty together form the outstanding example of the most prevalent model of the structure of teams and the ethics of team-mates.[4] A Roycean community is defined, in part, through the connections of three terms: a *cause*, *individuals* related to the cause, and the *relation* which binds a cause and the individuals. "[A] cause," Royce writes, "means . . . something that is conceived by its loyal servant as unifying the lives of various human begins into one life."[5] For example, a cause may be curing cancer, and the individuals related to the cause are those doctors and others that work together to see their cause to fruition. United through their service, these individuals constitute a single entity: a community. Loyalty is Royce's description of the relation between individuals and their common causes. In *The Philosophy of Loyalty*, Royce gives a series of definitions of loyalty, each intended to deepen and extend its import. His first definition reads: "The willing and practical and thoroughgoing devotion of a person to a cause."[6] A person is loyal when she *consciously intends* to serve the cause, actually *performs concrete actions* aimed toward it. Royce's mention of "thoroughgoing" is intended to add that true loyalty suffuses the whole person: intellect, emotion, will, and action must be aligned and harmonized in relation to the cause for true loyalty to exist. Royce's last definition of loyalty emphasizes its metaphysical and metaethical import: "Loyalty is the will to manifest, so far as is possible, the Eternal, that is, the conscious and superhuman unity of life, in the form of the acts of an individual Self."[7] This is not the place for a full explication of Royce's final definition of loyalty; I mention it only to exhibit a cause's centrality and importance with respect to its willing servants and their relations. As Royce says, they lie at different levels.

The doctrine of the two levels of a community finds a full articulation with respect to the Christian community in Royce's *The Problem of Christianity*.[8] But the clearest expression of this doctrine is found in a logical formulation written in a letter to a colleague.[9] In the letter, Royce argues that, formally, loyalty is the relation "being a member of," symbolized by Royce as "M" (currently by "M"). If one is loyal to a cause, then one belongs to the cause, or rather, belongs to community that is defined by, and is the expression of, the cause.

This relation has been studied closely by logicians and was used during Royce's time (and now) as the basis of what is now known as set theory. Its logical properties include the following: asymmetry, non-reflexivity, and intransitivity. In our context, the asymmetry of the M-relation is the most important, for it maps the two levels of a community. The individual's loyal relation to the cause is *not* the same as the cause's relation to the individual: the cause lies on a higher level than the individual. Royce argues this hierarchy implies that the cause and the community it forms are both more *real* and more *valuable* than the individuals which are loyal to it.[10] In one sense, these claims follow from the individual member's experience. Causes, since they call us to serve them and animate our life, appear as givers of purpose and meaning. In *The Problem of Christianity*, this gift of loyalty appears as *grace*, and also as the *origin of life itself.*[11]

While the great metaphysical and ethical importance of the cause with respect to loyal *individuals* is captured by the asymmetry of the M-relation, the formal difference, of the M-relation from other intra-communal relations captures the asymmetry of the *relation* of loyalty with respect to the *relations among members*. A similar metaphysical and ethical hierarchy exists here, as before. But here, it rests on the fact that intra-communal relations are logically *derived* from the loyalty relation. To see this formal difference, consider Royce's example in his letter:

> Consider, as a simple instance of what I mean, a "linear triad" of points in space. A linear triad in points in space, is a triad such as (p, q, r), when p, q, r, lie on one right line. In our ordinary "descriptive space, *one* of the members of such a linear triad lies *between* the two others. Now let T be used, for the moment, to name this linear triad as an assemblage or set of points. We can then say: "p M T," "q M T," and also "r M T." Notice how differnt is the relation of q to T from the relation of q to p and to r or the pair (p, r). q is *a member of* T. q is *between* p and r. The distinction is quite fundamental for the whole of geometry.[12]

Once these relations are adequately distinguished, it is possible, argues Royce to *define* all types of relations in terms of classes of individual members, and hence in terms of the M-relation.[13] Accordingly, not only do *individuals* pale in comparison to the cause that creates the community, but the *relations* among individuals appear to have a derivative and hence secondary status with respect to the relation of loyalty, or the M-relation.

This logical derivation cashes out in Royce's ethics in two distinct ways. First, the ethical relations among community members are determined with reference to, and in subservience of, the particular cause that unites them, and thus, one's duties towards others are derivative of one's logically prior loyalty to the cause. Second, since the relation of loyalty is of supreme metaphysical, logical, and ethic importance, Royce argues that our highest cause should be loyalty to loyalty itself. This means, concretely, that when judging and selecting causes, one should chose so that the cause also serves the cause of loyalty itself, that is, of preserving it and extending its field of connections.

With this rough sketch of Royce's theory in hand, we can return to the interpretation of the structure and ethics of the interior of a team. A team is a class of individuals loyal to a cause. Usually this cause is stated in terms of some competitive goal, such as winning a championship. One's individual ethical duties with respect to the team as a whole and its cause are determined by the needs of the cause. A player must train hard so as to help realize the goal, and play whatever position the team needs her to play in order to help secure the goal. She must be selfless, devoted, and dedicated. Her teammates are experienced *primarily* as coworkers united in their service to the cause. This calls for mutual respect and recognition, and perhaps support and encouragement in training and playing. Whatever other relations that may obtain between teammates, and that are not necessary to realize the cause, fade into the background and must not be allowed to interfere with competition and training. Loyalty to loyalty dictates that one respect the rules of competition, and do what one can to ensure the integrity of the game. For this ensures that other teams may form, train, and compete. The concern for fair play and sportsmanship is therefore an expression of loyalty to loyalty.[14]

CONCLUSION: THE FAILURE OF ROYCE'S MODEL AND NEW DIRECTIONS

That Royce's model of community is unconsciously adopted by many, if not most, Americans as the primary model of competitive athletic teams should not be controversial. Most anyone who has played on a competitive team is asked to do whatever it takes, within the confines of fair play, to help the team achieve its goals. "Be a team player!" "Sacrifice for the team!" And when conflicts arise between teammates, coaches usually say things like the following: "I don't care if you *like* each other or if you *hate* each other, but you will respect one another enough to *work* together to achieve our common cause!" In short, relations among teammates are important and worthy of care and nurture *only* to the degree that these relations contribute actively to the cause of the team. Their value *is* only insofar as they derive from loyalty to the team cause. By far the more important relation, formally and materially, is that of loyalty to the cause.

Royce's account of loyalty and community, therefore, is not merely descriptive; it is also normative. It serves as an ideal that all sport's teams should strive to achieve. Certainly some of Solo's teammates, and Solo herself, understood their situation in this manner. Commenting on what she sees as a transition from a non-Roycean to a Roycean team, US soccer team member Abby Wambach said, "Things are changing. The younger players have a little bit of that emotional attachment to each other, but less so than in the past. You don't have to like each other, but once you cross that line [enter the game], if you can like each other for at least 90 minutes, then I think you can be successful." Statements like these belie tacit acceptance of the normative force of Royce's model. Relations among teammates, if thought about at all, are typically categorized as those that that help the team, and those that don't. Those that don't are considered immature, irrelevant, and are often cast, like Wambach does, in emotional terms. And the lack of professional scholarship on the team-mate relation is only a natural consequence of conceiving it as "second-class citizen."

The force of Solo's situation, however, and other situations like it, should give one pause. Certainly, my own experience coaching and play-ing with both men's and women's teams has caused me to reflect upon the descriptive accuracy, normative force, and logical validity of Royce's model of community as it applies to competitive sports teams. For what is apparent is that Solo's teammates clearly thought her actions violated norms governing their relations as teammates, and further, that these relations were somehow *more* valuable (and perhaps more *real)* than whatever loyalty they possessed to the cause of winning the gold.[15] In my own experience as a professional coach over a period of ten years, I have seen this phenomenon, and not only on women's teams. Other coaches I have discussed this with have witnessed it as well.

It is *possible* to understand the experiential primacy of intra-team rela-tions as a failure on the part of Solo's teammates to properly evaluate and modify their relations to one another and to their cause, as Wambach seems to do. But we might also question the ability of the dominant Roycean model to explain the phenomena accurately, and its elevation to an ideal. A radically empirical philosophical methodology, one that takes its cue from the primacy of the phenomena, would seem to dictate this. This is a path I believe worth pursuing, and there are other resources within the American philosophical tradition from which to draw.

To conclude, I want to specify the general shape of such an inquiry. In order to successfully describe the phenomena of the primacy and ethic of the teammate relation I suggest the following two part program: (1) At the level of the logical analysis of relations, pursue a theory of relations that avoids defining them in extension (that is, as Royce does, as a class of individuals defined by the all-important M-relation). Charles Peirce, for instance, follows this path with his conception of a relation *as such.*[16] Making relations of all kinds logically primary, and not derivative from the relation of loyalty, appears to be a promising way to be formally faithful to the phenomenal importance of the teammate relation. (2) At the level of ethics, such a shift toward the primacy of inter-personal rela-tions suggests a turn toward a more overtly care based ethic, and a move away from deontological and consequentialist ethics (of which Royce's ethic is a unique blend). The version of care ethics developed by Jane Addams might prove to be an important resource in this context. For as Maurice Hamington notes, "while Addams employed caring in response to the needs of others, she contributes an active, even assertive, dimen-sion to care ethics not commonly found in feminist theory."[17]

A pragmatic care ethic with an emphasis on action, combined with a logic of relations, is a promising lead into an alternative model of intra-team ethical relations.

NOTES

1. Quotes taken from Grant Wahl, "Hard Return," in *Sports Illustrated*, June 30 2008.
2. See as evidence for this claim such texts as: *Ethics and Sport*, ed. M.J. McNamee and S.J. Perry; *Ethics in Sports*, ed. William J. Morgan, Klaus V. Mein, and Angela J. Schneider; *The Erosion of the American Sorting Ethos: Shifting Attitudes Toward Competition*, by Joel Nathan Rosen; *Sports Ethics: An Anthology*, ed. Jan Boxill, *Fair Play: The Ethics of Sport*, by Robert L. Simon.
3. There are, to date, no philosophical articles on the nature and ethics of the teammate relation. So far, the only research on intra-team relations has focused upon the coach-athlete relation.
4. Indeed, Royce himself used these theories to analyze various aspects of sports in "Football and Ideals," and "Some Relations of Physical Training to the Present Problems of Moral Education in American." Josiah Royce, *Race Questions, Provincialism, and Other American Problems* (New York: McMillan, 1908), p. 227 ff.
5. Josiah Royce, *The Philosophy of Loyalty*, p. 252.
6. Ibid., p. 17.
7. Ibid., 357.
8. Cf. Royce, *The Problem of Christianity*, pp. 50, 122, 139, 218, 268-269, 194.
9. Royce to Fite, July 20, 1913, *Letters*, ed. John Clendenning, 604-609. Royce often used symbolic logic as a means to clarify relations. Indeed, he argued that this was the sole purpose of symbolic logic! Royce writes: "'Symbolic Logic' I use, not as an end in itself, but merely as a means to state some exact relations so that one sees them for what they are, and gets clear of all this desolating pragmatistic psychologizing tendency which now undertakes to save us the trouble of having any thoughts at all." Royce to Fite, July 11, 1911, p. 556.
10. Royce, *The Problem of Christianity*, 125.
11. Ibid., 57-58.
12. Royce to Fite, *Letters*, 608.
13. "In brief, *a relation is a character that an object possesses as a member of a collection* (a pair, a triad, an n-ad, a club, a family, a nation, etc.), and which (as one may conceive), would not belong to that object, were it not such a member." Royce, *The Principles of Logic*, 339.
14. From this perspective, we can see that Solo's public criticism emerged from her loyalty to the cause of winning the championship, but that it was *not* an expression of loyalty to loyalty.
15. It is also doubtful that all the negative interactions between Solo and her teammates derived from some perceived violation by Solo of the cause of the team, or the cause of loyalty to loyalty. For loyalty to a cause, whether of winning the championship or to loyalty itself seems, in this situation, irrelevant. The issue appears to be centered on the relations among Solo and her teammates alone.
16. Robert Burch attempts a Peircean analysis of relations *as such*, what he calls *relation-simpliciter* in his work *A Peircean Reduction Thesis: The Foundations of Topological Logic*. To what degree his results might aid the present inquiry deserves attention.
17. Maurice Hamington, "Jane Addams," *Stanford Encyclopedia of Philosophy*.

EIGHT

Dick Butkus, Pragmatism, and Performance Art

Douglas Anderson, Southern Illinois University

Ralph Waldo Emerson and John Dewey are not the chief intellectual progenitors of what has come to be called "performance art." But they might have been insofar as they both, in somewhat different ways, argued for the carrying out of art in ordinary settings. Emerson says in his essay "Art," "All works of art should not be detached, but extempore performances."[1] And in *Art as Experience* Dewey maintains that "Works of art that are not remote from common life, that are widely enjoyed in a community, are signs of a unified collective life."[2] It is from this simple perspective that I want to examine the relationship between two American cultural phenomena: professional football and performance art. Moreover, within these two general phenomena I want to narrow our gaze in paying attention to two specific genres: the act of "linebacking" in football and the act of "performance" in performance art. And, finally, in order to hold our gaze at this level, I shall draw on the particular experiences of Dick Butkus, former University of Illinois and Chicago Bear football player whose mode of play essentially defined the role of "middle linebacker." On the other side, I will explore the works of several of the most noted performance artists of the last quarter century, including, for example, Linda Montano and Yves Klein.

It is a cultural commonplace for us that football and performance art should stand in stark contrast to one another. Artists and perhaps especially art theorists in the U.S. generally segregate their actions and the object of their study from the "business" and the "entertainment" that is football. Even in one instance where this seems not to be the case—the aesthetic of "kitsch"—the point is still to be made that the kitsch theorist *understands* the art-ness in ways that seem inaccessible to the ordinary person. In short, the arts and aesthetic theorizing in the U.S. operate from a standpoint of cultural superiority—football is its antithesis.

Football culture, unlike the culture of the fine arts, celebrates its down-to-earthness, its lack of pretension, and its blue collar—and consequently anti-intellectual—attitude. If there is a strategy in play-calling and game-calling and if there are "graceful" performances on the field, these are not to be mistaken for what is essential in football—what is essential is hitting other people. Football, especially at the higher levels, is "played for keeps." Linebackers, the primary "hitters," characterize and exemplify this violent essence of football. Football is not about what William James called "soul-flights"; it is about brutality, sheer and simple. Whatever one thinks of the moral issues involved in the recent "bounty" scandal of the New Orleans Saints, no one has questioned the centrality of violence and brutality for the game.

My aim is not to deny or reassess the basic aims of football and performance art. Nor am I likely to undo the deep cultural antagonisms that grow out of these differences. But I do think something can be said to show that the polarization is underwritten by severe caricaturing. Emerson and Dewey provide a lead here that I will follow. That is, the relationship between the ordinary and practical (say, football) and the extraordinary and theoretical (art and art theory) is significantly more complex than we let on. Rethinking this relationship requires us to reorient some of our cultural categories. At present, we employ some traditional and in some ways outmoded distinctions—fine art vs. *techne,* mind vs. body, thought vs. action—to blind ourselves to the ways in which football might be intrinsically artistic and the ways in which performance art may involve both spectacle and brutality. Performance art is often understood as "breaking frame"—as overcoming the traditional "framing" of art works to see the *process* of artistic creation as itself a work of art. My aim is to break the frame of traditional conceptions of football and performance art to try to illuminate what both are—or at least how they function for us—as human practices and experiences.

Performance art developed in the U.S. in the 1960s and '70s at the same time that Dick Butkus was playing college and professional football. An outgrowth of conceptual art, performance art was alternatively called body art, event art, or action art. Jackson Pollock's active style of painting foreshadowed the inauguration of performance art in the '60s. And Yves Klein's use of his models' bodies to apply paint to canvas in his "blue" works helped generate the full "breaking of frame" in which the body and its environment became the medium. Allan Kaprow, John Cage, and others created "happenings" in which individuals undertook loosely scripted roles in a communal performance that was more than random behavior but considerably less than fully choreographed theater.

In performance art, the body moved from instrument to medium; it became the site of testing, reflection, provocation, and judgment, as when German artists Marina Abramovic and Ulay performed "Light/Dark," a work in which "they slapped each other in the face until one of them stopped. Enduring such protracted physical pain was a part of their work."[3]

Performance's kinship with conceptual art meant that it was not what the idealists had come to call "art for art's sake." Whatever its intrinsic virtues, performance art also served to generate and explore meanings. Much performance was intent on revealing us to ourselves through actions that would awaken us to our own possibilities. "Light/Dark," for example, confronted us with everything from abusive relationships to the cultural prevalence of the "slap" in American film. Performance art reveals various features of human experience. Linda Montano and Tehching Hsieh tethered themselves to each other with a six-foot cord for one year; for Montano, the performance helped disclose elements of sexism in personal and cultural relations that might ordinarily go unnoticed. Thus, performance art explores the ambiguity of the border between the "real" and the "enacted." Performance is "real" insofar as it occurs in ordinary venues at ordinary times and is performed by apparently ordinary persons, including the sons of blue collar Lithuanian families in Chicago. But it is also "unreal" just insofar as it is a performance or exhibition; though not closely choreographed, it is always scripted in some general way.

In revealing our situatedness to us, performance art can have the secondary effect of triggering the exploration of issues in their relations to ourselves and to society generally. Montano, for example, "was interested in issues like claustrophobia, and ego and power relationships — Life issues."[4] Others have investigated the limits of the self. Gina Pane's legendary projects of self-mutilation, for example, tested not only short run pain but also the self's long run construction of an identity. Pane, one critic notes, "frequently pushed herself to her physical and psychological limits."[5]

Performance art such as Pane's and Montano's naturally raised issues that had implications beyond their individuality. The revelation of human possibilities and the public exploration of one's own limits provoked both social commentary and considerations of the transformation of cultural practices. Even if unintended, performance art inevitably has a political edge. Those performance artists who still view themselves as working in the genre of conceptual art usually do intend the political edge. Pane, and others like her, openly aim "to communicate ethical and philosophical concerns" through their performances. We need only note current explorations of tattooing, piercing, and branding in the last few decades to see that Pane's apparently marginal art work projects streams of influence that reach to the core of Western culture. Likewise, Korean-American artist Park Kum Young has used her art to explore the tensions in living across cultures as an adopted Korean woman living in the United States. Young, adopted by an American family as a child, now explores her Korean heritage from an outsider's view; she believes her status as outsider in all of her roles allows her performances to reveal things that often get overlooked. In general, then, performance art explores the reciprocity between self and society from a variety of angles of vision, always while blurring the distinction between the real and the enacted. Performance is almost always meant to be provocative and evocative— otherwise it might blend in too well with the ordinary and lose its efficacy.

I am hoping that those readers who are familiar with the football career of Dick Butkus will have heard phrases in my discussion of performance art that in a general way are transferable to Butkus. Phrases such as "provocative and evocative," "self-mutilation," "the body as a medium," and "finding one's limits." To see Butkus' practice of linebacking as an "art of the ornery" is to see him as carrying out a project similar in kind to those I have been describing as exemplary of performance art. In taking this line of thinking my aim is not to reduce Butkus to the status of avant-garde artist or artistic dilettante. Rather, my belief is that if we try to understand Butkus as a performance artist we might illuminate both features of his actions that we might otherwise overlook and features of our own relations to his performances to which we might occasionally be blind. I follow Dewey and Emerson in thinking that art is more revelatory than explanatory, and I join them in believing that something as ordinary as playing a football game on Sunday afternoon might be the site of artistic performance.

Butkus' field performance for nine years as a professional linebacker with the Chicago Bears is pragmatically equivalent to a variety of art performances. That is, the two share a wide range of actual effects in the world and are thus functionally the same. Most notably, Butkus used his body as a medium and means of expression. He employed extensive body language almost constantly while on the field and his body-in-motion was, ontologically speaking, the performing of linebacking. The similarity is simple and striking, despite the distinctions our cultural categories of "art" and "sport" try to maintain. Performance artists and linebackers do things with their bodies in public fashion for an audience. This affinity between the two is underwritten by a more general shared trait: art and sport create their own worlds *within* our everyday world. As T. R. Martland suggests: "To be in play is to be in an illusion. But illusion is not delusion."[6] Butkus and the performance artist create and work in an illusion that is not merely delusion—or perhaps in an illusion that self-destructs when it becomes delusion. Without any significant stretch, we can think of Hsieh's 1981-82 performance, in which he lived outdoors *as if* homeless for one year, as on a continuum with Butkus' nine seasons of performing on the football field *as if* he were genuinely ornery.

Butkus' particular self-chosen task was to embody, both literally and figuratively, bruteness and orneriness. In being self-chosen and intentionally created, this was a performative and artful embodiment—like an action artist, Butkus routinely blurred the distinction between the real and the enacted. Butkus was ornery and brutal but not merely so—his body's expression was both less and more than sheer brutality. It was less because it was a performance. Instead of just *being* ornery and brutal, Butkus had to prepare himself to perform. He would work during the week to get himself into an attitude of "nastiness" suitable for his performance on Sunday: "By the time I got to Wrigley Field on game day," he says, "I had psyched myself into a state of pure hatred of the enemy."[7] The process of preparation took place right until game time: "When I went out on the field to warm up," he said, "I would manufacture things to make me mad. If someone on the other team was laughing, I'd pretend he was laughing at me or the Bears. I'd find something to get mad about."[8] Although this may seem obvious to some, it has never been obvious to many. Butkus, because of the ambiguity of his role, is often understood to be his on-field persona—a nasty, mean, and brutal human being. This may be true of some athletes—Ty Cobb comes to mind—but it wasn't true of Butkus. "I am not mean by nature," he says almost defensively; indeed, that is the point of his preparation. During his senior year at Illinois, Butkus became the focus of a *Sports Illustrated* article by Dan Jenkins in which Jenkins described him as a "brute" and a "lover of violence." Butkus was genuinely offended and incensed by the article. Although performance art blurs the distinction between the real and the artful, it only functions if the distinction is maintained. If we saw Ulay and Abramovic slapping each other and were unaware that it was a performance, our reaction would be quite different. Butkus understood this very clearly and our failure to do so will blind us to the artfulness of his performances.

In saying that Butkus is a performance artist, however, I need to be clear that his art of the ornery is not merely "acting" in the conventional sense. This is true of all performance artists. In the many years since his retirement, Butkus has repeatedly demonstrated his ability to be an actor. His list of roles, large and small, is extensive; he can even be found on the old NBC television show *Hang Time* as Coach Katowinski. As a linebacker, however, he not only "acted" but he "performed." As the curator for the Van Abbe Museum maintains, "the performance artist does not play a role, like an actor, but carries out an act which has not been rehearsed."[9] Thus, in the film *Unnecessary Roughness* Butkus plays a specific role that is scripted, directed, rehearsed, acted, and edited. As a linebacker, in contrast, he performed the task of stopping opposition ball carriers. There are of course defensive schemes and practices, but the actual event of the game is both spontaneous and extemporaneous.

In performance art the "role" is generic rather than specific; there are ground rules but no blueprint for every action. Thus, Hsieh and Montano are left to explore what to do in living with the constraint of their tethered bodies; there are parameters but no script. The reason for this distinction is important. Because performance art intends to blur the distinction between the real and the enacted, it requires the freedom to do so. Performance takes us even closer than does acting to real human situations and thus creates an enhanced capacity for revelation and provocation. It is, as Jenkins' article and the actions of Cleveland Browns fans indicate, more difficult for the *observer* to suspend disbelief and maintain a critical distance. The power of performance art and Butkus' linebacking resides in this proximity between reality and performance that at the same time maintains their distinctness.

Thus, the fact that Butkus' performances are less than sheer brutality is precisely what allows it to be *more* than brutality. As a performance, the art of the ornery evokes a response that is quite unlike our responses to actual acts of brutality and orneriness. This distinction, which Butkus carefully cultivated, is clearly revealed in an episode involving another legendary linebacker, Lawrence Taylor. In a game against the Washington Redskins, Taylor flew around left end and zeroed in on quarterback Joe Theisman—he was the embodiment of linebacking, agility and strength permeated with a solid dose of meanness. When Taylor hit Theisman, Theisman's leg buckled under him. As Taylor heard the snapping of Theisman's leg, he immediately transformed to "concerned citizen," calling for medical assistance from the sideline. He hovered over Theisman like a worried parent. The sudden transformation reveals to us the performative nature of Taylor's role as professional linebacker. In considering our reaction to this event and to the two Lawrence Taylors, we see that our response to the linebacking of Taylor would be quite different if he had not switched persona but instead, say, had started celebrating the snapping of Theisman's leg. As it is, we respond to Taylor as performer, not as a mere brute.

What are our other responses to Taylor and to Butkus as artfully ornery linebackers? They are, I think, intellectual and aesthetic responses of the same sort we would have to performance art should we encounter it. The art provokes and evokes these responses in us. Let us consider for a moment Ulay and Abramovic's 1976 performance "Relation in Space." In it the nude artists begin in opposite corners of a room and walk back and forth toward each other until they touch lightly and, finally, collide. A kind of sensitivity to the two performers is immediately evoked because of their nudity and vulnerability; this will stand in tension with an impulsive embarrassment or discomfort for those not attuned to performance art. And yet we may be fascinated by the scene. As the action develops, the brute encounters of the performers will stand in such tension with the vulnerability that we will be provoked to consider its meaning. Thus,

"Relation in Space" confronts us with, among other things, our underlying human tendency toward violence, and forces us to consider it.

At first glance, it may seem that our responses to Butkus are not so intellectually deep or conceptual. But this is where seeing Butkus as a performance artist makes a difference. The art of the ornery does generate intellectual and aesthetic responses—everything from "did you see that" (as we might say of a Monet) to essentialist claims such as "Butkus is what linebacking means." This latter response is one that Butkus himself sought to create: "When they say 'all-pro middle-linebacker', I want them to mean Butkus."[10] On the one hand this is ridiculously obvious. In our ordinary conversations about Butkus-like performances, in television and radio sports talk, we routinely discuss our conceptual and aesthetic responses. ESPN has now, for years, shown us "highlights" whose aesthetic virtues and vices are in question. Unhappily, our cultural categorial division between art and sport makes us apologetic or makes us dismiss such talk as non-intellectual—the philosophy or aesthetics of sport are lower-tier precisely because the object of their attention is sport, in our case linebacking. Because it is about what happens on a football field and takes place in a football culture, we habitually segregate such talk from anything we might consider conceptual or aesthetic. The conservation of the cultural division seems more important than thinking about what it actually is we, as observers, are doing and what it is Butkus is actually performing.

When Butkus crosses scrimmage on a particular play and pounds a running back into the ground, we, as audience, are drawn into the performance. It is strictly analogous to a happening—the observers become active participants as audience and have the "responsibility" for interpreting what a work will mean or convey. We begin perhaps with a simple aesthetic ejaculatory response: "What a hit!" This is nevertheless an articulate response of the sort we might have to an artistic performance: "What a show!" But as we begin to consider not only one play, but other plays, games, and perhaps the whole of Butkus' career, we begin to reflect on a wider range of possibilities. Butkus reveals to us human traits both familiar and unfamiliar, such as the joy and intensity of tackling well and definitively. He shows us his—and vicariously our own—orneriness; he shows us what we might be capable of, as do Ulay and Abramovic in the slapping performance of "Light/Dark." Similarly Pane patiently and methodically cuts her arm with a razor and then sutures the cuts until she has a row of woven welts up each arm. Butkus, in his seventh season, prepared for games not only mentally but also physically. "Dr. Fox," writes Butkus, "was giving me shots of hydrocortisone after each game, then maybe another during the week, on Tuesday or Thursday. After a road game, he would come down the aisle to my window seat on the plane and sink a syringe-full into my knee at 30,000 feet."[11] He would limp to the field and punish running backs, in the process punishing his own swollen and offset knee. We see the limp and the deadened expression of pain; as in "Relation in Space" we are confronted with violence and its effects, we are pleased at and we even enjoy his ability to perform, and at the same time we wonder about the sanity of such a performance. What are we to think of these intentional disfigurements of Pane and Butkus? Is this really part of what it means to be human? In both cases, the body has become a site of the test, a medium for considering our own limitations and possibilities. Butkus and Pane, both willing to accept permanent bodily pain and alteration, evoke wonder in us and provoke us to consider our existence.

And as we consider Butkus' life and growth as a linebacker, we are drawn into an exploration of the wider implications. Hsieh and Montano tested the limits of personal endurance and proximity as a way to explore social rules about human relations. Butkus does the same. How much pain should Butkus endure in cortisone shots or in playing the game? When will the bumping of the nude artists stop; who will be the first to stop slapping? Through Butkus' performance we are led to consider the likes of football players such as Lyle Alzado and Mike Webster whose lives ended roughly and prematurely—what sort of endurance underlies this art of footballing? And for whom does Butkus endure—or Pane? We are the audience of the art of the ornery—and we have been drawn into "the happening." The sharpness of Butkus' performance keeps us from seeing too clearly the borders between the real and the enacted; we watch, enjoy, cringe, cheer, and revel in the use and abuse of the body artfully displayed in a performed orneriness. Performance artists routinely risk their own well-being as a way of raising questions concerning art and its uses—in this way they challenge the conventional notion that observers, spectators, or audience members are not complicit in the art and its consumption. Behind the scenes Butkus openly questioned the Bears' attention to his knee. But for us, the public, he performed. We are complicit as witnesses—complicit in the brutality, the orneriness, and ultimately in the testing of the limits of endurance and pain. As most of us know from experience and as studies have indicated, we actually are affected physically by our watching. In short, Butkus cannot help but make us think—he intends through his performance to pressure us into awe, into moral concern, and into aesthetic judgment. Should we transform our practices? Should we refuse to enjoy some features of each performance? Like "Relation in Space," Butkus' performances thematize the ornery, the violent, and the spectator's complicity.

One reason for taking performance art and not theater as the appropriate analogue for the art of the ornery is that it provides us no relaxing distance. This is not about abstractions. It is about an encounter with actuality that is loaded with conceptual possibilities—it is about the aesthetic dimensions that confront us as intelligent observers, our pretense to blue-collared earthiness notwithstanding. Butkus' performances are permeated with moral questions both inside and outside of the rules of the game. They are thoroughly revelatory of the Dionysian dimensions of our existence. If this seems too heavy-handed or intellectualist, let me close by paying attention to our aesthetic responses. We *know* a good hit when we see one; we are connoisseurs. We know an exemplary linebacking persona when we watch Butkus' play; NFL Films has no problem identifying him as the "number one toughest man" in the history of the sport. A myth? Perhaps. But no more nor less a myth than the various assessments of Hsieh's and Montano's year in human traction. The qualitative immediacy of Butkus' performances is ineffably beautiful—there is a kind of felt perfection in his particular forms of excess. We are stimulated by his incessant trash-talking, we anticipate anxiously his next crushing blow, and we are nostalgic as he becomes an aging warrior. Dick Butkus discloses the aesthetic complexity of the art of linebacking. If we sought sheer brutality, we would be happy to watch gorillas tear apart running backs. But despite our best intentions to be low-brow and ordinary, his art brings our aesthetic commitments home to us.

If Butkus were not a performance artist—and I believe many professional athletes are not—we would not respond in these ways. We might be indifferent or disgusted. With a Michael Vick or a Plaxico Burress, whose off-field experiences may raise questions, we might be even more uncertain about the distinction between the art and the real. When the distinction fully collapses, we respond quite differently. We would want to untie and provide therapy for Hsieh and Montano; we would want to re-educate Pane to the dangers of self-mutilation, and we might want to tell Butkus to be careful. But, as Emerson and Dewey saw, there can be depth in athletic performance—a depth that elicits conceptual and aesthetic responses. We should not dogmatically treat athletic performance as less than art. Nor should we treat art as somehow thoroughly transcendent of the ordinary. They are not mutually exclusive categories. Rather, as Montano, Pane, and Ulay/Abramovic illustrate, art can be created and discovered in bodily movements and encounters. And as Butkus exemplified, art can be found on the premises of Wrigley Field.

NOTES

1. Emerson, "Art," http://www.vcu.edu/engweb/transcendentalism/authors/emerson/essays/artessay.html.

2. Dewey, *Later Works, Volume* 10, ed. Jo Ann Boydston (Carbondale, SIU Press, 1987), p. 87.

3. Ulay, http://www.vanabbemuseum.nl/chroot/htdocs/archief/1997/972-1_en.html.

4. Carr, Cynthia, *On Edge: Performance at the End of the Twentieth Century* (Middletown, CT: Wesleyan University Press, 2008), p. 5.

5. Arnolfini, http://arnolfini.adatabase.org/index.php/objectui/type,vra.vraevent/id,2368.

6. Martland, T.R., "Not Art and Play, Mind You, nor Art and Games, But Art and Sport," *Journal of Aesthetic Education*, vol. 19, no. 3 (Autumn 1985), p. 69.

7. Butkus and Smith, *Butkus: Flesh and Blood* (New York, Doubleday, 1997), p. 154.

8. Schwartz, Larry, "Butkus Was One Mean Bear," http://espn.go.com/sportscentury/features/00014131.html.

9. Ulay,   http://www.vanabbemuseum.nl/chroot/htdocs/archief/1997/972-1_en.html.

10. Schwartz, op. cit.

11. Butkus and Smith, p. 208.

NINE

Toward a Somatic Sport Feminism

Joan Grassbaugh Forry, Vanderbilt University

I. INTRODUCTION

"Female golfers are handicapped by having boobs. It's not easy for them to keep their left arm straight, and that's one of the tenets of the game. Their boobs get in the way." Ben Wright, a golf commentator for CBS Broadcasting, made these statements in 1995 in an interview with Valerie Helmbreck of the *News Journal* of Wilmington, Delaware.[1] Wright made several other comments about female athletes during the interview, including remarks about lesbians "ruining" golf. When the interview was published, a short-lived controversy followed in which Wright denied making the comments (the interview was not recorded). CBS fully supported Wright, despite his record of politically inflammatory remarks, including a reference to his former editor as a "raging fag" during an interview with *Sports Illustrated*.[2] Later, while drunk at a dinner party, Wright proudly confirmed to sportswriter Dan Jenkins that he did indeed make the remarks in question. In a follow-up interview with *Sports Illustrated*, Wright speculated that Helmbreck was "possibly a lesbian" to explain why she would "maliciously" attribute such remarks to him.[3] Wright later admitted to CBS that he did indeed make the remarks in question, and CBS quietly suspended him.

Wright's remarks attributing female golfers' supposed inferiority to their breasts provide one of many examples of how the physical features of women's bodies are thought to be impediments to athletic performance. But, Wright's remarks do more than that. They reveal an underlying normative claim about how body movements in sport ought to be performed. Tied to this claim are implicit claims about which sporting bodies are most compatible with this imperative on how bodies ought to move, and claims about what features determine a body's ability or inability to perform movements in sport. Underlying claims about how bodies ought to move and execute sporting activities are deeply gendered. Wright's remarks provide a candid illustration of the normalization and idealization of male embodiment in sport. (These remarks also illustrate the idealized embodiment in sport is not only inherently male, but also able-bodied. The claim that having breasts is a handicap participates in the ableist erasure of disability, as if *having breasts* is somehow similar to a movement-impairing disability.) This normalization and idealization is such that the body postures and movements commonly attributed to exceptional male players are not just evaluatively good, but have become "tenets of the game." What is remarkable about this example, however, is that the normalization of male embodiment extends to such precise postures as how one holds one's elbow. Examples such as this one are part of a broad interpretive framework in which women's bodies are deemed inferior to men's bodies.

Body movement and comportment are meaningful in that they constitute recognizable, communicative patterns of being and embodiment. These patterns express a subject's orientation or intentional direction toward the world and the situations the world presents. Body movement and comportment express conformity to, and negotiation with, social norms. Gender is recognizable, in part, through body movement and comportment. Gender is a determinant factor in establishing patterns of body comportment and movement, such that gender shapes experiences of embodiment, and hence, embodiment itself. How do patterns of body movement and comportment, which are socially determined to some extent, produce particular kinds of bodies? How do these bodies resist and reinforce the power relations that produce them? What subjective experiences of movement, comportment, and embodiment accompany these bodies? These questions are important for sport because the manipulation of body movements is a fundamental feature of sport and sport practices, which are themselves coded as masculine and feminine, and work to produce masculine or feminine bodies. The underlying problem for sport is the normalization, idealization, and standardization of body movements and performances of some male bodies, and hence, male embodiment. This idealization not only affects interpretations and perceptions of the human body, but there are practical, physical effects as well.

Despite the volume of recently produced feminist body studies scholarship, there is a gap in the literature when it comes to the gendered sporting body. Feminist scholars have analyzed sport as a site of gender oppression, but the focus has been on issues of equality and access, leaving body movement, comportment, the gendered sporting body undertheorized. While there has been significant work performed under the rubric of somatic philosophy, which largely takes on a phenomenological flavor, this work has largely ignored body movement and comportment. Of the scholarship that has taken up body movement as a site for humanistic academic analysis, this work has largely failed to address how body movement is implicated by gender.

Iris Marion Young's 1980 piece, "Throwing Like a Girl: A Phenomenology of Feminine Body Comportment, Motility, and Spatiality," stands out at the intersection of scholarship on the human body, body movement, and gender as an incisive analysis of how patriarchy not only shapes how women inhabit and experience their bodies, but also shapes women's physical bodies. Young's essay has long functioned as a cornerstone feminist analysis of the body. Her argument is important for sport feminism because its emphasis on embodiment captures a dimension of gender and sport that goes unexamined by other sport feminist views. While feminist scholars have lamented how beliefs about women's bodies have served to justify women's lot in sport, feminist scholars have largely failed to articulate the connection between somatic experience in sport and socio-political empowerment. Young's argument offers one interpretation of this connection and in doing so, Young does some of the things that I argue are necessary for sport feminism. In this chapter, I bring together a set of philosophical moves to provide the groundwork for what I call 'somatic sport feminism,' drawing liberally from several lines of thought to address gendered somatic experience in sport. This work is important for pragmatist approaches to sport because it builds and expands upon pragmatist conceptions of experience, habit, and habituation.

II. THEORIZING GENDERED BODY MOVEMENT

Feminist theory has taken women's bodies to be a locus of oppression, thus, one of feminism's central projects is to understand how patriarchal power structures variously affect women's bodies. Feminist work in the burgeoning scholarship that can be collectively referred to as 'body studies' has produced incisive criticism of the theoretical elision of women's bodies in humanistic scholarship while also advancing new ways of theorizing gendered bodies. To clarify what I mean by 'somatic feminism,' I borrow Elizabeth Grosz's distinction between theoretical approaches to the body. Grosz locates recent scholarship on the body in one of two theoretical approaches. The first approach is the "lived body approach" and "refers largely to the lived experience of the body."[4] This approach takes bodily experiences, and the body schemas produced by bodily experiences, as its objects of analysis and is concerned with rendering bodily *experiences* meaningful while also treating meta-level questions of *how* bodily experiences become meaningful. Because bodily experiences and schemas are informed by socio-political power structures, this approach addresses these structures as they figure into bodily experiences.

The second approach is an "inscriptive approach" which conceptualizes the body as a "social object" or "receptive surface" that is "written upon by various regimes of institutional (discursive and nondiscursive) power."[5] This approach takes the effects of social structures, ideology, and power on the body as its objects of analysis, and is exemplified by Foucault's work on disciplinary power, and subsequent feminist appropriations of Foucault's work in explaining the effects of patriarchy upon women's bodies. Though both approaches focus on the body's interaction with socio-political power structures, they each have different analytic starting points. The first approach begins with bodily experience, while the second approach begins with external power structures. In this chapter, I focus on the first approach.

There is certainly overlap between these two approaches, and in some ways, the distinction is contrived. However, I think this distinction is methodologically helpful because it carves out a space for analyzing subjective experiences of movement. For my purposes, I will revise Grosz's 'lived body' label because I draw from diverse interdisciplinary resources that do not mesh neatly with the phenomenological associations connoted by 'lived body.' For example, later in this chapter I draw from research in kinesics, the study of communication via body movement and comportment, which focuses less on subjective experience and more on the conveyance and interpretation of meaning through movement. I refer to the approach that begins from bodily experience as the 'somatic' approach. 'Somatic,' from the Latin root *soma*, means 'of or relating to the body of an organism.' 'Somatic feminism,' then, is feminist inquiry that is explicitly concerned with articulating and theorizing how the systematic restrictions on women's freedom shape bodily experiences. What I am referring to as somatic feminism is identified by an implicit methodological claim, namely, that articulating and theorizing gendered bodily experiences is necessary for understanding women's oppression. Thus, the articulation and subsequent interpretation of somatic experiences forms the basis for advancing strategies with the political goal of alleviating restrictions on women's freedom.

'Somatic sport feminism' is then concerned with gendered bodily experiences as they occur in the context of sport and fitness practices. While many practices and activities fall under the rubric of 'sport and fitness practices,' I am concerned with 'proprioceptive' and 'kinesthetic' bodily experiences. 'Proprioceptive' experiences are those bodily experiences of spatial orientation and movement (as opposed to 'interoceptive' experiences which are experiences of pain and internal occurrences, or 'exteroceptive' experiences, which are those that involve experiencing the external world through sight, taste, hearing, smell, touch, and balance). The Greek root *kīnein*, which means 'to move, or to set in motion,' is the base for 'kinesthesia,' which refers to the sensation of movement as it is perceived by the muscular-skeletal system, and 'kinesthetic,' which means 'of or referring to the sensation of movement.' While 'proprioceptive' and 'kinesthetic' are often used interchangeably as synonyms, proprioceptive connotes spatial orientation, while kinesthetic connotes movement. 'Comportment,' another term I use frequently, is defined as styles of postures and movement.

How are particular bodily experiences of spatial orientation and movement informed by gender ideology? What is the relationship between particular movement experiences and socio-political gender empowerment? How does the context of sport and fitness enable the particular kinds of spatial orientation and movement that feminist sport theorists take to be important for resisting oppression? To respond to these questions, I outline several concepts to facilitate philosophical discussion and analysis of proprioceptive and kinesthetic experiences and their relationship to gender and sport. These distinctions function as signposts within a discussion of body movement experiences that follows the thread from descriptions of subjective experiences of movement, to recognizable meanings of movement, to arguments about how social structures shape body movement.

As we navigate the world, our bodies develop patterns of movement and posture that are more or less unified into a schema. The body schema is the unified set of past perceptions upon which present and future bodily experiences are built. As each new perception of movement experience is added to the set, the set changes. In walking down a sidewalk, an action I have performed many times, my body draws upon past perceptions of walking down a sidewalk. In building upon past perceptions, my proprioceptive experience is synchronous with a recognizable pattern of movements that is characteristic of how my body performs tasks. The specificity of this particular incident of walking down the sidewalk is incorporated into my body schema. Grosz characterizes the body schema as follows:

> The body schema is plastic. It is comprised both of the record of past bodily postures and movements and of the last posture or movement undertaken. On the basis of this history, it provides the context or horizon of current or future actions. It is thus able to function as a standard against which all subsequent changes of posture are measured.[6]

Every body has a distinct body schema, and thus a distinct "standard" that is specific to every particular body. Particular biographical elements, such as the past and present conditions, physical features, and possibilities of a body construct a body schema that is unique to each human body. While there are as many unique body schemas as there are bodies, there are similarities between schemas due to the social environments in which we are situated. The social values of these environments shape not only what our bodies do, and thus the patterns of movement we develop, but also how we perceive and assign values to our bodies.

Paul Schilder was the first to elaborate on a conception of the body schema as a multifaceted phenomenon, arguing for "a biopsychosocial approach . . . to examine its neurological, psychological, and sociocultural elements."[7] Feminist philosophers draw from Schilder's work in particular because his emphasis on the body image as constituted via physiological, psychological, and social exchanges provides a foundation for feminist interpretation and reconstruction of mind-body relations without sacrificing the unifying concept of self. Grosz uses Schilder's understanding of body image in arguing for the interdependence of the biological/material body and its "psychosocial domain," which has implications for conceptualizing gender, gender-based oppression, and resistance. This coordination is a "necessary precondition" for voluntary action, and is "the point at which the subject's intentions are translated into the beginning of movement, the point of transition in activating bones and muscles."[8] Similarly, Weiss uses Schilder's account to advance a view of embodiment as "intercorporeal." Weiss claims, ". . . the experience of being embodied is never a private affair, but is always already mediated by continual interactions with other human and nonhuman bodies."[9]

For Schilder, the construction and reconstruction of the body and its accompanying schema is achieved through movement. The body image and schema are manipulated through the "tension and relaxation of muscles, moving the body with and against gravity, with and against centrifugal forces."[10] Most of the time, the body occupies what Schilder calls "primary positions" or "primary attitudes," which he defines as "positions of relative rest."[11] Schilder writes, "We always return to the primary positions of the body."[12] Through patterned responses to situations and environments, the body acquires a style of spatial orientation. Thus, the manner in which space is occupied, or the performance of primary positions, is unique to each body. Primary positions or attitudes collectively form a "primary picture" of the body image or schema, and function as the background or horizon for manipulation of the body schema through future movement experiences. Schilder writes, "When we move, we depart from the comparatively rigid primary picture; it seems in some way loosened and partially dissolved until the body returns into one of the primary attitudes."[13]

This conceptualization of the relationship between the body, the body image or schema, and movement experiences is important for analyzing how social structures are corporeally manifested. But, while this discussion articulates how movement experiences *function* with regard to the body schema, the term 'movement' is still vague. Schilder seems to be making an assumption about the nature of the movement experiences that challenge the "primary picture" of the body schema. Certainly not all movement experiences affect the body schema in the same way. Distinguishing between different body movement experiences is important because movement experiences, as they occur within social exchanges, each carry particular meanings.

But how do body movements acquire meaning, thus becoming part of an axiological system? In her 1965 book, *Connotations of Movement in Sport and Dance*, Eleanor Metheny offers a vocabulary for identifying forms of movement. Metheny's vocabulary attempts to capture how we perceive body movement and the meanings attached to forms of movement. Metheny describes a "dynamic, somatic form" of a movement event as a 'kinestruct,' and characterizes it as a "patterned physical whole of a movement event."[14] Metheny elaborates:

> A kinestruct results from the synchronization of changes of tension in countless muscle fibers, but man [sic] cannot deliberately isolate the action of any one of these fibers in such a way as to direct its contraction or relaxation. He can only conceptualize the general pattern of the movement as a whole, and attempt to create that pattern. His execution of the kinestruct involves the exquisitely intimate interplay of sensory and motor units, the whole being coordinated at appropriate levels of the brain, but it is not given to the mind of man to comprehend these details while he is executing the movement. He thinks about 'wholes' of movement; his mind conceptualizes kinestructs, not the thousands of changes of muscle tension which go into the process of kinestruction.[15]

Metheny makes a distinction between the *form* and the *feeling* of a movement experience. The feeling of a movement experience is, like a kinestruct, perceived as an organized whole. Metheny names the feeling of a movement a 'kinecept,' and explains, "A kinecept is defined as a dynamic perceptual form resulting from the integration of all kinesthetic perceptions associated with a kinestruct. A kinecept is the form in which the mover experiences his own movements."[16]

Ivo Jirásek builds upon Metheny's work to explain the meanings of movements as they occur in particular contexts of movement culture. Jirásek claims that the meaning of movement experiences is dependent upon the context in which kinecepts and kinestructs occur. The situational elements that affect the meaning of movement include not only the setting in which the movement is performed, but also the emotional and intellectual perception of the person performing the movement. Jirásek uses the example of bending the knee while jumping, as performed by a soccer player in a game and a ballet dancer during a rehearsal. The perception and subsequent meaning of this movement is radically different for the soccer player, as opposed to the dancer, even though they are performing "identically executed movement activities."[17] Though the meaning of movement is context dependent, Jirásek posits that movement perception is "transformed into an abstraction that serves as a symbol of meaning that a given person gives to these perceptions" and this meaning is "nontransferable to any other cognitive forms."[18] The form (kinestruct) and feel (kinecept) of a movement establishes kinesthetic knowledge, or embodied knowledge of movement. When kinesthetic knowledge is abstracted into what Metheny and Jirásek call 'kinesymbolic knowledge,' such that kinesthetic knowledge is changed into a "symbol of meaning," knowledge about movement experiences becomes socially recognizable.

While this vocabulary applies to all body movements, these theorists seem to attribute more importance to dynamic movement. Dynamic movements expand the space the body claims as its own, may be performed with speed, or may require the performance of a physical skill. This emphasis on dynamic movement is useful for somatic sport feminism, especially in interrogating the assumption that particular somatic experiences, namely, those that involve dynamic movements in the context of sport, are connected to socio-political empowerment.

In reworking the relationships between mind, body, the body schema and image, movement experiences, and knowledge, this discussion imports another set of assumptions regarding the relationship of these components to the self. Drawing from John Dewey's work, Shannon Sullivan uses the concept of 'habit' to explain the relationship between body and self in her 2001 book, *Living Across and Through Skins: Transactional Bodies, Pragmatism, and Feminism*. Sullivan explains that by 'habit' she is referring to a "style or manner of behaving that is reflecting throughout one's being," and thus, this style involves both thinking and acting.[19] Sullivan eschews the colloquial connotation of habit as bad, or as "something to be eliminated from the self," rather, she argues that habits actually "constitute the self."[20] Sullivan writes, "They constitute one's identity as the particular self that one is, and they are the means by which one engages and transacts with the world."[21] For Sullivan, habits are not just embodied patterns of behavior, but habit structures the self and its corporeal life. Sullivan explains:

> Thinking of corporeal existence as composed of habit recognizes that the gendered and other habits that structure a person *are* that person. Habit makes human existence possible, as well as constrains it to the particular forms of existence that constitute it.[22]

Because our bodies determine, in part, our potential responses to particular situations, the body and its constitutive habits both produce and limit our possibilities as selves. Habit thus has the dual function of simultaneously enabling and constraining the self.

> For example, when I sit, I respond to the chair I sit on with a particular posture, that of slumping slightly and curving my shoulders forward. This posture is a readiness to comport myself in a particular fashion whenever I am presented with a situation involving sitting. As a man-

ner by which I respond to and engage with my world, it is part of my bodily constitution of self. As constitutive of the self, habits are both will and agency. Habit is how one is powerful and efficacious in the world.[23]

Sullivan's view of the self as intertwined with habit is important in three ways. First, her view subverts mind-body dualism in a way that avoids simply valorizing the body (as many somatic philosophical views are wanton to do) without challenging the way the body has been defined throughout the philosophical canon. Second, by emphasizing the role of habit in constituting the body/self, Sullivan goes beyond simply claiming that the mind and the self are embodied, and offers an explanation of the symbiotic relationship between body, self, and action. Third, Sullivan's account of habit as a set of predispositions concerned with our responses to situations in the world grounds the other concepts I have described in this section. Taken together, the concepts I have described in this section provide a framework for explaining how body movement and comportment are gendered.

The physical features of my body are materially determined, but the material of my body is also determined by my habits and activities. My body schema and image are produced through the performance of habits and activities. Social prescriptions assign meanings to body movements and comportment, such that when I perform my habits and activities, my perception of my movements and comportment, both kinestructs and kinecepts, are informed by these social prescriptions. My perceptions and the meanings I assign to the kinestructs and kinecepts are integrated into my body schema and image, and thus into my self as my overall *physicality*, which, at its most basic level, refers to the general manner in which one physically experiences oneself. In many ways, physicality is a learned phenomenon. This understanding of physicality as learned is consistent with the other concepts I have explored in this section, which attempt to adjudicate between the material, subjective, and social components of movement experience without privileging one over the other.

III. THROWING (AND WALKING, STANDING, SITTING, AND RUNNING) LIKE A GIRL

Somatic sport feminism's project is to expose and interrogate the underlying assumption that somatic experiences in sport are connected to socio-political empowerment. Iris Marion Young's work implicitly adopts this assumption. Her project in "Throwing Like a Girl" is largely devoted to articulating this version of the assumption, namely, that a *lack* of somatic experience in sporting contexts is connected to women's sociopolitical *dis*empowerment. Iris Marion Young's phenomenology of gendered body movement and comportment appears in three essays. Her first essay, "The Exclusion of Women from Sport: Conceptual and Existential Dimensions," was published in 1979 in *Philosophy in Context.* "Throwing Like a Girl: A Phenomenology of Feminine Body Comportment, Motility, and Spatiality" was first published in *Human Studies* in 1980, and represented the culmination of three years of Young's thought on gendered bodily experience. Young's reflection on this essay, "Throwing Like a Girl: Twenty Years Later," was published in the 1998 anthology *Body and Flesh: A Philosophical Reader,* edited by Donn Welton. I draw from each of these essays to analyze Young's major claims and I use Young's major claims to construct a cohesive somatic sport feminism view.

Young's major claims are most carefully articulated in "Throwing Like a Girl: A Phenomenology of Feminine Body Comportment, Motility, and Spatiality." Young opens this essay with a discussion by phenomenological psychologist Erwin Straus, who notes the differences between the sexes in the act of throwing a ball. Straus writes:

> The girl of five does not make any use of lateral space. She does not stretch her arm sideward; she does not twist her trunk; she does not move her legs, which remain side by side. All she does in preparation for throwing is to lift her right arm forward to the horizontal and to bend the forearm backward in a pronate position. . . . The ball is released without force, speed, or accurate aim. . . . A boy of the same age, when preparing to throw, stretches his right arm sideward and backward; supinates the forearm; twists; turns and bends his trunk; and moves his right foot backward. From this stance, he can support his throwing almost with the full strength of his total motorium. . . . The ball leaves the hand with considerable acceleration; it moves toward its goal in a long flat curve.[24]

Straus speculates on the cause of such a "remarkable difference," claiming that because this difference was observed at such a young age, what determines how a girl will throw a ball must be "the manifestation of a biological, not an acquired, difference."[25] However, Young notes that Straus is at a loss to pinpoint the responsible biological feature. Because the difference is noted in young girls, he cannot attribute it to the presence of breasts. Young faults Straus for failing to elaborate on his observations: "If there are indeed typically feminine styles of body comportment and movement, this should generate for the existential phenomenologist a concern to specify such a differentiation of the modalities of the lived body."[26] In the remainder of "Throwing Like a Girl," Young takes up the project of delineating the gendered modalities of body movement and comportment, noting that throwing is "by no means the only activity in which such a difference between masculine and feminine body comportment and style of movement can be observed."[27]

To explain feminine embodiment, Young defines femininity as "a set of structures and conditions that delimit the typical situation of being a woman in a particular society, as well as the typical way in which the situation is lived by the women themselves."[28] On this view, there is no necessary connection between biological sex and the qualities and behaviors that constitute femininity. This anti-essentialist definition is advantageous because it allows for the examination of conditions, qualities, and behaviors independent of the gender of the person operating within the conditions, possessing the qualities, and performing the behaviors in question. This definition is also problematic because it is culturally determinist, allowing 'woman' to be defined by the culture that oppresses women on the basis of their identities as women, which is, in turn, constructed as a biological given. Nevertheless, some women resist conventional femininity and thus, conventional definitions of 'woman.' However, resistance to conventional femininity does not preclude description of what it means to be a woman in a particular situation. Commonalities across situations invite extrapolation such that it is possible and reasonable to discuss what Young calls "feminine existence," and for her to make the following assertion, "There is a particular style of bodily comportment that is typical of feminine existence, and the style consists of particular modalities of the structures and conditions of the body's existence in the world."[29]

Using Straus's account as a starting point, Young describes several differences between men and women with regard to body movement and comportment:

> Women generally are not as open with their bodies as our men in their gait and stride. Typically, the masculine stride is longer proportional to a man's body than is the feminine stride to a woman's. The man typically swings his arms in a more open and loose fashion that does a woman and typically has more up-and-down rhythm in his step. Though we now wear pants more than we used to and consequently do not have to restrict our sitting postures because of dress, women still tend to sit with her legs relatively close together and their arms across their bodies. When simply standing or leaning, men tend to keep their feet farther apart than do women, and we also tend more to keep our hands and arms touching or shielding our bodies.[30]

Young argues that these differences are not due to differences in strength or size, but rather due to each sex's perception of bodily capabilities and to the way each sex makes use of the body. Young claims that women's body movement and comportment is generally characterized by a failure to make full use of their bodily potential. Young claims, "Women often do not perceive themselves as capable of lifting and carrying heavy things, pushing and shoving with significant force, pulling, squeezing, grasping, or twisting with force."[31] Young is careful to note that these assertions do not apply unilaterally to all women, claiming that the connection between these sorts of body comportments arise not from being a

biological female, but "from lack of practice in using the body and performing tasks."[32] Young is thus describing a feature of femininity, which
can be embodied regardless of biological sex.

From these observations, Young posits that there are three "modalities" of feminine body movement and comportment. In engaging with
the world through body movement, the feminine body exhibits an *ambiguous transcendence,* an *inhibited intentionality,* and a *discontinuous unity.*[33]
In discussing the feminine modality of 'ambiguous transcendence,'
Young claims that all bodily existence can be characterized by transcendence and openness, "The lived body as transcendence is pure fluid action, the continuous calling-forth of capacities that are applied to the
world."[34] However, feminine bodily existence is characterized by a per-
petual awareness of the body as simultaneous acting and being acted
upon. This awareness of the body as passive material object is expressed
in the passivity of the feminine body, as only part of it extends into the
world to perform a task, while the rest remains in "immanence." Young
uses Merleau-Ponty's concept of intentionality as the possibilities of acting upon the world defined by the body's sense of capability, or the "I
can." Every bodily action is accompanied by an evaluation of whether the
body can complete the task, and such evaluations are most often not
conscious, and are conditioned by past patterns of physical engagement
with the world, which are determined both by certain physical features,
and by learned responses to situations that are in turn, shaped by social
norms. For example, I am confident in my ability to walk down a flight of
stairs because I have performed this task many times before. To the question, "Can I?" my body responds without hesitation, and thus answers
with, "I can." However, Young posits that there is a gendered difference
with regard to these evaluations. Young explains:

> Feminine existence does not enter bodily relation to possibilities by its
> own comportment toward its surroundings in an unambiguous and
> confident "I can" . . . typically, the feminine body underuses its real
> capacity, both as the potentiality of its physical size and strength and as
> the real skills and coordination available to it. Feminine bodily exis-
> tence is an *inhibited intentionality,* which simultaneously reaches toward
> a projected end with an "I can" and withholds its full bodily commit-
> ment to that end in a self-imposed "I cannot."[35]

Young argues that women's intentionality towards physical tasks, such
as those demanded by sport, is often characterized by hesitancy and
frustration. The third modality of feminine body existence, what Young
calls 'discontinuous unity,' refers to perception of the body not as a unified whole, but as an aggregate of separate, disjointed parts. Young
claims that women "tend to locate their motion in part of the body only,
leaving the rest of the body relatively immobile."[36] This discontinuous
unity is produced by inhibited intentionality, which "severs the connec-

tion between aim and enactment, between possibility in the world and capacity in the body" in the feminine body's movements.[37]

If we take Young at her word, we are still faced with the question of how these modalities come to manifest themselves in women's embodiment. According to Young, the self-reference that underpins all of these three modalities is rooted in women's social situation, namely, that central to the "social existence" of women's bodies is the fact that they are objects to be "looked at and acted upon."[38] The annihilation of women's subjectivity such that a woman's subjectivity is reduced to a "mere body," is a consequence of patriarchy.[39] Living the possibility of the annihilation of one's subjectivity is, for Young, a definitive feature of the situation of being a woman. The reduction of women's bodies, and subsequently their subjectivities, to "potential objects of another subject's intentions and manipulations" is perhaps the most profound effect of patriarchy.[40]

Patriarchy produces the modalities that characterize the social existence of women's bodies and these modalities, taken together, form a cohesive set of meanings, which are enacted and expressed through women's performances of practical, everyday embodied projects. Young explains:

> There is a specific positive style of feminine body comportment and movement, which is learned as the girl comes to understand that she is a girl. The young girl acquires many subtle habits of feminine body comportment—walking like a girl, tilting her head like a girl, standing and sitting like a girl, gesturing like a girl, and so on. The girl learns actively to hamper her movements. . . . The more a girl assumes her status as feminine, the more she takes herself to be fragile and immobile and the more she actively enacts her own body inhibition.[41]

This is, in part, due to a lack of opportunity for girls and women to develop physical skills to enable them to engage the world in particular ways.

Two themes emerge from Young's account of feminine movement and embodiment that deserve elaboration, namely themes of spatiality and comportment. Spatiality is gendered in that the amount of space a body inhabits depends upon the gender of one's body. This is not simply a function of men's bodies being, on average, larger than women's bodies. Rather, this is due to subconscious judgments regarding how much space one's body can and ought to occupy, which are informed by power relations. How much space does a body claim for itself, regardless of its actual dimensions, and why? The relationship between the body and the space it occupies and this relationship is usually cast in terms of 'ownership.' What is the nature of the claim a body makes to the space it inhabits?

Kinesics, the study of bodily movements and gestures as a systematic form of communication, is devoted to responding to the questions above. In particular, kinesics seeks to understand how nonverbal communication, via body movements, gestures, and facial expression, conveys socially relevant messages. Henley pays particular attention to how nonverbal communication is gendered, connecting spatiality to an array of social privileges, one of which is gender. She notes that in general, women 'own' less space, and their 'ownership' of space is generally more tentative than men's. Men usually take up more space than women, regardless of body size, something Henley explains as a function of femininity:

> Not only women's territory and personal space, but their very bodily demeanor must be restrained and restricted spatially. Their femininity is gauged, in fact, by how little space they take up, while men's masculinity is judged by their expansiveness and the strength of their flamboyant gestures.[42]

The little space that women occupy is easily conceded. Henley cites four studies that observed responses to the invasion of personal space in crowded social settings, such as crossing a busy crosswalk and walking along busy sidewalks. All four studies found differences according to gender. Women yield to men far more often than men yield to women, and women's yielding movements are more dramatic than men's. For example, if a man and a woman are approaching each other from opposite directions on a narrow sidewalk, the studies found that the woman almost always yielded to the man by moving out of the way, interrupting her gait and turning her body while the man's walk and body space remained uninhibited. In yielding, women move and manipulate their body space to accommodate men's bodies. Henley argues that these subtle concessions of space reflect a gendered power differential. Put simply, women's claim to personal space is less important than men's. This is not to say that men do not move out of the way for women, rather, the claim is about the nature of the relationship between a subject-body and the space inhabited by that body.

Comportment, the manner or style in which we carry out body movements and postures, is generated by the body's relationship to space, or one's spatiality. It follows that if women claim less personal space, their postures and movements will be less expansive. Photographer Marianne Wex attempted to verify this claim about the gendered relationship of individuals to the space that surrounds them in her 1977 exhibit, "Let's Take Back Our Space: Female and Male Body Language as a Result of Patriarchal Structures." Wex documented gendered comportment by taking roughly six thousand photographs of men and women, without their knowledge, as they went about their daily lives. Wex photographed men and women as they sat in the park, waited for trains, stood conversing, etc., and then sorted them according to sex. Wex then sorted according to particular postures, searching for gendered trends by body parts. The exhibit contained two thousand thirty-seven photographs, coupled with observational commentary.

Wex interprets her findings, noting:

> The general characteristics of women's body postures are: legs held close together, feet either straight or turned slightly inward, arms held close to the body. In short, the woman makes herself small and narrow, and takes up little space. The general characteristics of male body postures are: legs far apart, feet turned outwards, the arms held at a distance from the body. In short, the man takes up space and generally takes up significantly more space than the woman.[43]

However, when Wex compared the comportment of women she observed in everyday life with those portrayed in the media, particularly in fashion magazines, she found that women in the media were often portrayed in "masculine" poses, reclining with legs open, with hands on knees, etc. Wex writes, "In the media, women are shown in all 'masculine' poses, but then clearly in a sexual proferring position for man."[44] For women to comport themselves in a "masculine" way is for them to signal their (hetero)sexual availability. For women, comportment does not merely refer to the manner in which a body performs movements and tasks, rather comportment is also connected to sexuality, specifically sexual propriety. Despite the use of portrayals of women in masculine poses in the media, "masculine" gestures and postures are thus stigmatized and prohibitive for girls and women in real life. Though neither Wex nor Henley take up this point, the enactment of putatively masculine comportment by women's bodies can also be read not as an indication of heterosexual availability, but instead as a rejection of femininity, and thus, heterosexuality.

Feminine body comportment is accompanied by a difference in bodily awareness. To illustrate this point, Henley describes a consciousness-raising cartoon from 1971 entitled, "Exercises for Men." The cartoon prescribes six exercises intended to show men what it is like to move through the world as a woman. Some of these exercises include:

1. Sit down in a straight chair. Cross your legs at the ankles and keep your knees pressed together. Try to do this while you're having a conversation with someone, but pay attention at all times to keeping your knees pressed together.
2. Bend down to pick up an object from the floor. Each time you bend, remember to bend your knees so that your rear end doesn't stick up, and place one hand on your shirtfront to hold it to your chest.
3. Sit comfortably on the floor. Imagine that you are wearing a dress and that everyone in the room wants to see your underwear. Ar-

range your legs so that no one can see. Sit like this for a long time without changing your position.

4. Walk down a city street. Pay a lot of attention to your clothing: make sure your pants are zipped, shirt tucked in, buttons done. Look straight ahead. Every time a man walks past you, avert your eyes and make your face expressionless. Most women learn to go through this act each time we leave our houses. It's a way to avoid at least some of the encounters we've all had with strange men who decided we looked available.[45]

These exercises are not simply about the movements or comportment, but about the awareness of one's body as an object that appears to others that accompanies women's actions, and how this awareness manifests itself in body movement and comportment. Henley explains:

> The kinesics here are not absurd. They contribute to feelings of inferiority in the women who must perform them, and to impressions of inferiority in whose who observe them. It is more interesting to note that those 'undignified' positions that are denied women—such as sitting with feet on the desk, or backwards straddling a chair—are precisely those positions that are used among men to convey dominance. Thus, prescribed female postures are just those which cannot be used to get power—are ones that must convey impotence, submission.[46]

Henley's claim that female postures are those that cannot be used to obtain power contains an implicit claim about how power structures are embodied, and imbued in movement and comportment. How does putting one's feet on a desk help one to "get power"? It seems doubtful that putting one's feet on the desk or making oneself as large as possible will help one get power, but these postures are part of a language of interpersonal dominance and submission, a replication of socio-political power structures. Henley explains, "Nonverbal power gestures provide the micropolitical structure, the thousands of daily acts through which nonverbal influence takes place, which underlies and supports the macropolitical structure."[47]

How does this gendered dimorphism with regard to body movement and comportment come to be? While biological features determine the possibilities and limitations of body movement and comportment to some extent, body movement and comportment is largely a social product. But it is not as if boys have to take a course entitled "Moving Like a Man 101" in school. It is not as if boys are explicitly taught that their personal space is more important than girls' personal space. Rather, body movement and comportment are produced via the subtle cultivation of embodied habits, a cultivation that is guided by others around us, and by conventions of dress. Clothing and dress function to enable body movements of boys and men, and restrict girls' and women's body movements. Explicit instruction with regard to how to conduct oneself when wearing clothes such as skirts, dresses, and low-necked tops (keep your legs together, don't bend at the waist, don't lean over and expose your bra and/or breasts, etc.) is not uncommon in girls' upbringing. Clothes permit particular kinds of movement, which are performed within particular systems of cultural meanings, thus cultivating habits which work to shape physical bodies. In her 2004 essay, "Gendered Bodies and Physical Identities," Robyne Garrett claims:

> Through continuous bodily practice, gender is 'performed' and it is through the on-going process of gender performance that the nature and meaning of people's bodies are physically altered. Knowledge of gender becomes deeply inscribed in muscle and skeletal systems, postures, gaits and styles of movement. [48]

On Garrett's view, bodies become gendered via a process of interpreting socio-cultural prescriptions and then expressing this interpretation through one's body. In this way, an exchange or transaction is made between the situations presented and the values inherent in the situations in question, and the body's habits. Sullivan also offers an explanation of the transaction involved with regard to gender:

> Through bodily habits, one incorporates the gender and other constructs of one's culture. . . . I have learned to comport my bodying — that is, myself — as a woman is 'supposed' to do. This comportment is not some sort of act that I put on, nor is it, for the most part, something that I consciously try to do. I know how to be a woman because and to the extent that I can effortlessly, without thinking, do the things that a woman would do in the ways that a woman would do them. My gender bodily habits can be seen in my gestures, which express my bodily style. My style, which emerges from and appears as the gestures that I make, is not some sort of veneer that is layered over my body. Rather it is a fundamental characterization of bodily comportment and activity itself. [49]

Sullivan's view that the body and the self are inseparable has consequences for how we think about gender. While Sullivan highlights the performativity of gender with her emphasis on habit and activity, her claims about habit as constituting the self subsequently emphasizes the materiality of gender and the nature of the self, the body, and gender as utterly inextricable from one another.

The plastic character of body movement and the fact that people have agency and control over how they move their bodies provides the basis for both a set of objections to the claims presented by this account of feminine spatiality and comportment, and possible strategies for resisting gender oppression. One could object that women could use the movements that "get power" if they wished. Were a woman to meet with a colleague with her feet on her desk, she would have access to the power that accompanies this act. If women are so oppressed by constricted body movements, why don't they just move differently? Henley argues that this is part of a solution to disrupting old gendered kinesics and creating new patterns of embodiment. She offers a set of practical recommendations:

> Women can *stop* smiling unless they are happy, lowering or averting their eyes when stared at, getting out of men's way in public, and restraining their postures. Women can *start* staring people in the eye, being more relaxed in demeanor (seeing it's more related to status than morality). Men can *stop* invading women's personal space, touching them excessively, taking up extra space. Men can *start* displaying emotion, smiling, condensing their bodies. Parents and teachers can *stop* teaching boys to charge through the world as if they own it, interrupt, touch, and crowd with impunity; showing young girls how to take up little space, back down in conversation, move out of everyone's way, smile at any and everything. Parents and teachers can *start* helping boys to limit their territories where they impinge on those of others (especially of females); accepting assertiveness, expansiveness, and anger in girls.[50]

These strategies are helpful insofar as they make us aware of the gendered behaviors and habits we perform without conscious knowledge. And, they are helpful insofar as they provide some practical guidelines for what to do with this knowledge once it becomes conscious. But, there are also some problems with Henley's suggestions. First, the guidelines for women are problematic because they require women to perform actions that most likely push them outside of their comfort zones, and subject them to the harassment or negative labeling that they avoid through conventionally feminine comportment. Second, if comportment and body movement is deeply gendered, such that it is rarely the result of explicit, or even conscious action, then it's unclear how parents and teachers ought to go about teaching boys and girls to comport themselves.

One might also object that conforming to norms of 'appropriate' comportment is a subversive act that enables women to gain access to power that would not be available to them otherwise. Rendering oneself as nonthreatening through conventionally feminine comportment might afford a woman certain freedoms that would not exist if she comported herself in such a way that made her a cause for suspicion of usurping masculine power. Another objection to this account of feminine comportment is concerned with how power is embodied and imbued in particular movements and postures. Are those positions that men use to convey dominance necessarily oppressive to women? Are said positions and comportment oppressive if they are not directly infringing upon a woman's personal space?

Responding to these questions also allows me to respond to another objection, namely, that this account makes too much of the way bodies move, that it attributes too much power to comportment. This objection can be made in two ways. The first is an attempt to discredit the feminist analysis of gendered movement and comportment. Claiming that one is 'reading too much into' a particular phenomenon is a way of shunning one's reality and lived experiences, usually the experiences of the socially disenfranchised. The second is an attempt to question the efficacy of the feminist analysis. Put another way, the objection is that this account attributes too much power to movement and comportment, such that (1) the focus on body movement and comportment is misplaced given the continuing presences of blatant structural oppressions such as pay disparities between men and women; or (2) the focus on body movement and comportment offers a confused means to liberation, or to put it plainly, to move one's body differently does not constitute socio-political gender liberation. My response to both forms of this objection is as follows. The positions that men use to convey dominance are oppressive, even when they are not infringing upon a woman's personal space, insofar as they are part of a system, or a language of movement, that reflects and reproduces gender-based oppression and the restrictions on women's freedom. While the movements that comprise gendered styles of comportment do not explicitly restrict the freedoms of women, they symbolically construct a set of cultural requirements that dictate the distribution of social power.

IV. SOMATIC SPORT FEMINISM

What are the consequences of this account of gendered movement and embodiment for sport feminism? How do these modalities manifest themselves in women's comportment and bodily movements in sport? Can sport provide the means for negating and negotiating the oppressive features of gendered body movement and comportment?

For Young, sporting contexts do not provide immediate reprieve from the modalities of feminine body movement and comportment. She writes:

> For many women as they move in sport, a space surrounds us in imagination that we are not free to move beyond; the space available to our movement is a constricted space. Thus, for example, in softball or volleyball women tend to remain in one place more often than men do, neither jumping to reach nor running to approach the ball. Men more often move out toward a ball and flight and confront it with their own countermotion. Women tend to wait for and then react to its approach, rather than going forth to meet it.[51]

Women's movements in sport can certainly become more expansive through practice, but Young's point here is that there is an inherent contradiction between the movement and comportment habits endemic to femininity and those endemic to sport.

Young explicitly addresses sport in her 1979 essay, "The Exclusion of Women from Sport: Conceptual and Existential Dimensions," and begins with the claim that women and sport are incompatible. If sport is defined by masculinist values and privileges masculine physicality, sport necessarily excludes women.[52] More importantly, Young offers a description of the relationship between sport and embodiment:

> Sport is the achievement of a nonutilitarian objective through engagement of bodily capacities and/or skills. In sport, at least ideally, the body is spontaneous subject and the subject is wholly embodied. The identity of body and active subjectivity reaches its paradigm in sport; the very stance, muscles, movement and directionality of the athlete exhibit directly her or his intentions and projects. . . . Athletic activity abstracts the body's movement and accomplishment from its normal involvement in the complex web of natural and social goals; sport calls upon the body's capacities and skills merely for the sake of determining what they can achieve. By its nature, then, sport exhibits the essential body-subject.[53]

Young points out that all human activities are embodied, and that many activities require the same skills and capacities required in sport. But for Young, what is unique about sport is that sport functions as a cultural paradigm of physical activity and engagement with the world. Young notes that the sanctions against girls' and women's physical engagement, either in the form of lack of opportunity or in the form of cultural messages about how girls are supposed to occupy their bodies, which usually involves a version of objectification, compromises girls' and women's ability to experience their bodies as "wholly embodied" and "spontaneous" subjects. Young claims, "Exclusion from sport as the paradigm of physical engagement with the world is not merely something that *happens* to girls, however. We also actively choose ourselves as inactive bodies."[54]

Young is not blaming girls and women here for their supposed 'choice' to cultivate inactive bodies. Rather, she is claiming that in a sexist society where girls' and women's bodies are defined as objects, girls and women are compelled to conform to this definition in their own consciousness and embodiment. Young writes, "To the degree that we choose ourselves as body-objects, we find it difficult to become enthusiastic body-subjects and frequently do not desire to challenge our bodies in sport."[55] In connecting women's experiences and self-definition to her conception of sport, Young argues that sport, in its ideal form, is freely chosen, nonutilitarian, and spontaneous and thus represents human freedom. In connecting this ideal form of sport as a kind of freedom to women's bodily experiences, and women's exclusion from sport, Young draws from Merleau-Ponty to claim:

> If, as Merleau-Ponty argues, the basic structures of human existence — consciousness, intentionality, purposiveness, etc. — have their foundation in the body as acting and expressing subject, then the inhibition of women's development of our body subjectivity implies a profound inhibition of our humanity.[56]

Because women's bodies, and hence, women, are defined in opposition to the basic aims of sport, women are thus precluded from a certain fundamental freedom. Young continues:

> If the exclusion of women from the concept of sport symbolizes our exclusion from humanity itself, and if our exclusion from the institutions of sport contributes in a basic way to a sense of weakness, body-objectification and physical timidity among women, then the inclusion of women in the symbols and institutions of sport is a basic aspect of our full participation in humanity.[57]

This portion of Young's argument is valuable because it advances a definition of sport in its ideal form. Young connects the basic aim of sport, to cultivate one's bodily subjectivity through engaging one's bodily capacities and skills in a freely chosen activity that requires some degree of bodily spontaneity, to freedom and the relationship between bodily subjectivity and humanness.

However, several criticisms can be leveled against Young's argument. First, her argument is dated, given the vast improvement in the formal inclusion of women in sport, and thus her claim that women and sport are mutually exclusive may not hold as much weight now than it did in 1979. Second, Young's notion that bodily engagement in sport is spontaneous ignores the fact that bodies in sport are often heavily trained, thus making many movements into robotic responses to particular situations. This is connected to a larger criticism about her ideal of sport. Third, while the sporting ideal she posits is attractive, and certainly plausible, given the presence of other important factors, it is ultimately incongruent with highly rationalized, disciplined contemporary sport, imbued with arguably excessive emphases on winning, aggression, and competition. Jean Grimshaw criticizes Young's account for tending "to idealize masculine movement."[58] Grimshaw also notes that while women have certainly been disadvantaged, men's bodies, and their accompanying modes of embodiment, are not unproblematic.

Grimshaw questions the dimorphism of gendered body movement and comportment that Young espouses, claiming that perhaps this dimorphism is perhaps not so much a matter of gender, but of habituation and the gender coding of sport and fitness activities. Grimshaw shifts the movement context of Young's major example from throwing a ball to an aerobics class, commenting, "Commonly, men are ill at ease, inhibited in their movements, and above all stiff and rigid; they often find it very hard to engage in the kinds of coordinated or flowing movements which characterize parts of an aerobics class."[59] Such differences would likely not remain if the men were to consistently practice aerobics. This example also points to how sport and fitness activities themselves are gendered. Women are likely better at aerobics because aerobics is coded as an 'appropriate' fitness activity for women.

Grimshaw notes that the idealization of the male body and masculine movement risks two elisions. First, the freedom of men's movement may not be free by itself, but may depend upon the restriction of women's movement. Grimshaw explains, "Young fails to note the ways in which men's full occupation of the maximum possible amount of space around them may be oppressive and inhibiting to others."[60] On Grimshaw's view, if Young wants for women's patterns of movement and comportment to emulate men's, then her solution is problematic in that she calls for women to adopt patterns of embodiment that are oppressive to others. Second, Young's view is problematic in that it universalizes male embodiment, failing to recognize that there may be problematic aspects to male embodiment that extend beyond the phenomenon of infringement upon the bodily territories of others. Such problematic aspects are magnified in sport. The body is objectified in that it is made into a thing to be molded, and subordinated to the will of the athlete and often to the will of coaches or other sporting pressure, thus becoming an instrument for external ends such as winning. Though a male body may move with a relative freedom and possess a certain freedom in its comportment, a subject's attitudes toward his own body do not necessarily reflect the 'freedom' that his movement seems to express.

Fortunately, Young addresses some of these criticisms in her essay, "Throwing Like a Girl: Twenty Years Later." Despite being constructed as passive beings constrained by patriarchy, Young notes, "Women are, however, even under the oppressions of patriarchy, active subjects, full of wit and wile, with active projects of their own."[61] This is the basis for her criticism of her previous construction of feminine body comportment:

> The model of action that "Throwing Like a Girl" takes as paradigmatic, thus, may harbor masculinist bias that values typically masculine activities more than the typically feminine. This bias may count for another potential weakness of the essay, namely, that it constructs an account of women's body comportment only as oppressed.[62]

Young notes that her account of feminine body comportment as "only oppressed" does not mesh with current cultural norms, which more readily accept women's sport participation and greater freedom of bodily expression. Rather, women's bodily existence is a nuanced phenomenon characterized by a negotiation between agency and socio-cultural prescriptions. While Young admits to privileging male modalities of movement and comportment, she counters that this is not without good reason, because male embodiment does not simply refer to itself and its accompanying features of putatively masculine existence, but it also refers to a standard of universal humanity.

This leads Young to make two considerations and recommendations for further work. First, to remedy the account of feminine comportment as one-dimensionally restricted and oppressed, Young suggests, "A description of women's body comportment and motility might also look for specifically valuable aspects of women's experience." [63] Second, Young invites the elaboration on masculine comportment by asking, "Are there not comparably specific masculine modalities, and if so, what are they?" However, she expresses some skepticism about this project. If, assuming that there are values that can be characterized as universally human, and features of masculine existence come closer to approximating these values, then there is some question as to what distinguishes the masculine from the universally human. Young speculates, "If in male-dominated society the humanly universal standards of freedom and creativity tend to be expressed by masculine norms and behavior, then how can there also be specifically masculine modalities?" [64]

I want to use the concepts and arguments regarding feminine body comportment and movement I have outlined, namely in relation to sport, as the basis for somatic sport feminism. Sport certainly prompts the body to move in dynamic ways that resist the rigidity of the body schema and body image. However, the ways that bodies move in sport are influenced by the habits of gendered comportment as they are performed outside of sport. The tensions between the somatic experiences cultivated in sporting contexts and the restrictive norms of femininity continue to be problematic for girls and women. Somatic sport feminism is devoted to the project of describing and articulating the gendered features of spatiality, physicality, and movement as they operate within sporting contexts. Rather than take for granted that particular somatic experiences contribute to some kind of socio-political gender empowerment, somatic sport feminism is concerned with questioning this assumption. One major liberal feminist claim with regard to sport is that girls and women ought to have opportunities to explore the limits of their bodily capabilities and develop physical strength and skills, and these opportunities ought to be the same as those available to boys and men. This is consistent with the general liberal feminist claim that extending equal opportunities to women, and enabling them to cultivate the physical qualities deemed valuable by patriarchal society, will enable women to fully exercise their possibilities as human beings. Radical feminist claims about sport differ by arguing that participation in sport is not a good in itself, especially if it is permeated by masculinist values and patriarchal domination. However, radical sport feminist arguments offer the qualifying claim that if a sporting context is actively cultivated to be woman-friendly, then sport can be an effective tool for resisting male domination, particularly by helping women to regain control of their bodies through particular types of somatic experiences. Feminist arguments about sport generally assume that physical engagement and somatic experiences as they occur within sporting contexts are connected to liberation and the alleviation of the negative effects of male domination.

The concepts and arguments I have addressed in this chapter enable a closer examination of the connection between somatic experiences and socio-political empowerment. Bodily habits, and thus bodies themselves, are cultivated through the ongoing exchange between the material body, its material environments, and the socio-cultural values present in the environments the body occupies. The cultivation of habit constitutes the self, and shapes the self's bodily perceptions through the construction and continual negotiation of the body schema. These perceptions, imbued with evaluations regarding the body's capabilities and efficacy, reciprocally shape bodily habits. The collective pattern of body movements, dependent upon habits, forms a general style of spatiality, or the manner in which one takes up space, and comportment, or the manner in which one performs movements. Movements that depart from the primary positions of the body schema, such as those dynamic, active, spontaneous movements in sport, have two components. The form of the movement is the kinestruct and the feeling of the movement is the kinecept. Together, all of these components contribute to an overall physicality, or the collective bundle of experiences that form an overall picture of how one experiences oneself physically. The feminist scholarship I have discussed argues that, due to the intercorporeal exchange of socio-cultural values, women's body movements and comportment are limited and constrained, that women are ambivalent about their bodily capabilities, and that these features are incorporated into women's very subjectivity via the body schema and body image.

For somatic sport feminism, the inhibited nature of feminine body movement and comportment is constituent of women's oppression. The feminist struggle around women's bodies extends beyond access to various health-oriented services, rights to bodily integrity and safety, and opportunities to engage in particular body practices such as those in sport and fitness, to the details and modalities of bodily habits, movement, and comportment. While sport feminism generally advocates that girls and women cultivate their physical skills and explore their bodily limits, somatic sport feminism attempts to explain the connection between somatic experiences and socio-political empowerment. Because somatic sport feminism focuses on the manifestations of oppression at the level of embodiment and somatic experiences, the strategies for navigating oppression are considerably different than the other feminist strategies.

But what makes a somatic experience contribute to socio-political empowerment? In adopting the assumption that women's bodily experiences are connected to socio-political empowerment, somatic feminist arguments about sport also adopt an implicit assumption about the self-awareness of the subject engaging in sport and the role of conscious reflection upon movement experiences. Feminine embodiment in patriarchal culture can be generally characterized as ambivalent, contradictory, and restricted, however, because the body schema operates regardless of conscious reflection, then these modalities of embodiment are not always recognized as restricted. The first step in refiguring these features of embodiment is to become aware of them. Sullivan explains:

> One can become reflective of one's habits, bringing conscious thought to bear on them such that one is aware of and might change them. . . . By consciously thinking of my bodily comportment as a hypothesis, I can become consciously aware of the meaning that I offer others.[65]

Becoming aware of one's comportment through conscious reflection does not necessarily mean to acquire a sort of feminist consciousness, but such conscious reflection upon bodily habits as they are influenced by socio-cultural gendered structures contributes to the cultivation of a feminist consciousness.

But how does my increased awareness, which may prompt me to comport my body differently, result in socio-political gender empowerment? How does thinking about, and moving my body differently work to empower women as a social group? Sullivan comments on this problem:

> Taken individually, an adult's rigid habits bode ill for her potential to change the gender structures in society. Taken as a whole, however, her habits make up a complex web of overlapping habits in which individuals' habits begin to wear upon and challenge and influence each other. When they do so, the resulting friction and weakening of some habits disrupts the usual ways adults habitually transact with the world, opening up possibilities for reconfigurations of habit and thus of culture as well.[66]

Changing my habits in such a way as to counteract the restrictive modalities of femininity may open up possibilities for me by shifting my perceptions about myself and my body. I may gain a sense of personal empowerment and engage my body in ways that contribute to a greater sense of efficacy. However, this does not in itself constitute socio-political empowerment. But, on Sullivan's view, changes of habit create possibilities for shifts in meaning with regard to movement experiences, which may effect change not only in myself, but in the values and structures particular to my socio-cultural environment. Sullivan elaborates on the value of changing one's habits:

> To acquire a new habit is a positive accomplishment. It is to grasp a
> new significance and to establish a new form of power in and through
> one's bodying. To incorporate a new habit is for one's body to learn a
> new way of comporting itself, expanding, in new directions, the power
> and efficacy one has in the world.[67]

This claim that examining and changing one's habits is linked to power is
important for somatic sport feminism. When Sullivan links power to the
process of changing one's habits, she conceptualizes this linkage such
that power is expansive, thus countering the restrictive nature of feminine existence.

Sullivan's remarks here point to an implicit assumption, namely the
fact that the power that accompanies the cultivation of new habits has the
effect of expanding the efficacy one has in the world. This assumption
fails to consider the ways in which the cultivation of new habits might
increase the efficacy one might have in one area, while decreasing efficacy in another. We need a better account of the role of habit cultivation in
expanding one's efficacy in the world. Also, this assumption seems to be
problematically tied to the simultaneous acquisition of a certain kind of
consciousness and awareness about one's body and the cultivation of
new habits. Here, we need an expanded view with qualifying claims
about this acquisition of consciousness and awareness.

An exchange with the world prompts a shift in awareness that then
prompts one to change her habits. The impetus to change one's habits is
often a result of external motivation and this presents a challenge for
thinking about authority and agency in changing one's habits. Sullivan
acknowledges that we often need help from others to improve somatic
experience, and that this might be a cause for concern, especially for
feminism. According to Sullivan:

> Endorsing transaction with others . . . might seem opposed to feminist
> aims in particular because it appears to give other people in a woman's
> life too much power to establish the meaning, veracity, and even sheer
> existence of her felt experiences. The sort of situation in which women
> have little or no epistemic authority in their lives and over their experi-
> ences has been and continues to be a crucial factor in women's oppres-
> sion and thus is something that feminism seeks to combat.[68]

This negotiation with epistemic authority creates an interesting bind for
somatic sport feminism. In sport, we learn to comport ourselves in particular ways by watching others, by receiving instruction from coaches or
other authority figures, thus giving over our authority to another and
opening ourselves to the possibilities of new kinesthetic knowledge.
However, this giving over of authority, while often necessary for shifting
awareness and thus changing habits, may be problematic given women's
historic lack of epistemic authority. But, this negotiation captures an important element of the transaction between bodies and culture that is

absent in other views. An account of this transaction is necessary for somatic sport feminism, to explain women's oppression, and the embodied strategies for combating women's oppression.

I have problematized the relationship between sporting culture and women's bodies. The scholarship I have used largely conceptualizes this relationship as a contradiction, while also conceptualizing the exchange between socio-cultural structures, perceptions of material bodies, and material bodies themselves as transactional. However, in conceptualizing this exchange this way, somatic sport feminism lacks an adequate account of the power operations in this exchange. While somatic sport feminism offers an inroad for explaining the connection between movement experiences and socio-political empowerment, further work needs to be done to effectively explore this connection.

NOTES

1. Jane Gottesman. *Game Face: What Does a Female Athlete Look Like?* Ed. Geoffrey Biddle. (New York: Random House, 2001) 215.

2. Michael Bamberger. "Living With a Lie: When CBS Decided to Defend Announcer Ben Wright, It Attacked the Truth." *Sports Illustrated.* (December 4, 1995) 86-92.

3. Ibid.

4. Elizabeth Grosz. *Space, Time, and Perversion: Essays on the Politics of Bodies.* (New York: Routledge, 1995) 33.

5. Ibid. 116.

6. Ibid. 66.

7. Thomas F. Cash and Thomas Pruzinsky, eds. *Body Image: a Handbook of Theory, Research, and Clinical Practice.* (New York: Guilford Press, 2004) 4.

8. Elizabeth Grosz. *Volatile Bodies: Toward a Corporeal Feminism.* (Bloomington, IN: Indiana University Press, 1994) 83.

9. Gail Weiss. *Body Images: Embodiment as Intercorporeality.* (New York: Routledge, 1999) 5-6.

10. Paul Schilder. *The Image and Appearance of the Human Body: Studies in the Constructive Energies of the Psyche.* (New York: International Universities Press, 1950) 207.

11. Ibid. 270.

12. Ibid.

13. Ibid. 207.

14. Eleanor Metheny. *Connotations of Movement in Sport and Dance: A Collection of Speeches about Sport and Dance as Significant Forms of Human Behavior.* (Dubuque, IA: WM. C. Brown Company Publishers, 1965) 93.

15. Ibid.

16. Ibid. 94.

17. Ivo Jirásek. "The Space for Seeking the Meaning of Movement Activities and the Meaning of the Human Way of Being: Movement Culture." *Acta Universitatis Palackianae Olomucensis Gymnica.* 36.2 (2006) 98.

18. Ibid.

19. Shannon Sullivan. *Living Across and Through Skins: Transactional Bodies, Pragmatism,and Feminism.* (Bloomington, IN: Indiana University Press, 2001) 30-31.

20. Ibid.

21. Ibid.

22. Ibid. 9.

23. Ibid. 30-31.

24. Iris Marion Young. "Throwing Like a Girl: A Phenomenology of Feminine Body Comportment, Motility, and Spatiality." *Throwing Like a Girl and Other Essays in Feminist Philosophy and Social Theory.* (Bloomington, IN: University of Indiana Press, 1990).

25. Ibid.

26. Ibid. 142.

27. Ibid.

28. Ibid. 144.

29. Ibid.

30. Ibid. 145.

31. Ibid. 146.

32. Ibid. 147.

33. Ibid.

34. Ibid. 148.

35. Ibid.

36. Ibid. 150.

37. Ibid.

38. Ibid.

39. Ibid. 155.

40. Ibid.

41. Ibid. 154.

42. Nancy M. Henley. *Body Politics: Power, Sex, and Nonverbal Communication.* (New York: Touchstone/Simon & Schuster, 1986) 38.

43. Marianne Wex. *Let's Take Back Our Space: Female and Male Body Language As a Result of Patriarchal Structures.* (Berlin: Frauenliteraturverlag Hermine Fees, 1979)

44. Ibid. 13.

45. Henley 143-144.

46. Ibid. 145.

47. Ibid. 179.

48. Robyn Garrett. "Gendered Bodies and Physical Identities." *Body Knowledge and Control: Studies in the Sociology of Physical Education and Health.* Ed. John Evans, Brian Davies, and Jan Wright. (New York: Routledge, 2004) 141-156.

49. Sullivan 92-93.

50. Henley 202-205.

51. Young "Throwing Like a Girl" 146.

52. This claim is similar to Carole Oglesby's claim, made in the introduction of her 1978 book, *Women and Sport: From Myth to Reality.*

53. Iris Marion Young. "The Exclusion of Women from Sport: Conceptual and Existential Dimensions." *Philosophic Inquiry in Sport.* Ed. William J. Morgan and Klaus V. Meier. Second Edition. (Champaign, IL: Human Kinetics Publishers, 1995) 262-267.

54. Ibid. 263.

55. Ibid. 264.

56. Ibid. 264.

57. Ibid. 265.

58. Jean Grimshaw. "Working Out with Merleau-Ponty." *Women's Bodies: Discipline and Transgression.* Ed. Jane Arthurs and Jean Grimshaw. (New York: Cassell, 1999) 91-116. 105.

59. Ibid. 107.

60. Ibid.

61. Iris Marion Young. "Throwing Like a Girl: Twenty Years Later." *Body and Flesh: A Philosophical Reader.* Ed. Donn Welton. Malden, MA: Blackwell Publishers, 1998. 286-290. 287.

62. Ibid. 289.

63. Ibid.

64. Ibid. 288.

65. Sullivan 77.

66. Ibid. 105.

67. Ibid. 91.
68. Ibid. 130.

TEN

Living the Injury: A Phenomenological Inquiry into Finding Meaning

Jill Tracey, Wilfrid Laurier University

Through experiencing an athletic injury and subsequent recovery, a potential exists for athletes to have an opportunity to learn more about who they are and to find meaning through a painful experience. By no means does this imply that the very real potential trauma of experiencing significant pain and temporary or permanent loss of functioning is diminished; rather, it suggests that there is another way to view the experience of sustaining and recovering from an injury. For those who do not recover or have permanent disability this may or may not apply; however the focus of this chapter is on successful recovery. As philosopher William James said, "experience is a process that continually gives us new material to digest."[1] Experiencing an injury can indeed provide an opportunity for the 'digestion' of material which is exemplified by Alberto Contador, the winner of the 2007 Tour de France, who had recovered from a severe head injury as the result of a bicycle crash in 2004 that almost ended his life. He said his recovery gave him "another perspective" and made him value more deeply "the fact that I am here."[2] Taking the approach of injury recovery as an experience that can afford an opportunity for self-learning and for finding meaning seems a worthwhile venture and one to which I find myself increasingly drawn as it connects to the pragmatic ideas of James who also said of experience: "we handle this intellectually by the mass of beliefs of which we find ourselves already possessed, assimilating, rejecting, or rearranging in different degrees."[3]

The purpose of this chapter is to explore from a pragmatic perspective the lived experience of athletes who sustain an injury and progress through the rehabilitation process and to highlight the potential for self-cultivation and the finding of meaning through the experience of a moderate to severe injury. Viewing injury rehabilitation from this perspective is in contrast to the traditional view whereby injury is most often viewed and treated as a negative experience with a sole focus on the physical recovery. I have come to explore injury rehabilitation from a pragmatic perspective through my work as a researcher and sport psychology consultant who works with many athletes recovering from moderate and severe injuries. It is through my research and consulting that I have discovered that many people recovering from injuries possess tremendous potential for self-cultivation and come to view their injury experience as positive and deeply meaningful. The ideas of William James relate well to this perspective on injury rehabilitation. While exploring and discovering meaning through this experience is a conscious choice to pursue, the effort undertaken taps into what James referred to as the "second wind," [4] whereby a person perseveres through the difficulties associated with rehabilitation to reveal a new perspective. Working with injured athletes in this way offers an opportunity for them to explore aspects of themselves such as resiliency, inner strength, and motivation, and provides a way to go below the surface rather than, as James aptly put it, to "continue living unnecessarily near our surface." [5] Therefore, the Jamesian framework for working with injured athletes involves exploring what may be gained through living the injury experientially. The chapter highlights a reconceptualizing of the lived experience of injury, a forwarding of an alternate methodology for examining the experience of injury and recovering, and assists in translating the experience of injury in order to enhance understanding of the unique processes of injury rehabilitation.

I. FRAMING THE INJURY EXPERIENCE

Historically, particular attention was not focused on the emotions and psychological rehabilitation within movement studies (e.g., kinesiology and rehabilitation). Once scholars became interested in injury rehabilitation, the landscape of injury rehabilitation was illuminated and an enhanced understanding was gained concerning various psychosocial factors such as the role of personality, the history of stressors, coping resources, and cognitive appraisals. [6] Based on comments from numerous scholars, [7] there is a need to reframe the injury recovery experience as having the potential to be a positive learning experience ripe with opportunity for creating meaning and fostering self-development. It is possible for a negative event such as sustaining an injury to be considered a shared experience that could be meaningful, as James alluded to in *The*

Varieties of Religious Experience: "let our common experiences be enveloped in an eternal moral order; let our suffering have an immortal significance." Additionally, several published papers have demonstrated a strong commitment by reputable publishers to disseminating applied research and professional practice focused on the use of qualitative and phenomenological research,[8] as well as research within a philosophical framework.[9] Given this, there is a need for gaining further understanding through deliberate discussion with injured athletes about their experiences in order to understand the potential for injury to be a positive learning experience.

Examining the experiences of injured athletes offers exploration of a unique area in which humans can make meaning out of recovering from an injury. Scholars in sport science and rehabilitation have focused predominantly on mechanistic and reductive perspectives of the injury and rehabilitation process. However, remaining solidly grounded in empiricism and experimental methods has resulted in an insufficient explanation of the experience of injury, since reflection and subjective knowledge are not typically a part of this process. As has been noted by several scholars,[10] this view is overly simplistic and does not allow for meaning to be expressed in an alternate and perhaps a more significant way. Exploration through other methods such as interviews and self-reflection may provide a valuable contribution to the understanding the complexity of the recovery process.[11] While many disciplines have benefited from experimental methods, these methods do not constitute a panacea for all the limits on our knowledge. Some areas within kinesiology, such as sport philosophy, sport sociology, and sport psychology have explored the value of subjective knowledge; however the exploration of such knowledge remains somewhat marginalized in many areas of sport science. Fahlberg and colleagues noted the limiting nature of this view: "reducing the interpretation of human behavior to behavioristic and physiological approaches, and restricting inquiry to solely empirical methods, is an artificial restriction on the nature of reality that we choose to perceive, severely limiting the understanding that results."[12]

An alternate perspective is to view an injury from a phenomenological point of view. For the purpose of this chapter my consideration of phenomenology as a perspective is guided in part by Patton's[13] description of taking an individual's unique view and attempting to understand how people experience and interpret the phenomenon of interest from an experiential perspective. In the case of the present chapter, the topic of interest is recovering from an injury. The objective of this approach is to focus on what an experience (such as injury recovery) means to an individual. The idea of struggle and suffering as a worthwhile and enriching experience seems an odd concept in a traditional sport rehabilitation view; yet, as James elucidated, the strenuous life is the one people seek. James' description of life as being built on doing and suffering, and creating offers a relevant example of the idea of suffering and successfully recovering from an injury as a meaningful experience. Additionally, looking at injury recovery in a positive light demonstrates an example of Thoreau's notion of experiencing something where he could truly know that he had lived. He saw the value in experiencing something difficult as a means of illuminating and enhancing the richness of life. He described why he chose to live so deliberately on Walden Pond: "I wanted to live deep and suck out all the marrow of life."[14] This perspective may allow for greater opportunity for developing meaning and self-cultivation. The basis of self-cultivation stems from the self-development and movement literature and has been highlighted through the work of Howard Slusher,[15] Patsy Neal,[16] and Elwood Craig Davis.[17] "Self-cultivation" is a term used to describe a process of self-development that can be realized through various means such as movement, effort, or, as suggested in this chapter, dealing with challenges faced during recovery from an injury. When looked at phenomenologically with an eye toward examining their meanings, the experiences of the athletes are highlighted and the emphasis is on the individual descriptions of their experiences. The work of two qualitative researchers serves as a theoretical framework with respect to using phenomenology when working with injured athletes. Using Polkinghorne's[18] framework of phenomenology as a method, I work with athletes to provide an opportunity to describe their core meaning of their experience in as much detail as possible. Additionally, a rich dialogue can occur when injured athletes are asked questions that are centered on examining what the experience of being injured and going through the process of recovery means to them and what (if anything) they feel they have learned about life and themselves through the recovery process.

When athletes experience injuries, attention is automatically and logically focused on the physical site of injury. Unfortunately, the focus often remains solely on the physical, which can ignore the embodied experience of being injured and the numerous thoughts, feelings, and behaviors associated with an injury and the subsequent recovery process. The perspective under consideration has been brought to light through hundreds of hours of interviewing and consulting with injured athletes. In particular, the genesis of this chapter stems from qualitative studies I have conducted, together with my ongoing research and consulting practice. In both consultation and research with athletes from a wide variety of individual and team sports who have sustained moderate to severe injuries often requiring lengthy suspension from participation, I often talk with athletes about the experience of injury as being a pivotal moment for them. While being challenged, they learned they can handle difficult situations and persevere. James referred to the importance of suffering as a central part of life in *The Varieties of Religious Experience*: dealings with suffering of some kind "are pivotal human experiences" and essential components to life that, he suggested, we all must experience.[19] Experi-

encing an injury can be reframed as a positive experience in which athletes can acknowledge, and when provided with the opportunity, discuss
their emotional experience of the injury and recovery process of what it is
like to 'live' an injury. Recovering from an injury can be a lived struggle
through which there is a challenge posed to the athlete's meaning structure and sense of self, a struggle that can last throughout the journey of
recovery and be influenced by this journey. This impact on self is the
necessary struggle James believed to be vital for human prosperity and
meaning. Sustaining and recovering from an injury in part involves making sense of the world in an experiential way, not merely in a cognitive
way. The injury disrupts the athletes' worlds and forces them to find new
ways of dealing with their worlds because of the unexpected nature of
sustaining an injury. An example from Cheung and Hocking highlights
this point:

> As individuals interpret their world, they assign meanings; thus, mean-
> ing can be explicated from the person, who is situated in a world and
> for whom things matter, are of value, and have significance in a given
> time and space. When meaning is shattered, for example through loss,
> coping strategies are initiated to restore meaning. . . 'the goal of coping
> is restoration of meaning.'[20]

Providing a forum for injured athletes to describe their experiences offers
the potential for them to learn about themselves in ways that have the
potential to contribute to their self-development and to enhance their
overall well-being.

The suggestion has been made by sport psychology researchers Brewer, Gould,[21] and colleagues that the physical injury is not, in itself, as
crucial an issue for psychological adjustment as is the cognitive appraisal
and emotional response an individual has to the injury and rehabilitation
process. Through detailed description of the lived experience, scholars
have revealed a further understanding of the emotional experience of
being injured underreported in the past.[22] Injured athletes navigate
through a difficult terrain and emotional journey as they acknowledge,
accept, and cope with the injury and recovery process.[23] The injury and
recovery experience involves, among many things, learning from the series of challenges that may be faced during the recovery process such as
setbacks in rehabilitation, pain management, perceived or real fear of loss
of fitness or loss of position on a team, managing anxiety, frustration, and
loss of functioning for a sustained period of time. Many athletes I have
interviewed have dealt with the situation by reframing it from an event
they perceived as negative, even devastating, and attempting to turn the
reality of the injury into something positive by taking the perspective that
the experience was something to learn from and an opportunity for personal growth. The nature of the qualitative interviews allows athletes to
discuss the meaning of their injuries and the richness of what they

learned about themselves through the process. By tapping into the experiential nature of injury recovery, those invested in their well-being can
enhance understanding of the injury and rehabilitation process.

II. INJURY AS SHATTERED MEANING

Sustaining and recovering from an injury can be emotionally difficult for
athletes. A myriad of emotions have been identified from mild mood
disturbance to significant depression, and these may be experienced by
injured athletes from the onset of injury when pain is significant throughout the recovery process. Injury can, as Pelligrino noted, place an individual in a changed existential state whereby there is a "confrontation with
the fragility of our existence."[24] Sustaining an injury can be interpreted as
an assault on one's being, particularly for athletes whose identities are
often centered on their role as athlete. This temporary or permanent
change in physical functioning can be a tremendous loss to self and
meaning. In Marni Jackson's book *Pain: The Fifth Vital Sign*, she explores
the mysteriousness of pain and our relationship with it through experiencing injury and/or illness. She asks, "why do we persist in the distinction between mental and physical pain when pain is always an emotional
experience?"[25] A heavy reliance on empiricism within Western medicine
has served humanity well but has also created a disconnect that has been
fostered in the rehabilitation setting. If the goal is to heal a person or to at
least attempt to allow them to regain functional abilities and pain reduction based on proven protocols, then more attention needs to be centered
on the whole person. The essence of this concept is reflected in the work
of Thomas and Rintala:

> it is important to remember that our concern is not just with strength,
> flexibility, range of motion, or pain levels. The torn ACL is their inabil-
> ity to move; it is being removed from a significant part of their iden-
> tity. . . . It is feeling alienated from their own bodies and wondering
> whether they will ever be able to fully trust their knee to support them
> in movement again. [26]

Injury is often experienced as a loss, and not just a loss of physical functioning. The shattered state an injured person is experiencing has far-
reaching implications for her sense of being and her relationship with her
body—these implications should not be understated.

The reality of sustaining an injury affords athletes with a choice of
what mind-set to bring to recovery and to carry with them throughout
the rehabilitation process. The tendency is to look at injury as an exclusively negative event (which it certainly can be as far as the sudden
limitation and disengagement from sport participation, along with the
severity of pain that can be involved). Life, according to James, offers
endless risk, as well as endless possibility. Armed with this perspective, a

person can navigate through life and situations that involve potential danger, failure, and improvement with the attitude to experience opportunity, to struggle, and to engage in creating meaning about that lived experience. Thomas and Rintala highlight this point in the following: "The elite athlete who is faced with a serious long-term injury has the opportunity . . . to examine the sport experience from another perspective and to return to it with a broader, more objective point of view."[27] Viewing injury this way may allow for an athlete to return to sport in a more authentic way. Certainly it is possible to return with an enhanced level of gratitude towards a healthy self and an understanding of the vulnerability of the self to injury. In viewing injury recovery as a process of struggle, a Jamesian approach through which the struggle is embraced would involve using it as an opportunity through which growth and self-knowledge may be possible.

III. THE CULTURAL ACCEPTANCE OF PAIN, RISK, AND INJURY

Athletes are trained to deny pain, often to treat it as a natural part of being an athlete. Whether it is an injury or serious illness, athletes are taught to train through pain and to diminish the experience of pain to the point where there is a common normalization of pain in sport culture for both male and female athletes.[28] However, there is a more dominant acceptance of pain for males whom researchers note are socialized to believe they must deny and play in pain. There is also a pervasive tendency to reduce pain to its component parts, which serves to perpetuate the lived dualism of viewing the body as 'other.' This normalization of pain and a 'techno-rational' perspective discussed by Young and colleagues of viewing the body as individual and impersonal parts has impacted how athletes deal with being injured, as well as how athletes are treated by many interested parties (i.e., coaches, training staff, media, fans). What can be created is a blurry line between viewing pain and struggle as meaningful as opposed to viewing pain and struggle as meaningless, and this can be very confusing for those experiencing it. In many sports, playing through pain is often rewarded and cultural mottos such as 'no pain no gain' have been derived from this powerful message. While this attitude may have its genesis in professional sports, it has filtered down to most levels of sports, and examples are abundant in both competitive sports and recreational activities. Though perhaps surprising and disturbing, there are sports and recreational participants who buy into playing beyond the discomfort associated with physical exertion. While there may be benign pain or discomfort associated with sport participation, continued play is usually possible; pain associated with more serious injury typically means suspension from participation for a period of time. There can be an increased risk in pushing past personal limits, not for skill development or goal attainment, but rather adopting the 'no pain no gain' mantra and/or feeling that there is no other way to 'do sport.' Many athletes respond to this by pushing beyond their limits, which can increase their risk of serious injury and place them at risk for developing chronic problems. The pressure to buy into this mantra is alive and well within the NFL as evidenced in a *Sports Illustrated* article by Tim Layden[29] in 2007 highlighting the "Big Hits" along with many others in recent years and the powerful culture within professional football to play in pain, yet also recognizing the detrimental effects of serious injuries that can occur. The huge popularity of professional football may serve to augment this powerful cultural message of pain and prowess in sport.

Researchers from sport sociology and sport psychology in particular have written numerous papers highlighting the issue of the cultural influences leading to a culture of risk such as media, coaching practices, team subcultures, as well as treatment of injuries by the health care professionals. Injury in sport has become a locus in the media for fervent discussion. Sport has long celebrated athletes willing to take potentially high risks, to play in pain, and to deny the severity of an injury. A highly publicized example is that of professional football player Ronnie Lott who had part of a finger amputated during the 1985 season rather than miss the remainder of the season. This example, while extreme, serves to add to the culture of pain and risk in sport and further entrenches the idea that playing in pain is the right thing to do and tends to heighten the hero status of many athletes. Lott was often described as a 'true warrior' and his decision to remove his finger was viewed as a sign of 'dedication' to his team and to his sport.[30] Part of the danger of this and other examples in sport is that it filters out to all levels of sport (youth, recreational, competitive, and professional) and the risk of these athletes fostering rather than diminishing pain and injury has serious implications for sport and the health of all participants. The normalization of pain and the 'no pain no gain' mantra can minimize the experience of injury and has led to a powerful culture of pain denial by many athletes.

IV. MEANING AND SELF-CULTIVATION OF THE LIVED STRUGGLE

We do not willingly want people to be thrust into dealing with an injury, yet injury through sport occurs and occurs often. The challenge I pose to everyone is to consider the value and meaning that can be acquired from such an experience. The ideas of James in *The Energies of Men* are useful in this part of the discussion. He writes about how we tend to use only a small amount of the power we possess and that difficulties lame many people, yet when faced with an opportunity it is possible to 'wake up' and find resources we may not have known we possessed until such time when we are tested. While sport participation does not automatically mean an injury will occur, athletes understand the inherent risk of and potential for injury that can occur. However, if they sustain an injury, they can use the reality of dealing with the injury to parlay it into a strengthened belief that they can overcome a difficult situation. In one study I conducted examining the emotional response to injury and recovery, one athlete who had sustained multiple stress fractures in her foot said that being injured felt like being in prison and that if she had the chance to escape she would take it (for anyone who has been injured, this may be easy to relate to). The same athlete who was tempted to escape later discussed the fact that she was 'grateful' and that she learned more about herself because of the injury. Gratefulness could be just one of many possibilities that may be derived from injury recovery. Subjective knowledge can be an essential part of life yet there can be a tendency to de-emphasize the importance of subjective knowledge and the value of experience. Dealing with an injury tends to be viewed through a dominant physical focus without including the role of the subjective experience. Bain and Kerry and Armour[31] have noted the relevance of subjective knowledge in the synthesis of meaning of various experiences. As Bain has described, examining the true value of subjective knowledge requires more than merely knowledge of experience. Reflection on the whole experience is a more comprehensive and valuable way to use subjective knowledge. Subjective knowledge can be a powerful tool in the development of meaning of a lived experience, with the potential to foster a positive learning experience for those recovering from injury.

It is possible for athletes to discuss their lived experience of dealing with the injury to utilize subjective knowledge to reveal their self-knowledge, to foster self-cultivation, and to relate this idea to James' ideas of struggle as essential to existence. Athletes can describe the experiences of sustaining an injury and the recovery process, and can specifically be asked to express their interpretations of what it is like experientially to 'be injured' from both a physical and psychological perspective. As philosopher Merleau-Ponty[32] suggested, the possibility is available for becoming a new self through the reorganizing of self, and this idea can be applied during rehabilitation. Gaining subjective knowledge by providing opportunities for athletes to discuss their experiences can facilitate this reorganization and enhance understanding of the self. By employing a phenomenological perspective to the experience of injury, athletes can discover positive aspects of the experience, such as recognizing that they possess the motivation and perseverance to take on a physical and psychological challenge. Viewing recovery in this manner relates to a comment by McDermott[33] with respect to the idea of converting something challenging into something revelatory: "the fundamental challenge is to convert the personal weaknesses into strengths and to drive our strengths into the teeth of a personally neutral, but relatively pregnant world." Some athletes have told me that dealing with an injury enhanced their self-confidence and increased their sense that they possess the ability to overcome what they perceive as a significant physical and psychological challenge. The potential to gain subjective knowledge and meaning through an experience can be revealed by the narratives of those expressing their experiences of injury and the meaning they can derive from it.

George Sheehan,[34] in his classic book *Running and Being* relates the work of James and the concept of finding meaning through difficult experiences such as running a marathon. Sheehan said that it is not sufficient to "groove through life. [James] believed in effort." James also believed that humans lived far below the energy they possess and should be encouraged to reach to the depths of self where there is a reservoir of power. Subjective knowledge is at the core of experience and can play an important role for individuals to gain understanding and find meaning in the experience. Similarly, dealing with injuries tends to be viewed as a dominance of physical focus without including the role of personal insight, reflection, and the potential for learning from that experience. The following comment is from an athlete who suffered multiple stress fractures and clearly recognized the impact the injury had on her life and was conscious that she learned she was more resilient and self-assured than she thought she was prior to the injury:

> I think just from my past knowing that it [sport] isn't the biggest thing in my life. There were times when I was awful . . . and I was still a happy person. Just knowing that helps (me know) that it will pass and things will move into my life that will be different and lead me to a different focus.[35]

She approached the experience of injury recovery as a time to reflect on what she had learned and to recognize other things in her life that she valued such as supportive family and friends, and that she was moving into a new phase of her life that was going to be challenging (graduating and embarking on a career). The athlete later discussed that while she was disappointed that she was unable to compete in her final national championship competition, she felt she had learned a great deal about herself, her ability to persevere, patience, confidence, and motivation through the experience of being injured.

A significant component in the injury experience is that of the visible nature of the injury and the subsequent effect it can have on the experience of the individual. Many injured athletes I have interviewed through consultation and research have discussed the impact the type of injury has on them if there is a visual component to the injury such a swelling or bruising. Observing the reality of a reduction in swelling or bruising caused by a moderate to severe sprain (i.e., ankle) or tear (i.e., hamstring), for example, is reported as having a profound effect on how athletes feel emotionally and becomes part of what forms meaning from the experience. An athlete who broke her foot and was in a cast reported the lack of being able to have something visual as impacting her entire experience. Since she could not see her foot, she expressed the importance of looking at the calendar to mark off the days until the cast was removed. For her, the act of crossing off the days helped her to deal with the emotional experience such as the frustration she felt being physically restricted, as she had something tangible to see that she was getting closer to 'freedom' as she referred to it. Additionally, a rugby player who sustained a separated shoulder provided the following example of the visual aspect of injury and the impact it had on him:

> Well I have this huge bump on my shoulder, which doesn't look too nice and I look in the mirror and I say 'what are you doing?.' . . . If it was bruised and I could see the bruise going away I would have to say I would feel better knowing it is going away.[36]

Later in his recovery, he discussed that he relied on being keenly aware of his body and his internal feelings to help him determine how well he was healing. His subjective knowledge and experience was shaping how he navigated through his recovery:

> I don't know how I am healing, but I *feel* as though it is healing. . . . I can't obviously tell. . . . I can't see things healing and it impacts me every day, but I can feel it and I have better range of motion. I guess it's the range of motion for me that sort of takes the place of the bruising I can't see. I just know it's getting better even though I can't physically see it.[37]

Both athletes reported feeling frustrated and depressed, but used it to fuel their motivation to learn from these feelings to push them to deal with the injury and to recover successfully so they could return to sport.

Clearly, relying on subjective knowledge was important in the healing process for these and many other athletes. Another athlete reflected on the self-knowledge gained through his recovery: "It will make me a stronger person. I feel like the more hardships you have the stronger you become." This athlete's words relate to the idea forwarded by James in *The Energies of Men* regarding the use of energy. Using energy and pushing your limits do not in fact 'wreck' you; rather you adapt and it may be possible to reveal a strength you did not previously realize you had. As time passes for those experiencing injury, it becomes more about how their affective state serves to inform meaning of the experience through self-reflection and that struggle can lead to a realization of meaning and possibility. If we remained grounded in mechanistic reduction, we would only see the tip of the iceberg of the experience of injury. We would miss a significant and larger portion of the iceberg that is under the surface. As Fahlberg and colleagues suggested, "meaning, for humans, is like water for fish; meaning is the world we live in, move around in, and share."[38] We would be remiss if we ignored the expanse of the iceberg and should celebrate the meaning derived from the experience of injury.

V. THE LIVED EXPERIENCE

Living the experience of injury and recovery can indeed uncover not only a second wind, but a third or fourth wind as suggested by James. A positive and optimistic attitude held by injured athletes has been noted by several researchers to hold potential benefits in rehabilitation. For example, athletes in my 2003 study discussed at length their positive outlook toward recovering successfully and attributed much of it to their personal factors such as optimism, self-perceptions, motivation, and coping skills, and believed that remaining optimistic was essential to dealing with pain and recovering from an injury. They appraised the situation by reframing it from something purely negative and attempting to turn the injury into something positive by taking the perspective that the experience was an opportunity to organize this event in their lives as something to learn from. This group of athletes appreciated that they learned about themselves because of 'living the injury' and dealing with pain and injury. Some of what can be learned has also been highlighted by Udry [39] and colleagues who noted benefits reported by athletes including acknowledgment that they became "more mature," "learned patience," "more independent," and enhanced their outlook on life in general to be more positive.

A unique feature using a phenomenological method of inquiry is that it provides an opportunity for those going through the experience to discuss the meaning of the injury and to verbalize the learning that has taken place. As noted in the previous section, some researchers have identified athlete reflections of learning that has occurred through the recovery process. The work of Merleau-Ponty is based on the meaning of experience and centers on the belief that "human consciousness is an embodied consciousness." Each day our experiences through our 'lived body are embodied consciousness' and not simply about information and cognitive processes.[40] In the view of James, this enhances understanding that learning is possible through the experience of injury. While athletes accept inherent risk, they do not necessarily get injured each time they participate; however the potential for injury is always present. Since James viewed the world as being inherently filled with risk and believed that risk is necessary for a full life, then athletes can gain valuable insight about themselves through experiencing an injury, such that learning is illuminated. As James[41] stated in "Pragmatism and Religion":

> I find myself willing to take the universe to be really dangerous and adventurous, without therefore backing out and crying 'no play.' I am

willing that there should be real losses and real losers, and no total preservation of all that is. When the cup is poured off, the dregs are left behind forever, but the possibility of what is poured off is sweet enough to accept.

Viewing life this way may be in part what makes life worthwhile as it provides richness, and the opportunity to learn through experiences that may be dangerous or difficult. McDermott referred to this idea when discussing whether life is worth living and wrote of possibility as something that can be approached apprehensively or it could be enriching, "yet we have no guarantee of which direction our possibilities shall take . . . we move slowly . . . reading the consequences of our thoughts as they emerge in the crucible of existential experience."[42] Therefore, suffering, loss, pain, and injury are certainly real, but personal growth can emerge and help to create a meaningful experience for injured athletes through a concerted effort to reflect on, and attempt to make sense of, their injury and recovery experience.

Athletes I have interviewed through both research and consultation, acknowledged they reached a point when they recognized they had learned about their own inner strength, motivation, and belief in their ability to overcome a difficult physical and psychological obstacle; all of which they did not know they possessed prior to sustaining their injury. One athlete who had broken his foot four times, and was, at the time, dealing with a severe foot contusion, commented that "even if I broke it five more times, I would still come back and play baseball."[43] He approached his injury with the belief that his determination made him feel more confident in himself and his ability to overcome what he expressed to be an extremely challenging obstacle. Another athlete described how she learned to persevere in spite of the many times she was not sure she was capable: "if you get hurt, just keep going, it will pass (you will) get through it . . . that definitely got engraved this time, you just keep going."[44] Several athletes in my 2003 and 2007 studies discussed their injuries as a process of passing a challenge through which they felt there would be a tremendous accomplishment, with one athlete suggesting that the experience would be used to deal with future challenging events. The confidence and determination displayed by these athletes was indicative of many of the injured athletes interviewed and provides examples of learning through experience. The work of Merleau-Ponty and his ideas of phenomenology as a solid way of interpreting the lived experience seem particularly relevant when discussing the experience of injury and his ideas of experience as a provider of meaningful richness of human existence. This view is a direct opposition to the mechanistic view so pervasive when dealing with injured people.

Sport participation affords a tremendous opportunity to enrich life, as well as to experience the wide spectrum of fear, loss, exhilaration, and excellence. The inherent possibility of experiencing pain and injury through sport, as reflected through the experiences of the many athletes interviewed and consulted with, provides a different perspective of how injury can be a medium for self-discovery. Experiencing pain whether it is caused through injury, illness, or from extreme physical exertion can be empowering and enriching. A clear example of this has always been the challenges and triumphs of Lance Armstrong, seven-time winner of the Tour de France and a cancer survivor. Of pain and suffering he said:

> Pain is temporary. It may last a minute, or an hour, or a day, or a year, but eventually it will subside and something else will take its place . . . by now you have figured out I'm into pain. Why? Because it is self-revelatory, that's why. There is a point in every race when a rider encounters his real opponent and understands that it's himself. In my most painful moments on the bike, I am at my most curious, and I wonder each and every time how I will respond. Will I discover my innermost weakness, or will I seek out my innermost strength . . . you might say pain is my chosen way of exploring the human heart.[45]

It begs the question, should we deny pain, suffering, and the severity of an injury or celebrate it in some way? Perhaps at the very least living with pain can be viewed as something that can be learned from and that can be a source of pride. This is not to suggest an injured athlete should be elated to have sustained an injury; rather, it implies that recovery does not have to be purely a negative experience. In discussing the concept of courage, Corlett[46] highlighted an important tenet of sport involvement:

> Athletes choose to participate in the circumstances that produce fear that debilitates them. They actively seek the opportunity to challenge themselves beforehand that if the challenge were trivial, there would be no point. The difficulty of achieving is the reason for playing.

Since most people seem to view sport as a predominantly worthwhile venture, can we also see the possibility of injury as a positive event for enriching life? As I have noted in my previous research, possessing a positive attitude, resolve, determination, and inner strength were some of the qualities that the athletes did not know they possessed, yet believed they developed or discovered because of living the injury. Additionally, while positive qualities are not only derived through sustaining an injury, the experiences of the athletes highlighted in this chapter, along with other scholars have also noted that it is possible for injured athletes to realize numerous benefits to self through recovering from an injury such as clarifying priorities and becoming mentally tougher. By providing an opportunity for athletes to discuss their experiences of being injured, self-discovery and enhanced awareness of the self can be illuminated. Upon reflecting on the meaning of being injured and his realization of his physical vulnerabilities and limits, one athlete summed up his feelings by stating:

I have learned to take better care of myself. I think everybody takes all things for granted, like being able to walk. To use that in the future is making me think that anything bad can happen, like one day you could be paralyzed forever. I think it is very tough not to take things for granted because you still feel invincible and you're not – I have really learned that with this injury.

This athlete and others interviewed accepted and responded to their injuries with maturity and determination. They acknowledged that experiencing an injury was in fact a significant learning experience for them, as well as a very emotional one. Interestingly, they appreciated the opportunity to discuss their experience, and were extremely forthcoming with how much they enjoyed talking about it. Understanding people's experience and interpretation of an event reveals a recognition of the meaningfulness of the experience, and injured athletes who are offered the opportunity to discuss their experiences and organize them into rich narratives allow for greater understanding of the experience of injury.

VI. CONCLUSION

An alternative and appropriate perspective has been forwarded in this chapter to view people who experience injuries as more than a "knee," a "concussion," or a "hamstring." They are more than abstract objects bound by a dualism of the 'injury self' as different from the whole person, and more so, they are human beings who find profound meaning through suffering and living the experience of injury and recovery. A vivid example is to consider the extreme suffering witnessed and experienced by Victor Frankl, a psychiatrist and philosopher who survived a Nazi concentration camp. He believed that people could survive and deal with tremendous trauma of various kinds if they were able to derive meaning from the experience from it.[47] James posed this idea in his views on the value of living a strenuous life, on finding meaning through suffering, and on pushing boundaries to dip below the mere surface of living. He criticized humankind for continuing to fail to stretch their limits. And he worried that each person uses energy "below his maximum and he behaves below his optimum."[48] Experiencing something traumatic, such as an injury, offers an opportunity to tap into a new energy level, as James describes, and the possibility for self-cultivation and meaning may be derived through opening up the layers of the experience to discover a third or fourth wind.[49] While an injury is often a physically painful and traumatic experience due to the damage to the body, in many ways it can be an opportunity to learn about oneself in a holistic way. While it is often easy to adopt a mechanistic view and to treat a person as the injured body part, the continuous challenge is to remember that the whole person is dealing with the impact of the injury and rehabilitation and for

everyone working with injured athletes, as well as the athletes themselves, this must not be an oversight.

This chapter has utilized a pragmatic perspective forwarded by
William James among others and has highlighted the reconceptualizing
of the experience of injury and recovery by suggesting an alternative
method to view the process from a more positive perspective and as an
experience with potential for self-cultivation and personal learning. Increasing awareness and understanding of this perspective affords the
opportunity to incorporate some suggestions and techniques for those
who work with injured athletes and can be applied into their framework
of working with injured athletes. Firstly, it is important to be conscious
about not viewing the injured person as just a damaged body part. The
individual is dealing with physical damage, but the ripple effect of what
that injury impacts can be far greater than the physical component and
includes the psychological stress and emotional impact as well that is
often ignored. Secondly, we can discuss with them that it is possible that
something positive can come from this difficult experience. We can focus
on specifically asking injured athletes what can be gained from the injury
and recovery experience that can be positive, instead of always focusing
on the negative aspects of being injured. Thirdly, we can provide examples of other athletes (i.e., teammates, elite or professional athletes) who
have experienced an injury and recovered successfully to demonstrate
the potential to come back from adversity and can serve as a motivating
influence. Fourthly, taking the third point a step further within certain
environments where social support groups can be formed to provide a
forum for athletes to discuss with other injured athletes (at various stages
of recovery) about their experiences, to highlight the positive things they
have learned from the experience, and to share coping strategies. Fifthly,
we can provide more opportunities to consult with sport psychology
professionals where athletes can talk about their experiences and to verbalize what it means to go through the recovery process, to help them
develop coping strategies, and to help guide them to see the potential to
reframe the experience as something positive and personally meaningful;
a suggestion noted as potentially beneficial by others. Lastly, we can
discuss with athletes the possibility for them to use their injury experience as a challenge or test that they can transfer to other challenges they
may face in life, both in and out of the sport environment.

The experience of being injured and recovering affects the whole person in many ways (i.e., notions of loss and invincibility, disruption of
routine, questioning health, limits to physical abilities) and attention
needs to be paid to those experiences and the meaning derived from
them. By considering the perspective forwarded in this chapter we can
view injury and recovery as a place to embrace risk in a way that allows
for a meaningful learning experience. James believed that it is only by
risking in life that people truly live, so recovering from an injury pro-

vides an experience in which to do so. Eastern philosophical insight can assist in providing explanation of the role and meaning pain has in peoples' lives. In the *I Ching* it was stated that "the experienced person respectively appreciates the natural cycles of health and injury. One can do little to totally reverse this cycle, other than wait it out and to look for wisdom in acceptance of these times."[50] James offers an important contribution to finding meaning through experience as expressed by George Sheehan in *Running and Being:*

> We are all in the works of William James. He is the psychologist who tells us we can be more than we are. The philosopher who appeals to everyone who values his own experience. The thinker who saw happiness in the struggle and found the meaning of life in the marriage of some habitual idea with some fidelity, courage, and endurance.[51]

While Sheehan believed that James' description was as close to the definition of a marathon as was possible, it is also relevant for the experience of injury. People who get injured do more than just go to the seemingly endless rehabilitation sessions; they journey through an experience that can be full of emotion, frustrations, perhaps enlightenment of a kind, and meaning. While it is possible that for some the experience is fraught with hopelessness and futility, this does not have to be the case if we work with injured athletes to become more aware of the issues addressed in this chapter and pursue the alternative approach to specifically address the potential for finding meaning. For those who work with injured athletes during the rehabilitation process and are committed to assisting them, expanding awareness and understanding of the psychosocial processes can serve to facilitate a healthy recovery with various services that encompass physical, social, and psychological components in a holistic way. In this discussion of the experience and meaning of injury, the alternative perspective is to view it as a rich experience through which meaning is found that enhances the lives of those who experience injury (and work with those who do), along with the useful lessons derived from that unique lived experience.

NOTES

1. William James. "Humanism and Truth." In *The Essential Writings.* Ed. Bruce Wilshire. (New York: State University of New York Press, 1984) 264.
2. A. Murphy. "False positive." In *Sports Illustrated, 107*(5), 46-48.
3. William James. "The Energies of Men." In *The Writings of William James: A Comprehensive Edition,* 671-683. Ed. John J. McDermott. (Chicago: University of Chicago Press, 1977) 671.
4. Ibid. 671.
5. Ibid. 672.
6. B. U. Brewer, J. Van Raalte, D. Linder. (1991). "Role of the Sport Psychologist in Treating Injured Athletes: A Survey of Sports Medicine Providers." *Journal of Applied Sport Psychology, 3*(2), 183-190.; L. Ievleva, T. Orlick. (1991). "Mental Links to Enhanced

Healing: An Exploratory Study. *The Sport Psychologist, 5,* 25–40; S.A. McDonald, C.J. Hardy. (1990). "Affective Response Patterns of the Injured Athlete: An Exploratory Analysis. *The Sport Psychologist, 4,* 261–274; D. Gould, E. Udry, D. Bridges, L. Beck. (1997). "Stress Sources Encountered When Rehabilitating From Season-ending Ski Injuries." *The Sport Psychologist, 11,* 361–378; D.M. Wiese-Bjornstal, A.M. Smith, S.M. Shaffer, M.A. Morrey. (1998). "An Integrated Model of Response to Sport Injury: Psychological and Sociological Dynamics." *Journal of Applied Sport Psychology, 10,* 46-69.

7. L. L. Bain. (1995). "Mindfulness and Subjective Knowledge." *Quest, 47,* 238-253; D.S. Kerry, K.M. Armour. (2000). "Sport Sciences and the Promise of Phenomenology: Philosophy, Method, and Insight." *Quest, 52,* 1-17; L.M. Mainwaring. (1999). "Restoration of Self: A Model for the Psychological Response of Athletes to Severe Knee Injuries." *Canadian Journal of Rehabilitation, 3,* 145-156; C.R. Snyder, K.A. Lehman, B. Kluck, Y. Monsson. (2006). "Hope for Rehabilitation and Vice Versa." *Rehabilitation Psychology, 51*(2), 89-112; J. Tracey. (2003). "The Emotional Response to the Injury and Rehabilitation Process." *Journal of Applied Sport Psychology, 15*(4), 279-293.

8. William James. "The Sick Soul." *Varieties of Religious Experience.* 114-142. (New York: Touchstone, 1977) 124; G. Dale. (2000). "Distractions and Coping Strategies of Elite Decathletes During Their Most Memorable Performance." *The Sport Psychologist, 14,* 17-41; V. Krane, M.B. Andersen, W.B. Strean. (1997). "Issues of Qualitative Research Methods and Presentation." *Journal of Sport & Exercise Psychology, 19,* 213-218; R.M. Liberti. (2004)."Forbidden Narratives: Exploring the Use of Student Narratives of Self in a Graduate Sport Sociology Course." *Quest, 56*(2), 19-207; A.R. Nicholls, N.L. Holt, R.C.J. Polman. (2005). "A Phenomenological Analysis of Coping Effectiveness in Golf." *The Sport Psychologist, 19,* 111-130; T.V. Ryba, H.K. Wright. (2005). "From Mental Game to Cultural Praxis: A Cultural Studies Model's Implications for the Future of Sport Psychology." *Quest, 57*(2), 192-212; B. Smith, A.C. Sparkes. (2005). "Analyzing Talk in Qualitative Inquiry: Exploring Possibilities, Problems, and Tensions." *Quest, 57*(2), 213-242.

9. J. Corlett. (1996). "Sophistry, Socrates, and Sport Psychology." *The Sport Psychologist, 10,* 84-94. A. Poczwardowski, C.P. Sherman, K. Ravizza. (2004). "Professional Philosophy in the Sport Psychology Service Delivery: Building on Theory and Practice." *The Sport Psychologist,* 18, 4, 445-463.

10. J. Corlett. (1996). "Virtue Lost: Courage in Sport." *Journal of the Philosophy of Sport, XXIII,* 45-57; L.L. Fahlberg, L.A. Fahlberg, W.K Gates. (1992). "Exercise and Existence: Exercise Behavior from an Existential-phenomenological Perspective." *The Sport Psychologist, 6,* 172-191; W.B. Strean, G.C. Roberts. (1992). "Future Directions in Applied Sport Psychology Research." *The Sport Psychologist, 6,* 55-65.

11. T. Bianco, R.C. Eklund. (2001). "Conceptual Considerations for Social Support Research in Sport and Exercise Settings: The Case of Sport Injury." *Journal of Sport & Exercise Psychology, 23,* 86-107; D. Gould, E. Udry, D. Bridges, L. Beck. (1997b). "Coping with Season-ending Injuries." *The Sport Psychologist, 11,* 379–399; Mark Nesti. *Existential Psychology and Sport: Theory and Application.* (New York: Routledge, 2004) 38-50.

12. L.L. Fahlberg, L.A. Fahlberg, W.K Gates. (1992). "Exercise and Existence: Exercise Behavior from an Existential-phenomenological Perspective." *The Sport Psychologist, 6,* 172-191; W.B. Strean, G.C. Roberts. (1992). "Future Directions in Applied Sport Psychology Research." *The Sport Psychologist, 6,* 55-65.

13. M.Q. Patton. *Qualitative Evaluation and Research Methods* (3rd ed.). (Newbury Park, CA: Sage, 2001).

14. Henry David Thoreau. *Walden. A Fully Annotated Edition.* Ed. Jeffry S. Cramer. (New Haven: Yale University Press, 2004) 88.

15. Howard Slusher. *Man, Sport, and Existence.* (Philadelphia, PA: Lea & Febiger, 1967).

16. Patsy Neal. *Sport and Identity.* (Philadelphia, PA: Dorrance, 1972).

17. Elwood Craig Davis. *The Philosophic Process in Physical Education.* (Philadelphia; PA: Lea & Febiger, 1977).

18. D.E. Polkinghorne. "Phenomenological research methods." In R.S. Valle and S. Halling (Eds.), *Existential-Phenomenological Perspectives in Psychology* 41-60 (New York: Plenum Press, 1989).

19. William James. "The Sick Soul." In *The Varieties of Religious Experience* 114-142 (New York: Touchstone, 1977) 122.

20. J. Cheung, P. Hocking, (2004). "The Experience of Spousal Carers of People with Multiple Sclerosis." *Qualitative Health Research, 14*(2), 153-166.

21. B.W. Brewer (1994). "Review and Critique of Models of Psychological Adjustment to Athletic Injury." *Journal of Applied Sport Psychology, 6,* 87–100; D. Gould, E. Udry, D. Bridges, L. Beck. (1997). "Stress Sources Encountered When Rehabilitating from Season-ending Ski Injuries." *The Sport Psychologist, 11,* 361–378.

22. T. Pizzari, H. McBurney, N. Taylor, J. Feller (2002). "Adherence to ACL rehabilitation: A Qualitative Analysis." *Journal of Sport Rehabilitation, 14*(3), 201-214.

23. E. Udry (1997). "Coping and Social Support among Injured Athletes Following Surgery." *Journal of Sport & Exercise Psychology. 19,* 71-90.

24. E.W. Pelligrino. *The Healing Relationship. Proceedings of the NEH Health Ethics Institute* (Lexington, 1983) 77.

25. M. Jackson, *Pain: The Fifth Vital Sign.* (New York: Crown Publishers, 2002) 5.

26. C.E. Thomas, J.A. Rintala (1989). "Injury as Alienation in Sport." *Journal of the Philosophy of Sport, 16,* 44-58.

27. Ibid., 55.

28. H.L. Nixon (1996). "Explaining Pain and Injury Attitudes and Experiences in Sport in Terms of Gender, Race, and Sports Status Factors." *Journal of Sport & Social Issues, 20,* 33-44; P. Safai (2003). "Healing the Body in the 'culture of risk': Examining the Negotiation of Treatment between Sport Medicine Clinicians and Injured Athletes in Canadian Intercollegiate Sport." *Sociology of Sport Journal, 20*(2), 127-146; K. Young, P. White, W. McTeer (1994). "Body Talk: Male Athletes Reflect on Sport, Injury, and Pain." *Sociology of Sport Journal, 11,* 175-194.

29. T. Layden. (2007, July 30). "Big Hits: The Glory, Danger, and Repercussions." *Sports Illustrated, 107*(4), 52-62.

30. There have been anecdotal references through television broadcasts of NFL games over the years with athletes being compared to his level of 'bravery.' Internet sites highlighting Lott's career and Hall of Fame induction make reference to his amputation and use Lott to compare his 'toughness' as a justification for such an act and the story has been immortalized (Anecdotage, http://www.anecdotage.com/index.php?aid=15985; CNN Sports Illustrated 2000; Jelsoft, 2005).

31. L.L. Bain. (1995). "Mindfulness and Subjective Knowledge." *Quest, 47,* 238-253; D.S. Kerry, K.M. Armour. (2000). "Sport Sciences and the Promise of Phenomenology: Philosophy, Method, and Insight." *Quest, 52,* 1-17.

32. Maurice Merleau-Ponty, *Phenomenology of Perception.* C. Smith, Trans. New York: Humanities Press, 1962). (Original work published in 1945).

33. J.J. McDermott. "Experience Grows by Its Edges." in *The Drama of Possibility: Experience as Philosophy of Culture.* Ed. D. R. Anderson. (New York: Fordham Press, 2007).

34. George Sheehan, *Running and being.* (New York: Simon and Schuster, 1978) 202.

35. J. Tracey. Unpublished raw data.

36. Ibid.

37. Ibid.

38. L.L. Fahlberg, L.A. Fahlberg, W.K. Gates. (1992). "Exercise and Existence: Exercise Behavior from an Existential-phenomenological Perspective." *The Sport Psychologist, 6,* 177.

39. E. Udry, D. Gould, D. Bridges, L. Beck (1997). Down but Not Out: Responses to Season-Ending Injuries. *Journal of Sport & Exercise Psychology. 19,* 241.

40. Maurice Merleau-Ponty, *Phenomenology of Perception.* C. Smith, Trans. (New York: Humanities Press, 1962). (Original work published in 1945).

41. William James. "Pragmatism and Religion." In *The Writings of William James: A Comprehensive Edition*, 461-472. Ed. John J. McDermott. (Chicago: University of Chicago Press, 1977) 470.

42. J.J. McDermott. "Why Bother: Is Life Worth Living. Experience as Pedagogical." In *The Drama of Possibility: Experience as Philosophy of Culture*. 223-235. Ed. D. R. Anderson. (New York: Fordham Press, 2007).

43. Tracey. Unpublished raw data.

44. J. Tracey, Self-cultivation and Meaning through the Experience of Injury Rehabilitation: A case study. (Manuscript in review), *The Journal of Excellence*.

45. L. Armstrong. *It's Not About the Bike: My Journey Back to Life*. (New York: Berkley, 2001), 269-270.

46. J. Corlett. (1996b). "Virtue Lost: Courage in Sport." *Journal of the Philosophy of Sport, XXIII*, 52.

47. V. Frankl. *Man's Search for Meaning*. (New York: Washington Press, 1984).

48. William James. "The Energies of Men." In *The Writings of William James. A Comprehensive Edition*, 671-683. Ed. John J. McDermott. (Chicago: University of Chicago Press, 1977) 674.

49. Ibid 671.

50. J. Lynch, W. Scott. *Running Within*. (Champaign: Human Kinetics, 1999) 146.

51. G. Sheehan. *Running and Being*. (New York: Simon and Schuster, 1978) 203.

ELEVEN

Deweyan Pragmatism and Self-Cultivation

Richard Lally, Lock Haven University

I. INTRODUCTION: DEWEY'S ENDURING SELF

John Dewey's broad range of interests and vast catalogue of writings provide a fertile ground for commentators from many fields of inquiry. It is not surprising then that the avenues of access into Dewey's thought are numerous. I intend to add to this diverse tradition by applying Dewey's interest in human self-cultivation, which Roth says is implicit in all his writings, to my own niche area of interest—the lived experience of the endurance athlete.[1] For Dewey, the cultivation of the self meant the development of the individual's personality to its fullest potential and energies. However, Dewey's vision of how the individual was to attain this potential did not come complete with a detailed set of instructions one was to follow. This lack of specificity was intentional, and Dewey himself realized that it might be viewed as a weakness in his thought.[2] In its place Dewey described the conditions that could act as catalysts for the cultivating process, pointing us in the direction of improvement without attempting to lead us by the hand.

My plan for this chapter resembles Dewey's overall approach. First, I will examine the athletic self and the cultivating process in Deweyan terms. Second, I will examine Dewey's thought regarding the structure of experience, as this is central to his understanding of human development. Throughout the chapter I will utilize a radically empirical approach to build a case in support of Dewey's position regarding self-cultivation. This will be achieved in two ways. First, I will look directly to

Dewey's writing on the subject for philosophic support. Second, in keeping with radical empiricism's traditional reliance on narrative, I will refer to my own experiences as an endurance athlete.

II. SELFHOOD: AN UNENDING PROCESS OF ACTUALIZED POTENTIAL

In *Art as Experience*, Dewey asserts that the conscientious commentator on both artwork and the self must be concerned with the dynamic unfolding of the creative process that gave birth to that which he now judges. In making this point, Dewey speaks of an individual who aspires to understand the process of creation in all its varied manifestations. "It is quite possible to enjoy flowers in their colored form and delicate fragrance without knowing anything about plants theoretically. But if one sets out to *understand* the flowering of plants, he is committed to finding out something about the interactions of soil, air, water and sunlight that condition the growth of plants."[3]

With this in mind, we must realize that an examination of Dewey's thought regarding self-cultivation cannot be a straight-line undertaking, vulnerable to an aggressive frontline assault. We must walk the perimeter of the question, patiently gathering the full measure of the landscape, alert to all the undulations and false peaks. Less progress will be made by trying to vigorously wring the solution out of the riddle of athletic self-cultivation, and a strictly definitional treatment of self-cultivation would be foolhardy, an undertaking that Dewey himself warns us against. We would be better served to retreat to a distance that allows for an appreciation of the individual athlete within a historic landscape. From that vantage point we can assess changes that have taken place, complete with the normative assertions about self-improvement, but we should not hope to produce a complete picture of the individual that will exist with permanent accuracy.

If we do this, what becomes possible is a collage-like picture of the self, ripe with representations that aid in our understanding of the cultivating process, *snapshots* that contribute to, but never completely color in, the individual. And while we might prefer the comfort of a fixed version of the self, claims of its existence do not ring true given the dynamic environment it inhabits. As Dewey points out, "Perfect certainty is what man wants. It cannot be found by practical doing or making; these take effect in an uncertain future, and involve peril, the risk of misadventure, frustration and failure."[4]

This absence of a neatly categorized depiction is not a limitation. In fact, a composite view of the self, arrived at via a detour, is enough to justify love, friendship, distrust, and denouncement. Examiners of athletic self-cultivation are well served in exercising patience when assessing the dialogue that takes place between the self and the environment. If possible, we must guard against the arrogance that assumes that full knowledge of the subject is possible. In *Art as Experience* Dewey states: "The point is that no amount of ecstatic eulogy of finished works can of itself assist the understanding or the generation of such works."[5]

Despite being a Hegelian idealist in his youth, Dewey grew to be critical of philosophic conceptions that viewed the self as transcendental or supernatural. Along with Peirce and James, Dewey was heavily influenced by the work of Darwin and came to view the evolution of the human self as an ongoing, upward process that had no predetermined telos. For the pragmatists, the human self was best understood as the byproduct of an unending process driven toward the actualization of human potential. This belief is the reason that pragmatism functions well as a lens through which athletic self-cultivation can be viewed. A central theme within pragmatism is a belief in the power of the will to manage the challenging complexities of existence in a way that makes successful action possible. For Dewey, the individual's faith in her own ability to actualize latent potential made her a powerful player within the universe's functioning. More specifically, in the case of the endurance athlete, ability to create improved performance through the actualization of potential highlights the connection between the power of the will and self-improvement. Not only does the athlete come to appreciate the forcefulness of her will, she also becomes aware of the potential that remains untapped. In referring to this unending move toward potentiality Dewey stated that "without an awareness of potentials, we would be powerless to understand experience. All experience would be primary, or immediate, and persons would have no means to direct or control nature."[6]

Within the pragmatic conception, all human action involved a transaction with the environment, and thus caused a remaking of the momentarily established self. Dewey asserts that each of our exchanges with the world "creates new desires, instigates new modes of endeavor, brings to light new conditions which instigate new ends. . . . In the strictest sense, it is impossible for the self to stand still; it is becoming and becoming, and becoming for the better or the worse."[7] As a result, the self continues to unfold and develop as we live our days, collecting and being modified by experience.[8] As we are modified through lived experience, we realize to a greater extent the potentiality of our lives and come to recognize our own identity in this process of actualization. In Dewey's words: "Individuality itself is originally a potentiality and is realized only in interaction with surrounding conditions. . . . The self is both formed and brought to consciousness through interaction with environment."[9] In this regard, we can again see the importance of the power of the will in orchestrating positive outcomes for the developing self.

Through this ongoing process individuals work to overcome the limiting passivity of everyday existence in pursuit of an enlargement of the self. According to Roth, "this is not merely an extraneous addition to man's experience but something to which his whole being is directed."[10] Cunningham concurs, asserting that "individuality and the human self are based on his assertion that potentials are a legitimate aspect of nature. Revealed through the application of intelligence to experience, potentials provide us with concrete ends-in-view which infuse life with meaning and value.[11]

According to Dewey, the move toward greater actualized potential is not strictly a discretionary journey instigated by the autonomous actions of the individual. While the degree of cultivation that takes place along the life journey varies from individual to individual, Dewey felt that "it was not something that man could control, that he could handle intellectually. . . . It is something that man cannot shake off, or perhaps that man shakes off only to his own detriment so that his personality becomes isolated and stunted.[12] The resultant self then comes to life through its transactions with other things; individuals change because of the way they engage in a give and take with the universe that surrounds them. Individual cultivation begets greater cultivation.

Dewey believed people had the innate need, and the insight necessary, to seek out those future events or actions that offered the greatest possibility for increased cultivation. This ability to assess the growth potential of future actions allowed the individual to view personal existence as a journey along an infinite path rather than as a limited trip to a point of terminus. The following passage captures Dewey's view of the human self in this regard:

> Individuality is itself originally a potentiality and is realized only in interaction with surrounding conditions. In this process of intercourse, native capacities, which contain an element of uniqueness, are transformed and become a self. Moreover, through resistances encountered, the nature of the self is discovered. The self is both formed and brought to consciousness through interaction with environment. . . . The self is created in the creation of objects, a creation that demands active adaptation to external materials, including a modification of the self so as to utilize and thereby overcome external necessities by incorporating them in an individual vision and expression.[13]

It follows then that the pragmatic conception of the self emphasized a view of the human as a creature with "initiative, inventiveness, varied resourcefulness" and the "assumption of responsibility in choice of belief and conduct"; an entity moving forward as it engages the universe through experience.[14] Dewey's own description of the dynamic nature of the self confirms this view: "It is not something complete in itself, like a closet in a house or a secret drawer in a desk, filled with treasures that are awaiting to be bestowed on the world."[15] There is no intrinsic self, no "brute core of existence" that we could hope to attain at some point in the future, only the as yet unrealized possibilities.[16]

It is likely that this connection between action and self-identity is present in all humans, but it is easily recognizable in the endurance athlete. An example from endurance sport will help to clarify Dewey's understanding of the connection between self-identity and action. To know that an individual is a triathlete is to know a great deal of the total picture. A person who rises early, swims three thousand meters before breakfast, eats enough cereal for three people, completes a six-hour bike ride, takes a two-hour nap, runs six miles, eats a huge dinner, drinks a couple of beers, and is in bed by ten, is training for an Ironman. That's the athlete's day—that's everyday. When she eats, it is with an eye toward the next run. When she sleeps, she does so with the intention of recharging and restoring before the next workout commences. Her practice becomes the hub around which everything else spins. Her actions will tell us a great deal about her ever-developing identity. These are the habits that identify her as a serious triathlete. It is through these habits that we can come to know her.

In assessing this athlete we are applying the Deweyan conception that requires us when judging the product of a creative effort, be it a painting or the self, to have an appreciation of the forces that came together during its genesis. Likewise, an assessment based totally on the appearance of the current outcome is less than it might be if we fail to assess the environment in which it was generated. George Sheehan explains this process as it plays out in the ongoing generation of the athletic self in the following way:

> Jogging or whatever our sport is, therefore, is the way we move from actuality toward our potential, toward becoming all we can be. At the same time it will fill us with uneasiness, with what Gabriel Marcel called inquietude, the recognition that there is work to be done to fulfill our lives.[17]

As I attempt to build a case for viewing the endurance athlete as a fine example of the ever-developing Deweyan self, it is important to take a moment and reflect back on the key themes of pragmatism highlighted in the introduction to assess their relevance to the process of actualizing potential. In doing so, I hope to establish a continuity of thought and analysis regarding the connection I see between pragmatism and the self-cultivation of the endurance athlete.

In regard to the pragmatic faith in the experimental method, and Dewey's conception of the ever-developing self, a strong connection can be seen between the importance of testing and self-improvement. In the introduction I claimed that pragmatism's experimentalism is well suited to the examination of a practice such as endurance sport, which is itself inherently experimental. The athlete establishes goals and then employs methods to achieve them. In doing so, she continuously tests the validity of her beliefs and abilities, and thus meets the criteria Dewey proposed for the self.

In regard to the second pragmatic theme mentioned in the introduction, the acceptance of risk, similar evidence can be found in the athlete's experience to draw parallels with Dewey's understanding of the self. The Deweyan self is characterized by a forward movement through experience and a continuous attempt to actualize perceived potential. However, the advancement through experience is a risky endeavor due to the precarious nature of the universe with which the individual must converse. The hope of future improvement is tempered by the realization that future failure is also a possibility. The endurance athlete encounters failure more frequently than success. Goals regarding training and competition must be set at levels that make their attainment only occasionally possible. This process breeds a familiarity with the risks of failure, and generates within the athlete, a willingness to live with it each day.

The third pragmatic theme mentioned in the introduction, the power of the will, is also a part of Dewey's conception of the self. The will to believe in our potential can be a habit developed over time through a sustained commitment to a practice. The endurance athlete realizes significant improvement only after years of training. However, once that improvement is realized, the athlete gains an appreciation for the cultivating power of her will, and thus comes to personify the Deweyan self in action. Often, the individual's continued involvement with the practice is justified only by her desire to actualize what she perceives to be her latent potential. Other extrinsic motivators are fleeting, while her willingness to believe in her own future possibilities remains constant.

III. THE CULTIVATING PROCESS AS EMBODIED BY THE ENDURANCE ATHLETE

For a triathlete preparing for an Ironman competition, the training often consists of three hundred miles of cycling, sixty miles of running, and fifteen thousand meters of swimming each week. Training of that intensity requires the athlete to search for compelling reasons that justify the accompanying hardships. After all, six hours of pedaling up and down the hills of Pennsylvania cannot be explained by an expressed desire to lose a few pounds. In the words of two-time Ironman champion Scott Tinley: "When it's good, it's good. When it's bad, it's bad. . . . A 60-mile ride with friends on a warm sunny day is a blast. One hundred miles in the rain leaves a lot to be desired." [18] Even thoughts of future victories are not enough to sustain this type of arduous activity over the course of months or years. What is necessary is the profound feeling that such efforts improve the person, connecting the athlete to a world larger than himself, one that is rich in meaning. This realized improvement within training does not come to the athlete in the form of an epiphany, exploding in one's consciousness as a single moment of clarity. It is closer to Dewey's conception of self-realization, in which a deeper sense of meaning takes form in fleeting glimpses, as brief peeks into a larger universe to which we find ourselves inextricably connected.

The pragmatists would have referred to this athletic cultivation as an *unfolding*; a process through which the athlete moves "out of the diffuse existence of an ordinary life into something clearly beyond this and draws from the great store of our inchoate emotional experiences a circumscribed entity of passionate feelings." [19]

Evidence of this freshly cultivated skill can be found in the improved performance the athlete generates. The strengthened performer can recollect an earlier version of himself, when the apprenticeship to a chosen practice was embryonic. There is an awareness of what he once was, and an appreciation for the decisions that led him to improvement. Experience has demonstrated to him that a willingness to make active choices produces positive results. These, in turn, offer glimpses of a unifying meaning which would have been unrecognized previously. In many cases, what occurs is an abandonment of the role of spectator to life, which according to Dewey afflicts many individuals. The athlete may find that, after an extended apprenticeship, many self-imposed limits are left behind.

IV. THE CULTIVATING PROCESS: ASSESSING THE RESULTING SELF

As I have stated earlier, within Deweyan pragmatism the self is neither transcendentally divine nor metaphysically doomed—we are therefore as good or bad as the habits by which we live. Individual actions of the self are the foundation on which moral assessments rest. To quote Dewey in this regard:

> continuity and character are strictly correlative. Continuity, consistency, throughout a series of acts is the expression of the enduring unity of attitudes and habits. Deeds hang together because they proceed from a single and stable self. Customary morality tends to neglect or blur the connection between character and action; the essence of reflective morals is that it is conscious of the existence of a persistent self and of the part it plays in what is externally done. [20]

Assumptions about the self that the athlete makes are always subject to the acid test of the athletic lifestyle. An inflated judgment regarding ability, preparation, or toughness is quickly exposed. In this regard, training and racing serve as unique and consistent forms of self-measurement. Each may allow for a more accurate appraisal of one's own character and ability. While training can help to prevent exaggerated estimations of one's abilities, it is the race that allows for the truest estimation of the endurance athlete's character. Extreme distances and brutal conditions can strip away all but the most basic aspects of the individual's identity. The social costumes often worn during everyday life tend to disappear in such extreme conditions. When that silt of socialization is removed, what remains is a version of the individual in a more unadorned incarnation, unprotected from what might be the harsh judgments of the universe. An example may help to better explain this phenomenon.

Miles thirteen through twenty of an Ironman-distance run can be a time of psychological darkness. That stretch of internal darkness occurs between miles 129-136 of the overall race. To reach that point the athlete has often suffered through years of training, ruined relationships, ignored responsibilities, and financial hardship. Yet with all these sacrifices, thoughts of abandoning the race enter the competitor's mind. The athlete questions his reasons for being there. The cracks in his character which he normally attempts to keep hidden from sight are now impossible to hide, or for others to overlook. It is at that point that the desire to abandon the fight and return to the comfort of the hotel room bed can be nearly overwhelming. At that moment the athlete is faced with a choice of the self; his actions will tell the world all it needs to know about the quality of his character. It is the type of choice Dewey considered the parent of virtue, one made through the exercise of the will. He describes it in this way, "the choice of what kind of self one is to be is always a moral choice, for it involves the choosing of habits and motives having tendencies to produce certain types of consequences." [21]

If the athlete is able to make the virtuous choice in the late stages of that race the internal debate will stop. What he will experience is a quiet acceptance of the work that remains and a comfort that comes with the willingness to complete what he has started. At that moment, the race surrenders its last bit of romantic pretense, becoming only a journey to an endpoint. The athlete may find himself speaking out loud, listing those things that he is thankful for, primarily, the opportunity to be in that spot, on that day, at that moment. And while not normally a religious being, he may find himself thanking an unknown creator for his ability to move well through space and time. His fellow competitors, were they not offering up similar benedictions of their own, might assess these ramblings as merely the byproduct of severe dehydration. Each competitor, who makes what Dewey called a virtuous choice, is purified to a degree, having earned the opportunity to converse with the universe in the unadorned language of the weary. It is one of those rare moments that Dewey felt gave the individual access to his greater potential.

VI. CULTIVATION AND A PORTRAIT OF DEWEYAN CHARACTER

In *Human Nature and Conduct* Dewey writes, "Character is the interpenetrating of habits. . . . A man may give himself away in a look or a gesture. Character can be read through the medium of individual acts."[22] The following autobiographical account will help to illustrate the close connection between habit, action, and assessments of the self that the athlete learns through direct experience. In 1995 I was living in Hawaii and had recently become interested in multi-sport endurance events. Each weekend a local group of athletes held an informal race in Ala Moana Beach Park that consisted of a 3.1-mile run, a 1-mile ocean swim, and a second 3.1-mile run. The same thirty individuals tended to show up each weekend to test themselves.

I knew few people on the island and decided to enter the event in an attempt to find a friend or two. The first morning I kept to myself, going about the business of appearing unconcerned with the distances and the depth of the rough ocean waters. The regulars were either better at hiding their fear or more legitimately unconcerned.

As the group amassed at the starting line (which was nothing more than the spot on the sand where they always started), I placed myself in the middle of the pack and waited for the gun. A senior member of the group shouted, "Go"—and everybody ran away from me. It was obvious that the lighthearted banter of the morning was now over for at least the next hour. I caught the pack and hung on to the leaders as the familiar burning sensation filled my lungs and legs. The pace was quicker than I had imagined it would be, and I struggled to hold it. Since the course was unmarked, and I risked getting lost if I dropped back, there was little choice but to push on. We completed the first of the running segments and headed for the surf. I was somewhere in the top ten but hurting badly and unsure of my chances of completing the swim.

My arms were lead-like, my legs so full of lactic acid that they refused to kick, and my breathing became spastic gasps taken between strokes. With an ocean thousands of miles wide, the lead pack swam within a space no larger than a backyard plastic pool. Despite the acres of unused water, we crawled over each other in a fight for six feet of space.

I struggled to regain my breath as we approached the turnaround buoy. To my great relief, the other members of the group had not quickened the pace. We moved as a single unit, eventually finding a rhythm. I began to envision the second transition and the sand-encrusted shoes that awaited my arrival.

We exited the swim and I was pleased to have held my ground in the group. I struggled to replace my running flats on wet feet as two other men did the same. A spectator informed us that we held positions four through six— the leaders having just exited the transition area. The three of us shuffled back onto the course, desperate to be done with what forty-five minutes earlier had been some weekend fun. Our breathing was labored, our strides unified, and our faces similarly twisted in pain. We were thirty yards behind the lead pack and unable to close that gap by even a foot. It became obvious that the battle was only between us.

We arrived at the final quarter mile together. The leaders were still in sight, approaching the access road to the park. All that remained was a right-hand turn and a thirty-yard sprint to the finish. It was at that moment, gazing at the leader's backs through a lactic acid haze, that I was struck by what I saw. The front-runner left the road, stepped up on grass and cut the corner, taking a more direct line to the finish. The second and third athletes also left the pavement, eliminating the corner and at least fifteen yards. Even in my hypoxic state I had an appreciation for the *wrongness* of their actions. None of the men had hesitated. For a moment I wondered if this was possibly the accepted behavior for the group. After all, this was a weekly event and I was a first time participant.

As we approached the same turn I was in sixth place and unsure of what to do. The man in fourth place, only feet in front of me, had no doubts; he cut the tangent and ran directly toward the finish. I did not hesitate, fully aware that I was cheating, I stepped up on the grass, happy to be ending the ordeal as quickly as possible, while moving up in the standings by one. The third member of our group made a different choice. He continued on the paved surface, ran around the corner, and completed the full course.

As I crossed the finish in fifth a sense of guilt enveloped me. I turned around to face the honest man. He walked toward me as my glance shifted toward the ground in shame. I expected to be reprimanded for my actions. Instead the honest man extended his hand and asked me if I was new to the group. When I mumbled that I was, he said welcome and walked away smiling.

His simple choice to honor the racecourse told me all I needed to know about his character. I have never seen the man again, but I could testify to this day to his extraordinary excellence. In a single moment that was an acid test, I learned a great deal about each of us. Dewey's assertion that "every act has potential moral significance, because it is, through its consequences, part of a larger whole of behavior" was validated.[23] In addressing this aspect of Dewey's thought, Murphey makes this point clearly when he writes

> Our moments of present choice are significant for just this reason; they may make the world other than it is, or would have been had we acted otherwise. . . . This moral choice is an effective agent in the world, and it is this fact which gives meaning and zest to life. Indeed this is Dewey's call to the heroic life.[24]

VII. THE ELEMENTS OF EFFORT AND WILL

Within the pragmatic conception a key element to any cultivating process, be it the raising of crops or the production of an improved self, is the ingredient of effort. Peirce, James, and Dewey believed people are in a competition of sorts with the universe. Our victory or defeat is dependent on the level of effort we expend in confronting the challenges presented. Living within the confines of an endurance practice requires a consistent level of effort that helps to insure that the individual will avoid the lassitude that limits cultivation. The athlete reorders her priorities and expends her energy to meet the demands of the practice. Commitment toughens her, making her less prone to roll over in the face of adversity, while rendering previously acceptable standards undesirable.

In this way, the athlete is allowed to see that the limitations of her current existence are not permanent. She may become dissatisfied with her current powers, determined to make a greater investment of time and effort, in the informed belief that excellence is attainable. This new commitment, if sustained, finds permanence in the form of a cultivating habit. To quote from Murphey's introduction to Dewey's *Human Nature and Conduct*: "All habits are demands for certain kinds of activity; and they constitute the self. In any intelligible sense of the word will, they are will. They rule our thoughts determining which shall pass from light to obscurity."[25] I can reflect back to a time before my apprenticeship to endurance sport began when I struggled to complete a two-mile loop around the Chestnut Hill reservoir near Boston College. Each day I would leave the comfort of my apartment to again fight the shortness of breath, the tired legs, and the powerful desire to return to the soft warmth of my couch. I can now appreciate how that daily effort allowed me to overcome my past laziness and lack of direction. I am able to look back on that version of myself, aware that cultivation has taken place.

This assessment has little to do with a loss of weight or an increase in aerobic capacity. The cultivation I refer to is one of character brought about through the exercise of the human will. In completing a two-mile jog each afternoon, I had initiated a complete reordering of my existence that continues uninterrupted to this day. My act of will, as impotent as it may have appeared to the outside observer, altered my dialogue with the universe.

My experience is common to many endurance athletes. George Sheehan, in recounting his mid-life return to running described his own transformation:

> I became bored with medicine. When I applied for the faculty at Rutgers Medical School, citing boredom as my only qualification, the application was rejected. I then turned to a higher ambition. To become a forty-four-year-old miler. And, in an absolute, unreasonable, single-

minded dedication to that absurd project, discovered my body, my play, my vision and eventually a new life. I found my truth. [26]

In exercising the power of the will while surmounting the resistances of daily training, the athlete achieves a new and improved equilibrium that Dewey refers to in *Art as Experience*:

> Life itself consists of phases in which the organism falls out of step with the march of surrounding things and then recovers unison with it— either through effort or by some happy chance. And, in a growing life, the recovery is never mere return to a prior state, for it is enriched by the state of disparity and resistance through which it has successfully passed. [27]

Increases in ability are made possible by hardships met and overcome on the road toward a new sense of balance. Dewey described the growth in this way: "In the process of living, attainment of a period of equilibrium is at the same time the initiation of a new relation to the environment, one that brings with it the potency of new adjustments to be made through struggle." [28] As a result, there is never a static life for the growing athlete; resistances are met with effort and the force of individual will and become the fertilizer for continued improvement. The third pragmatic theme mentioned in the introduction, the power of the will, prevents complacency in regard to one's own development. Effort is expended in an attempt to attain equilibrium, which in turn is challenged by the desire for greater development, thus leading to increased effort yet again. In this way, the power of the will acts as a continuous catalyst for growth.

With each reclaiming of the equilibrium, a new challenge comes to the fore. Even during periods of fulfillment, during which the growing athlete is at rest, there is an awareness of the future challenges to be met. If the process of self-cultivation is viewed as a forward moving process, then our struggles with resistance are the transforming tunnel through which we must pass. The words of Sheehan regarding his life as a runner make this point powerfully: "The intensity of my physical life tells me all the old sayings are true. Sin is the failure to reach your potential. The answer to life is more life. You must seek limits of the possible and then go beyond. Guilt is the unlived life." [29]

While the individual is continually confronted by threats to the equilibrium, there is still a remembrance of what stability feels like, along with a desire to return to that state. It is for this reason that a conception of the self can never be complete, each moment is an attempt to make something permanent out of the ever-shifting sands of experience. According to Roth, "the individual is not finished, closed, complete; there is an individual still to be made; human personality unfolds and develops; an old self is put aside and a new self develops in and through its interactions with the environment." [30] Dewey's metaphorical use of the man stirring a fire highlights the manner in which athletic self-cultivation functions through endurance sport: "The man who poked the sticks of burning wood says he did it to make the fire burn better; but he is none the less fascinated by the colorful drama of change enacted before his eyes and imaginatively partakes in it."[31]

The athlete undergoes change as she acts on behalf of such change. The process is never a linear one, in which a single alteration follows a single action. Rather, it is a multi-dimensional event in which change and action converse, molding each other as the fire is altered by the man with the stick. When engaged in such an event, we are carried forward like the reader of Coleridge's poetry, unconcerned with an endpoint or destination, interested only in riding the process as it unfolds through us. To further support this assertion, Dewey uses the example of the ballplayer whose tense grace is appreciated by the fans in the seats.[32] The crowd is swept up and carried forward by the player's grace just as the art audience is touched by the uplifting power of the painting. The tension, present in the moment of expectancy before a pitch is thrown, creates a heightened sense of living for both the outfielder and the crowd. This tenuous relationship between the present, and the yet unborn moment, inspires the artist to create works of art on both the canvas and the playing field. All that has come before, and all that is now, is subject to the transformative powers of the future. The pregnancy of the moment is never ending.

It is also important to note that within everyday life the human organism engages in dual tasks. First, she attempts through an effortful exercise of her will to re-establish the equilibrium of the habitual self that is lost through the transactional exchange with the environment. Second, she attempts to actualize her unmet potential, aspiring to grow, hoping to enlarge the scope of her current abilities. Roth describes Dewey's thought regarding the process in the following way:

> Through effort, the organism acts upon the environment and is acted upon by it. When equilibrium is reached the organism attains satisfaction. Life becomes a series of disorientations and reintegrations with the environment, resulting in restored equilibrium, satisfaction, consummation, fulfillment.[33]

These two tasks incorporate the three pragmatic themes mentioned previously in the introduction. First, the athlete utilizes the experimental method in her transactional dialogue with the environment. Various approaches are tested and the most effective are adopted. Second, the athlete willingly welcomes the risk of setback that accompanies all attempts at growth and improvement. And lastly, she demonstrates a powerful willingness to believe in her own potential by faithfully returning to the rigors of the practice each day.

This movement forward through experience in search of improvement is propelled by the individual's imagination. Since the cultivating process consists of realizing previously unmet potential, the imagination becomes fired with what the future may hold. The ties that once bound the possible are loosed, freeing the individual to envision future excellence. Our endeavors are now imbued with a sense of purpose and the future's most striking characteristic is now potential improvement. The individual can then "shake off his isolation which will only stunt his personality, that he may strive to develop his full potentialities for the unfolding of the human person."[34]

The resulting self is not a transcendental constant or a metaphysical entity. In effect, the athlete is what she does. If we desire to know her we must simply observe her as she lives her days. Her habitual actions will provide a window to the self, allowing us to make a judgment about her character. All that must be learned can be culled through direct observation. And while the self is a plastic-like entity capable of many transformations over the course of a human life, we can gain an appreciation for its identity at a particular moment by observing the dialogue that takes place between the individual and the environment via her habits.

An example might help to clarify the point in relation to athletic self-cultivation. If I were to encounter a collegiate cross-country athlete in the middle of his season, I could make a partial, yet worthwhile, assessment of him at that point in time. It is likely that the individual who stood before me would have spent years running by the time I met him. His identity would be inextricably intertwined with his practice. In many ways it would represent how he thought of himself and how others viewed him. Physically he would appear almost gaunt. Lean by nature, the years of training would have sharpened his natural design, giving him legs of cabled muscle and an upper body free of all speed-stealing tissue. He would resemble the fictional miler Quenton Cassidy from Parker's novel *Once a Runner*.

> There were no inefficient corners or bulges; the form was simply chiseled as if from sand worn driftwood, fluted with oblique angles and long, tapering ridges, thin products of his core. Even now, standing perfectly still in the early morning glow, inverted teardrop thighs and high bunched calves suggested only motion: smooth effortless speed.[35]

Mentally he would be a creature most comfortable when exploring the inside of his own head. He would most likely be a thinker, having developed the ability to sit with himself over the course of thousands of training miles. His best friends (possibly his only friends) would be his teammates, those few who had suffered beside him during four years of morning runs while the world slept. They alone would know the price he had paid. While aware of the exclusivity of that tight-knit group, a collection of hardened individuals with little time for the non-running world, he would be unconcerned.

His days would be habitual. The secondary components of life: eating, sleeping, studying, socializing, and sex would orbit around the hub that is running. Few actions would be undertaken without a perfunctory cost-benefit analysis in regard to the training and racing schedule. Classes would be selected that did not interfere with afternoon practice or demand the athlete to expend more than the allotted portion of the mental energy on academics. The bulk of this particular organism's energy would have been spent on what it truly valued—covering miles at a high rate of speed.

VIII. THE STRUCTURE OF EXPERIENCE WITHIN DEWEY'S PRAGMATISM

In *Art as Experience*, Dewey detailed the relationship he saw between the creation of art and the cultivation of the artist within the context of experience. In the section that follows I will apply Dewey's thoughts on the production of artwork to my own concerns regarding the cultivation of the self through sport. Like all people, the artist and the endurance athlete are immersed in the flow of experience while they strive to create. In speaking to this point Dewey states: "An experience is a product; one might almost say a by-product, of continuous and cumulative interaction of an organic self with the world. There is no other foundation upon which esthetic theory and criticism can build."[36] This constant flow of experience works on the individual in the same way a stream does as it passes over a stone, wearing down and reshaping, making certain unnoticed beauty within both the athlete and the stone apparent. The stone, the work of art, and the individual are each engaged in a dynamic conversation with externalities that will transform their nature. As a result, the final appearance of the entity being washed by experience can be predicted with some degree of accuracy, but it cannot be foretold with certainty until the dialogue between the stone and water, or athlete and the practice, has taken place.

Within Dewey's system, experience is understood to be an uninterrupted flow of events through consciousness. There are various types of these events ranging from the unorganized that are *inchoate,* to the intelligently organized *real* experiences. Our ability to organize general experience into more meaningful units is dependent upon the perception of sensuous and emotional feelings. As a result, the power of perception is critically important within the Deweyan system and will be discussed in detail.

Inchoate experiences lack the demarcations of perception that would unify them. These are the unnoticed moments that fill a human life. An example from the athletic realm would be a swimmer who completes the latest in a long string of tedious mid-season workouts. There is nothing remarkable about the day's practice. The swimmer's high level of fitness prevents him from being physically taxed, and he is able to mentally disengage from the task. He passes through the practice as if lobotomized, swimming the meters, hitting the intervals, unengaged by the activity.

For Dewey, *an experience* is a period of time denoted through articulation, gathered into a meaningful order, unified by a conclusion, and emotionally felt by the individual participant. *An experience* offers us a sense of conclusion that serves to unify events into a whole that produces an emotional feeling of harmony. It is this emotional feeling that constitutes the aesthetic quality for Dewey.[37] The intensity of *an experience* is never encountered apart from the ordinariness of *experience* in general, but rather, is a biopsy taken from a greater organism.

Dewey stresses the inseparable connection between what we call the extraordinary moment and the ordinary constant. There is no actual separation, only those moments of creation that we layer upon the backdrop of experience as a whole. The person who lives through *an experience* has the sense of passing through time and a forward movement toward a moment of consummation. There is a sense of vested meaning that comes from "problems worked to a solution, a game played through or, some chosen objective achieved." Active participation in this process is critical. Dewey's clever example of the cook making good soup effectively emphasizes the vital importance he placed on an individual's active participation with the world. The cook tastes his creation as it is being born, adding ingredients as the process unfolds, modifying the soup as he converses with it. The process is a dynamic transaction that modifies both the creator and creation.[38] As Mitchell points out, sporting events operate in a similar fashion, and thus are well designed to facilitate the creation of *an* experience.[39] These events usually begin with a ritual such as the tossing of a coin or kickoff that mark the beginning of the movement. The series of events that follow tend to be highly structured and are monitored continuously by players, fans, and officials. A clock is often used to keep track of the length of the experience—concluding at the sounding of a gun. This organization allows the involved individuals to perceive the actions as parts of a unified whole.

IX. DEWEY'S STRUCTURE OF EXPERIENCE: THE ROLE OF PERCEPTION

Within Dewey's system, a human's ability to grasp the aesthetic qualities within experience is dependent on her ability to perceive. Perception is a power unique from all others that allows an individual to grasp the unifying string that runs through life's moments. According to Dewey, we use perception as a tool to assess our transactional dialogue with the environment. Through perception, we are able to recognize our standing as first-person actors within the universe. Therefore, no subject-object dichotomy exists between man and the environment within the Deweyan system—we are agents who act within the unified whole of existence.

Dewey believed that individuals are socialized to ignore their powers of perception. We tend to rush from event to event, determined to accumulate unnoticed activities at the expense of *real* experience. Dewey described the existence of most individuals as the "crowding together of as many impressions as possible." [40] Rarely is the individual appreciative of the aesthetic beauty present in lived experience. The endurance athlete differs in some important ways from the modern person Dewey describes. The athletic lifestyle offers daily exposure to an intensified brand of living. *Real* experiences are more readily available to the athlete who relies heavily on her powers of perception to monitor performance. The ever-changing relationship between the individual and the environment is something that must be *felt* if effective performance is to result. For the athlete in action, there is an immediately perceived connection to the moment that is lacking in the disconnected existence of Dewey's modern human. And it is through this heightened feeling that the individual "has a sense of being comprehended and sustained in a universal situation." He has become a living example of *The Inward Morning*'s man most alive, for whom "there is no separation of meaning for the act in which it is realized." Through the adoption of the endurance lifestyle, the athlete may come to believe, as Bugbee did, that "If you believe profoundly in what you are doing, the doing itself is a mode of being relevant, and it constitutes your manner of being articulate." [41]

In endurance sport, this transactional account between athlete and environment makes the birth of *an experience* a common occurrence. A marathoner converses with his fellow competitors, the environment, the course, and his own abilities and limitations. In the early miles of the race, the runner is strong, easily covering distance with light legs and an optimistic outlook. As the race progresses fatigue becomes a factor, leaving the runner with a new set of environmental conditions to which he must adjust. If he is to succeed, he must converse with new circumstances that change the dynamic of the interplay. In describing the challenge presented by the Boston Marathon's legendary Heartbreak Hill, George Sheehan emphasized the sudden change in conditions and his attempt to adapt.

> And now at the seventeen-mile mark comes the Newton hills, a two-mile stretch which includes the four hills that make up the world-renowned Heartbreak Hill. . . . Quite suddenly, what in the beginning seemed like something I would accomplish with ease and even distinction comes down to survival. . . . Descending the hill from Boston College. . . . And I know that the last six miles at Boston will be the

worst six miles I will ever run. . . . I experiment with strides and body
positions to see if there are any muscles still willing to respond.[42]

In the later miles the runner relies on the force of his own will and the
desire to complete what he has started. His environment is continuously
altered. The muscles of the leg ache each time the foot strikes the ground,
the stomach threatens to erupt, and the mind begins to dim. The marathoner may feel the almost overpowering desire to sleep, which leads
him to scan the street's side for a shady tree under which to nap. The
internal voice of the mind, that in the early miles offered nothing but
encouragement, now utters negative proclamations. Mile-markers on the
road's edge, which skipped by only an hour beforehand, now must be
earned through pain. The runner shuffles along head down, hoping that
he overlooked the sign for mile twenty-three, while in the same moment
aware that it must still be awaiting his arrival down the road. This ever-
changing drama forces the athlete into new decisions and actions, gener-
ating the type of vital interaction that Dewey spoke of:

> only occasionally in the lives of many are the senses fraught with the
> sentiment that comes from deep realization of intrinsic meaning. We
> undergo sensations as mechanical stimuli, or as irritated stimulations,
> without having a sense of reality that is in them and behind them; in
> much of our experiences different senses do not unite to tell a common
> and enlarged story . . . we see without feeling.[43]

For Dewey, *an experience* becomes a *real* experience when it is imbued
with profound meaning. In *Running and Being*, Sheehan describes the
creation of his own *real* experience as a competitor:

> The start is all laughter, talking, and wishing people well. This pace is a
> pleasure. Smooth, comfortable, and little more than a trot. . . . Down the
> long hill out of Hopkinton and through Ashland and over the gentle
> slopes of Framingham, I coast along. The running is automatic. I feel
> nothing but the elation of being in this company. The miles pass as if I
> was watching them out of a train window. . . . But the miles change,
> somewhere the holding back must end. I pass the ten-mile mark and
> enter Natick. The miles no longer effortless become an effort that comes
> easily. . . . Soon I am in Wellesley, the halfway point. The miles again
> change. Now each mile I am running at my best. It is now becoming
> hard work. . . . No longer child's play. Not just a long run in the sun. . . .
> But somehow I reach Beacon Street and I know I have made it. Like a
> horse who smells a barn, I am suddenly refreshed . . . .The last mile
> brings with it a joy, an elevation of the spirit, that makes everything
> that went before worthwhile.[44]

For both Sheehan and Dewey, the meaning generated by *real* experiences
is never something that is bestowed on us; it is a problem worked, a
solution sought, and a vitality generated through active participation.
Standing on the starting line of an Ironman distance triathlon qualifies as

an experience that Dewey would label *real*. These races start in the early morning hours on the sandy shores of a large body of water that is normally tranquil. On Ironman morning all that changes.

The coastline teems with several thousand athletes and spectators, all shifting from foot to foot, aware that months of preparation have led to this moment. The competitors in the crowd are easy to spot, clad only in racing swimsuits, their bodies trimmed of all but the essential flesh required of forward movement. The large crowd is quiet. The athletes are both focused and tentative. The families only whisper, afraid to say the wrong thing—their day will be the longest and most difficult.

The fear of dehydration is so great that the competitors seem to consume more fluid in the two hours leading up to the start than they have in the preceding two months of training. Equipment that has been ignored for weeks is checked and rechecked. Goggles are cleared, cleaned, put in place, removed, cleared, cleaned, repositioned, and then removed once again. Watches that will be forgotten during the race, that have not been worn during a single six-hour training ride, are fastened to wrists.

Only in the final minutes before the gun goes off, when they fear being left behind, do the athletes leave the company of their loved ones and wade into the water. Individuals known for their endless supply of physical endurance shuffle to the water's edge as if exhausted, heads down, eyes fixed on the sand, not a word passing between them. Nervous energy seeps out of the guy standing next to you. A thousand individuals share a tiny swatch of sand and no eye contact is made. The same internal monologue reverberates in each of us, "Stay calm, let the race unfold, stay within yourself, get to that first buoy near the front and settle into your rhythm. When it gets ugly, maintain your composure. You have done the work, have faith in your preparation."

The call of the race officials breaks the silence: "Thirty seconds—Stay behind the line!" A quick word of encouragement is shared with the individuals at your sides. A few final deep calming breathes, and almost to your surprise, the explosion of the starting cannon. The herd charges into the surf. Your heart rate leaps as you try to lift your knees. The strongest swimmers begin to "duck-dive" their way under the rollers as the water reaches waist height. Arms and legs batter you. Quicker swimmers climb over your back, pushing you beneath the churning surface. The unfamiliar fear of drowning enters your mind. Between strokes you search for the first large orange navigational buoy. On faith you follow the swimmer directly in front of you—to stop even for a moment guarantees that you will become a hit and run victim of the equally myopic gang that is incessantly slapping at your feet.

Over the next two miles the crowd thins, bodily collisions diminish but never disappear. You get your first hint of what the day will bring. By the end of the swim, if you are going to have a bad day, you know it. Confirmation of a good day will not be possible for several hours. You approach the shore and can make out the exit chute. Your mental focus switches from swim technique to all that needs to be done to guarantee a smooth transition to the bike leg. Once again you remind yourself to stay under control and relaxed. The nervousness of the morning is replaced by a workmanlike attention to detail and a gratitude for the sensation of sand between your toes. The triathlete exiting the water is familiar with each of the three pragmatic themes mentioned in the introduction, but at that moment, as he rushes from the surf, none is more familiar than the willing acceptance of risk.

X. DEWEY'S IMPULSIONS AND SELF-CULTIVATING EXPERIENCE

In Dewey's conceptualization of experience, aesthetic events come about as the result of an impulsion that engages the whole organism. These specialized intentions drive the organism to action, creating complete experiences, giving human existence an anticipatory, future-focused edge, defined not by the long-sought discovery of some underlying origin, but rather, through a forward search for the originary. As a person addresses surrounding circumstances, alters her actions to meet the challenges presented, and advances along a chosen path in accordance with motivating impulsions, she fulfills the Deweyan requirements of creative living. Dewey describes the process in the following way:

> Every experience of slight or tremendous import, begins with an impulsion, rather as an impulsion. . . . It is the fate of a living creature, however, that it cannot secure what belongs to it without an adventure in a world that as a whole it does not own and to which it has not native title. . . . If, and as far, the organism continues to develop, it is helped on as a favoring wind helps a runner. . . . Blind surge has been changed into purpose; instinctive tendencies are transformed into continued undertakings. The attitudes of the self are informed with meaning.[45]

The first-time marathoner standing on the starting line is an example of Dewey's purposeful adventurer, long driven by an impulsion that has propelled her to a moment rich with originary potential. Countless miles of solitary training, numerous physical setbacks, personal sacrifices made at a high cost, all contribute to the production of meaningful experience. Her initial desire to run, whether generated by a need for community or solitude, fitness or freedom, competition or pleasure, acted as the catalytic force that led her to this place. Her first motivations have been continually re-infused by concrete self-improvements, realized on the journey from novice to marathoner.

The cultivating process she has lived through has never been independent of the energizing fuel of the initial impulsion, nor can it disassociate itself from the originary spark that gave the evolutionary process life. Her involvement with the practice owes its history to that initial impulsion, regardless of how legendary or anonymous that history may prove to be. Dewey's reflections on the process are of particular relevance for this athlete. The following excerpt is a fine example:

> The only way it (the self) can become aware of its nature and its goals is by obstacles surmounted and means employed; means which are only means from the very beginning are too much one with an impulsion, on a way smoothed and ordered in advance, to permit of consciousness of them. Nor without resistance from surroundings would the self become aware of itself; it would have neither feeling nor interest, neither fear nor hope, neither disappointment nor elation. Mere opposition that completely thwarts creates irritation and rage. But resistance that calls on thought generates curiosity and solicitous care, and, when it is overcome and utilized, eventuates in elation.[46]

The incredible power of sport to cultivate the self is derived from the impulsions the athlete lives with each day. Unlike the passive spectator who may shy away from cultivating experience, the athlete often rushes toward the encounter, welcoming the struggle and its power to create aesthetic meaning. When the runner accepts the challenge of the hill, or the cyclist fights a headwind, the cultivating power of the impulsion is at work. Sheehan speaks of how the athlete recommits to the initial impulsions in accepting the hardships of competition.

> But then comes the Hill and I know I am made for more. I am challenged to choose suffering, to endure pain, to bear hardship. . . . At first the gentle swell carries me. . . . But gradually the Hill demands more and more. I have reached the end of my physiology. The end of what is possible. And now it is beyond what I can stand. The temptation is to say, "Enough." This much is enough. But I will not give in. I am fighting God. Fighting the limitations He gave me. Fighting the pain. Fighting the unfairness. Fighting all the evil in me and the world. And I will not give in. I will conquer this hill, and I will conquer it alone.[47]

I would guess that the committed practitioner of piano experiences both physical and mental discomfort as the result of long hours of required drill, yet returns to the instrument the next day as he did on the second day, to take up the challenge once again. The initial impulsion is reaffirmed with each hour spent before the instrument.

There is a group of runners I train with on my occasional trips home to Marshfield, Massachusetts, who continue to obey their initial impulsions. These practitioners have run together for years and constitute a tight-knit community. During the course of a two-hour early morning run each individual will experience the discomfort brought on by the resistances of distance, terrain, and pace. Rather than retreating from that which awaits them, they gladly go to greet it, once again obeying an impulse that requires effort and promises hardship. They have all suffered together in the past, having forged the bonds of strong friendship that fellow sufferers share. Similar histories of effort, achievement, and failure unite this group. To an individual they will testify to the unmatched joy two hours of arduous exercise can produce.

I first learned of the immense power of athletic impulses not from Dewey, but from these seasoned athletes. To this day, after years of obeying the same motivating force, I do nothing with more originary meaningfulness than run along a very familiar tree-lined road in Marshfield, Massachusetts in the company of this group. The familiar sights and smells, the steep hills and long straightaways, the texture of the running surface, the love of the childhood days spent running beside my father over the same course, have produced a strong emotional connection to an otherwise unexceptional place. It is during these runs that I gain an appreciation for what Dewey intended when he spoke of *real* experiences. On those early weekend mornings we runners, "are, as it were, introduced into a world beyond this world which is nevertheless the deeper reality of the world in which we live in our ordinary experience. We are carried out beyond ourselves to find ourselves."[48] It is our practice of running, and the suffering we welcome on those mornings, that makes this possible. These two components are vital to the cultivating process undergone by the athlete. Each is also a tenet of pragmatism and needs further explication within a philosophy of sport.

NOTES

1. Robert T. Roth. *John Dewey and Self-Realization.* (Westport: Greenwood Press, 1978), v.

2. John Dewey. *Individualism Old and New.* (New York: Capricorn, 1962), 99.

3. John Dewey. *Art as Experience.* (New York: Minton, Balch and Company,1934), 4.

4. John Dewey. *The Quest for Certainty.* (New York: Minton, Balch & Company, 1929), 21.

5. Ibid. 12.

6. Cited in Craig Cunningham. "Unique Potential: A Metaphor for John Dewey's Later Conception of the Self. *Educational Theory.* 44:2. (2005), 216.

7. John Dewey. *Ethics.* (New York: H. Holt and Company, 1932), 340.

8. Robert T. Roth. *John Dewey and Self-Realization.* (Westport: Greenwood Press, 1978), 31.

9. John Dewey. *Art as Experience.* (New York: Minton, Balch and Company,1934), 282-3.

10. Robert T Roth. *John Dewey and Self-Realization.* (Westport: Greenwood Press, 1978), 8.

11. Craig Cunningham. "Unique Potential: A Metaphor for John Dewey's Later Conception of the Self." *Educational Theory.* 44:2. (2005), 213.

12. Robert T. Roth. *John Dewey and Self-Realization.* (Westport: Greenwood Press, 1978), 131.

13. John Dewey. *Art as Experience.* (New York: Minton, Balch and Company,1934), 286-7.

14. John Dewey. *Reconstruction in Philosophy.* (New York: H. Holt and Company, 1920), 194.

15. John Dewey. *Individualism Old and New.* (New York: Capricorn, 1962), 168.

16. John Dewey. *The Later Works, 1925-1953.* (Carbondale: Southern Illinois University Press, 1981- 89), 110.

17. George Sheehan. *Running and Being.* (New York: Simon and Schuster, 1978), 69.

18. Scott Tinley. *Finding the Wheel's Hub: Tales and Thoughts from the Endurance Athletic Lifestyle.* (Palo Alto: Trimarket, 1995), 46.

19. Michael Polanyi. *Meaning.* (Chicago: University of Chicago Press, 1975), 88.

20. John Dewey. *The Later Works, 1925-1953.* (Carbondale: Southern Illinois University Press, 1981- 89), 172.

21. John Dewey. *Human Nature and Conduct.* (Carbondale: Southern Illinois University Press, 1988), xvii.

22. Ibid. 30.

23. John Dewey. *The Later Works, 1925-1953.* (Carbondale: Southern Illinois University Press, 1981- 89), 169.

24. John Dewey. *Human Nature and Conduct.* (Carbondale: Southern Illinois University Press, 1988), xix.

25. Ibid. 21

26. George Sheehan. *Running and Being.* (New York: Simon and Schuster, 1978), 99.

27. John Dewey. *Art as Experience.* (New York: Minton, Balch and Company, 1934), 14.

28. Ibid. 17.

29. George Sheehan. *Running and Being.* (New York: Simon and Schuster, 1978), 237

30. John Dewey. *Art as Experience.* (New York: Minton, Balch and Company, 1934), 31.

31. Ibid. 5.

32. John Dewey. *Art as Experience.* (New York: Minton, Balch and Company,1934), 5.

33. Robert T. Roth. *John Dewey and Self-Realization.* (Westport: Greenwood Press, 1978), 38

34. Ibid. 41.

35. John Parker. *Once A Runner.* (Tallahassee: Cedarwinds, 1997), 7.

36. John Dewey. *Art as Experience.* (New York: Minton, Balch and Company, 1934), 220.

37. Robert T. Mitchell. *A Conceptual Analysis of* Art as Experience *and Its Implications for Sport and Physical Education.* (Eugene: Microform Publications, College of Health, Physical Education, and Recreation, University of Oregon, 1976), 51

38. John Dewey. *Art as Experience.* (New York: Minton, Balch and Company,1934), 37.

39. Robert T. Mitchell. *A conceptual analysis of* Art as Experience *and its implications for sport and physical education.* Eugene: Microform Publications, College of Health, Physical Education, and Recreation, University of Oregon, 1976. 50.

40. John Dewey. *Art as Experience.* (New York: Minton, Balch and Company,1934), 45.

41. Henry Bugbee. *The Inward Morning.* (Athens: University of Georgia Press, 1999), 52.

42. George Sheehan. *Running and Being.* (New York: Simon and Schuster, 1978), 209.

43. John Dewey. *Art as Experience.* (New York: Minton, Balch and Company,1934), 27

44. George Sheehan. *Running and Being.* (New York: Simon and Schuster, 1978), 209.

45. John Dewey. *Human Nature and Conduct.* (Carbondale: Southern Illinois University Press, 1988), 58-59.

46. Ibid.

47. George Sheehan. *Running and Being.* (New York: Simon and Schuster, 1978), 12.

48. John Dewey. *Art as Experience*. (New York: Minton, Balch and Company,1934), 195.

Selected Bibliography

Alexander, Thomas M. *John Dewey's Theory of Art, Experience, and Nature: The Horizons of Feeling* (Albany: State University of New York Press, 1987).

Anderson, Douglas R. *Philosophy Americana: Making Philosophy Home in American Culture* (New York: Fordham University, 2006).

Bannister, Roger. *The Four Minute Mile* (New York: Dodd, Mead & Company, 1955).

Bugbee, Henry. *The Inward Morning: A Philosophical Exploration in Journal Form* (Athens: University of Georgia Press, 1976).

Butkus, D. and Smith, R. *Butkus: Flesh and Blood* (New York, Doubleday, 1997).

Carr, Cynthia. *On Edge: Performance at the End of the Twentieth Century* (Middletown, CT: Wesleyan University Press, 2008).

Carville, James *Stickin': The Case for Loyalty* (New York: Simon & Schuster, 2000).

Conroy, Phil. *My Losing Season* (New York: Nan A. Talese/Doubleday, 2002).

Dewey, John. *Later Works*, Volume 10, ed. Jo Ann Boydston (Carbondale, Southern Illinois University Press, 1987).

Fraleigh, Warren. *Right Actions in Sport: Ethics for Contestants* (Champaign, IL: Human Kinetics, 1984).

Frankl, Viktor. *Man's Search for Meaning* (New York: Washington Square Press, 1984).

Gale, Richard. *The Divided Self of William James* (Cambridge: Cambridge University Press, 1999).

Gavin, William J., ed. *In Dewey's Wake: Unfinished Work of Pragmatic Reconstruction* (Albany, NY: State University of New York Press, 2003).

Gibson, John. *Performance versus Results: A Critique of Values in Contemporary Sport* (Albany: State University of New York Press, 1993).

Jackson, Phil. *Sacred Hoops: Spiritual Lessons of a Hardwood Warrior* (New York: Hyperion, 1995).

Jackson, Phil and Rosen, Charley. *More Than a Game* (New York: Seven Stories Press, 2001).

James, William. *The Essential Writings,* ed. Bruce Wilshire (Albany: State University of New York Press, 1984).

The Principles of Psychology (New York: Dover, 1907).

———. *The Writings of William James. A Comprehensive Edition,* ed. John McDermott (Chicago: University of Chicago Press, 1977).

———. *The Varieties of Religious Experience* (New York: Touchstone, 1977).

Lynch, J. and Scott, W. *Running Within* (Champaign: Human Kinetics, 1999).

MacIntyre, Alasdair. *After Virtue* (Notre Dame, IN: University of Notre Dame Press, 1981).

Menand, Louis. *The Metaphysical Club: A Story of Ideas in America* (New York: Farrar, Straus and Giroux, 2001).

Merleau-Ponty, Maurice. *Phenomenology of Perception*, trans. Colin Smith (New York: Humanities Press, 1962).

Morgan, William J., ed. *Ethics in Sport* (2nd ed.) (Champaign, IL: Human Kinetics, 2007).

Nesti, Mark. *Existential Psychology and Sport: Theory and Application.* (New York: Routledge, 2004).

Novak, Michael. *The Joy of Sports: End Zones, Bases, Baskets, Balls, and the Consecration of the American Spirit* (New York: Basic Books, 1976).

Peirce, Charles S. *The Essential Peirce: Selected Philosophical Writings*, Vol. 1, eds. Nathan Houser and Christian Kloesel (Bloomington, Indiana: Indiana University Press, 1992). Vol. 2, eds. Houser et al. (Bloomington: Indiana University Press, 1998).

Royce, Josiah. *Lectures on Modern Idealism*. [1919] (New Haven, CT and London: Yale University Press, 1964).

———. *The Philosophy of Loyalty*. [1908] (Nashville, TN: Vanderbilt University Press, 1995).

Sheehan, George. *Running and Being* (New York, NY: Simon and Schuster, 1978).

Simon, Robert. *Fair Play: Sports, Values & Society* (Boulder, CO: Westview Press, 1991).

Slusher, Howard. *Man, Sport, and Existence* (Philadelphia, PA: Lea & Febiger, 1967).

Smith, John E. *Experience and God* (New York: Oxford University Press, 1968).

Smith, Ronald A. *Sports and Freedom: The Rise of Big-Time College Athletics* (New York: Oxford University Press, 1988).

Thoreau, Henry David. *The Portable Thoreau* (New York: Penguin, 1982).

———. *Walden: A Fully Annotated Edition*. ed. Jeffrey Cramer. (New Haven: Yale University Press, 2004).

Valdano, Jorge, ed. *Cuentos de Fútbol* (Madrid: Alfaguara, 1995).

Whitehead, Alfred N. *Adventures of Ideas* (New York: Free Press, 1961).

———. *Process and Reality: An Essay in Cosmology* (New York: Free Press, 1969).

Index